# SHAKESPEARE AND THE IDEA
# OF THE BOOK

# Shakespeare and the Idea of the Book

CHARLOTTE SCOTT

OXFORD
UNIVERSITY PRESS

# OXFORD
## UNIVERSITY PRESS

Great Clarendon Street, Oxford OX2 6DP

Oxford University Press is a department of the University of Oxford.
It furthers the University's objective of excellence in research, scholarship,
and education by publishing worldwide in

Oxford New York

Auckland Cape Town Dar es Salaam Hong Kong Karachi
Kuala Lumpur Madrid Melbourne Mexico City Nairobi
New Delhi Shanghai Taipei Toronto

With offices in

Argentina Austria Brazil Chile Czech Republic France Greece
Guatemala Hungary Italy Japan Poland Portugal Singapore
South Korea Switzerland Thailand Turkey Ukraine Vietnam

Oxford is a registered trade mark of Oxford University Press
in the UK and in certain other countries

Published in the United States
by Oxford University Press Inc., New York

British Library Cataloguing in Publication Data

Data available

Library of Congress Cataloging in Publication Data

Data available

Typeset by Laserwords Private Limited, Chennai, India
Printed in Great Britain
on acid-free paper by
Biddles Ltd., King's Lynn, Norfolk

ISBN 978–0–19–921210–1

# Acknowledgements

There are many people who have been central to the evolution and execution of this book, not least of all the Shakespeare scholars and book historians who appear throughout these chapters. To each of them I am grateful for the diverse ways in which they have sustained, contested, and lighted my passage with Shakespeare's books.

I would particularly like to acknowledge and sincerely thank Jonathan Bate, whose guidance, scholarship, discipline, and patience have influenced and supported me in this project. Alice Hunt, Richard Scholar, David Margolies, Emma Mason, Kevin Sharpe, Carol Chillington Rutter, Peter Mack, Jay, my sister Sophie, and Chris Jones have all, and in different ways, provided conversations, challenges, resources, and refuges at various stages on this journey. My thanks also to Margaret Kean, Tiffany Stern, and Laurie Maguire.

I am very grateful to the staff at the Bodleian Library, who have been both a support and a resource; and to Goldsmiths College, London.

But my greatest thanks goes to my mother, Emma Lambe, who not only taught me Shakespeare, but taught me the book of the heart, and it is to her that I dedicate this book.

# Contents

# 1

# Introduction: 'Give me that glass, and therein will I read'

In Shakespeare's Sonnet 23 the poet imagines what it is to be silenced by the need to speak. Comparing this feeling to an actor's stage fright, or 'some fierce thing replete with too much rage', he pleads for the written future of his voice. 'O'er charged with [the] burthen of mine own love's might', he declares:

> O let my books be then the eloquence
> And dumb presagers of my speaking breast,
> Who plead for love and look for recompense
> More than that tongue that more hath more expressed.
> Learn to read what silent love hath writ.
> To hear with eyes belongs to love's fine wit.[1]

The sentiment is love, the image is the stage, and the expression is the book. Even within the written form of the sonnet, the idea of the book becomes the place in which not only can the tongue express more, but the inexpressible—the silence—will eventually be translated into pages to be read and heard by the eyes of the beloved. These books reassure the burdened poet and promise not only a definitive place of expression but 'recompense'. The book both reflects and receives a version of what it represents. Sonnet 23 maps an idea of the book on to the requisites of the stage, where the acute relationship between an actor and his part replicates the relationship between the voice and the heart. The sonnet's synthesis of the book and the stage provides a significant starting-point from which to engage with ideas and images of the communicable. Here, the book conjures a form through which the actor and the poet move in the hope of compensation for the inadequacies of their response to the present. As the sonnet shifts through some of the inexorable frailties

[1] Stephen Booth (ed.), *Shakespeare's Sonnets* (New Haven and London: Yale Nota Bene, Yale University Press, 2000), Sonnet 23, ll. 9–14.

of our relationship to expression—the stunned inarticulacy of fear, the suffocating weight of emotion, or the absolute desire for lucidity—his books, as ambiguous and elliptical as they are, alleviate the pressure of the moment. The books of Sonnet 23 celebrate the luxury of a second chance, and promise, in all their shapelessness, an eloquent narrative of the soul. It is books like these, which speak, signify, shape, and presage that Shakespeare places on the stage of his dramatic imagination.[2]

As recent work on the history of the book has shown, the book is central to the development and dissemination of the human consciousness and its self-reflexivity, affecting and reflecting the social and personal movements that we make. Equally central to the evolution of the media, the transmission of ideas, and the widening of geographical boundaries in the transactions between the cultural and the political, are the quieter revolutions of the book: the essay, the diary, the margins, and the library; the pocket book, the quarto, and the folio. In conjunction with the material book, the metaphoric book took hold of Elizabethan consciousness to become a token of the world, or what Montaigne called 'la condition humaine'. Yet, where Montaigne's book became a synecdoche for his experience, Thomas Heywood's world became the stage:

> If then the world a theatre present,
> As by the roundness it appears most fit. . . .
> And chief determiner to applaud the best,
> And their endeavours crown with more than merit
> But by their evil, actions dooms the rest
> To end disgrac't, while others praise inherit
> He that denies then Theatres should be,
> He may as well deny a whole world to me.[3]

The metaphoric function that both the book and the stage were able to provide for the world was supported by their dual ability to accommodate and represent the self. Both the book and the theatre

---

[2] 'Presagers' is often considered an awkward description of the books' activity and has led to various rereadings of 'books' for 'looks'; however, as Stephen Booth explains, given the extended theatrical analogy through which the sonnet moves, it seems that books here operate in a similar way to prologues or choruses. See Booth (ed.), *Shakespeare's Sonnets*, 172. In other words, the books anticipate the narrative, establish the context, or expose the art. All these functions centralize both the dramatic and the narrative role of the books, which signify their ability to both transcend and accommodate the limitations of the stage and the 'speaking breast'.

[3] Thomas Heywood, *An Apology for Actors Containing Three Brief Treatises* (London: Nicholas Okes, 1612), A4v. I have modernized both spelling and typography.

actively recognized, organized, and verified their observers, and the 'world' became a far more capacious symbol than the sign over the Globe may have suggested. Yet, unlike Heywood's idea of the stage, the book does not provide a composite image; rather, it becomes a gesture or an inflection, a thought or its 'local motion'. The idea of the commonplace book frequently suggests a relationship between the book, the individual, and the world; drawing in quotations and observations as the mind and body grow up with an expression of their graphic self. The commonplace book provides an image of the way in which the book and the mind interact. Thinking about the commonplace book may provide us with a picture of the way in which the book develops in both subjective and social conditions. The introduction to Thomas Cooper's *Thesaurus* of 1578 states: 'A studious yong man . . . may gather himselfe good furniture both of words and approved phrases . . . and make to his use as it were a common place booke.'[4] John Marston in his collection of satires, *The Scourge of Villanie* (1598), writes: 'Now I have him, that . . . . Hath made a commonplace booke out of playes, and speakes in print'.[5] Whereas, for Cooper, the commonplace book suggests a sensible and close companion of 'approved' quality, for Marston it signifies a superficial stockpile betraying ignorance and cursory experience. For Peter Ramus, however, the commonplace was neither random nor discursive, but an acute reduction of the journey between thought and reason. Yet Cooper's analogy to furniture is important, since, for good or bad, the book houses a portable mind and a social imagination that may move independently of the body and in conversation with experience. For Ann Moss the history of the commonplace book is 'an integral part of the history of Renaissance culture in general, because it is the history of its technical support system, and consequently of one of the most important factors contributing to its intellectual paradigms'.[6]

The most significant writers on the commonplace included Erasmus, Agricola, Melanchthon, and (in English) Henry Peacham. Whereas Erasmus offered a complex and philological structure, Melanchthon proffered a sustainable inventory specifically designed to accommodate and augment both real experience and esoteric endeavour. Peter Ramus,

---

[4] Thomas Cooper, *Thesaurus Linguae Romanae & Britannicae* (London, 1578).

[5] John Marston, *The Scourge of Villainie*, ed. G. B. Harrison (Edinburgh: Edinburgh University Press, 1966), 'Satyre. X. Humours', 107.

[6] Ann Moss, *Printed Commonplace-Books and the Structuring of Renaissance Thought* (Oxford: Clarendon Press, 1996), 134.

however, in his propounding of 'method' and 'order' for the reduction of
' "general principles" to "specials" by means of definition and dichoto-
my', looked to a process in which 'everything could be "methodised"
after this fashion, and the process had a close link with that whereby
language could be "reduced" to writing'.[7] Yet, 'The whole theory of
"common places" as propounded by Agricola, and later by Ramus,
represents, says [Walter] Ong, not a "settled philosophical outlook",
but an "inexorable disposition to represent thought and communication
in terms of spatial models and thus to reduce mental activity to local
motion".'[8] The 'local motion' of writing within the 'spatial model' of
a commonplace book reflects the mind's capacity to interact with its
world in a way that simultaneously comprehends and controls this relationship. The knowledge that the book may accommodate is supported
by the knowing that the bringing together of the book reflects. Such a
dynamic relationship between knowing and knowledge often sustained
an interrelationship between the book and memory. Johann Sturm's
treatment of the commonplace is linked to the art of memory appropriated by Renaissance humanists, in which he devises 'places' for 'things'
as a route-map to discovery and definition, plotting the co-ordinates
of both nature and knowledge onto a book of life; and 'as Cassiodor-
us declared, "wherever the human mind turns, whatever thoughts it
considers, it refers of necessity to one of the commonplaces" '.[9]

Generically, we may consider the idea of the book to belong, at
this point, to the nexus between the metaphorical landscape of the
world, signifying the knowing mind and a sensible presence, and the
individual body, testing its subjective wit against consensual impressions.
Shakespeare draws his books from this grand arena, and sets them as
'furniture' or 'local motions' upon his stage. Yet outside the figurative
realm, books have a powerful place within religious, political, legal, and
pedagogic discourse; but as we move through Shakespeare's books, we
become aware that they do not always retain their shape, sanction their
context, or reproduce their histories. Whilst the book may suggest a
grandiose commitment to certain ideologies or a peculiar friendship
with the self, it emerges on Shakespeare's stage as a dynamic challenge

---

[7] Terence Hawkes, *Shakespeare's Talking Animals: Language and Drama in Society*
(London: Edward Arnold, 1973), 39.

[8] Ibid. 39–40.

[9] See Moss, *Printed Commonplace-Books*, 195; and Sister Joan Marie Lechner, OSU,
*Renaissance Concepts of the Commonplaces* (Westport, Conn.: Greenwood Press, 1962),
48–9.

to both thinking and seeing. The purpose of *Shakespeare and the Idea of the Book* is to explore the idea of the book within Shakespeare's plays. Specifically focusing on seven of his plays, I examine the book, both materially and metaphorically, as it is manifest on Shakespeare's stage.[10] Working from the plays outward, I trace the book from its immediate theatrical impact to its broader implications within Elizabethan or Jacobean discourse. The chapters are devised chronologically, to expose the various definitions and significations through which the book moves during Shakespeare's dramatic career. The vagaries, subtleties, and paradoxes of interpretation and mimesis begin to emerge as we follow the interrelationships between two complex media of expression and reflection. The book both betrays and belongs to the representational body of the theatre.

## 'AND NOW I WILL UNCLASP A SECRET BOOK'

The word 'book' occurs in thirty-six of Shakespeare's thirty-eight plays.[11] Although the 'book' is used to cover a number of written articles, including a single page, a tablet, a manuscript, lettering, and the printed volume, I follow Shakespeare's use of the word 'book' under the general definition of something that is written. Shakespeare refers to approximately twenty-six different types of book, which span both the metaphorical and the material. Within these references the book ranges from the specific—the Bible, instruction manuals, conduct books, law books, almanacs, books of heraldry, hawking, or arithmetic, and the Book of Common Prayer—to generic signs of learning, pedantry, education,

---

[10] The texts of the seven plays, which this book focuses on, will be based on the First Folio. I am deeply conscious of the ongoing debate that surrounds the relationship between a Shakespearean text—quarto, folio, fair copy, or foul paper—and ideas of authenticity, authorship, and value, be it the single unblemished genius, collaborative artist, or flawed memorial constructions of audience members and actors. I have chosen to use the First Folio as my 'control text' not in the belief that the versions of the plays therein necessarily reflect a stable authorial or dramatic decision, but rather because the First Folio is a book in which the culmination of Shakespeare's work first became available as a material object, and as this project is about his theatrical books, it seemed best to start with the one in which all the others came to rest. I have, however, for ease of reference and style, chosen to use modern editions, rather than a facsimile of the Folio itself. All deviations from the Folio will be noted.

[11] This number includes *The Two Noble Kinsmen* and *All is True*; whilst I recognize Shakespeare as the 'author', I do not preclude the probability of collaboration on a number of plays, including *Titus Andronicus*.

art, and experience. Similarly, the book surfaces on a figurative level in reference to faces, hearts, beauty, conscience, inner consciousness, 'trespasses', 'nature', 'misfortune', 'virtue', memory, 'the secret soul', and character. The word 'character' often plays upon the ambivalence between the book and the body, as it moves between constructions of reading and writing, the graphic face, and the letter type.

Although *The Comedy of Errors* and *All's Well that End's Well* are Shakespeare's only plays to avoid the word 'book', we still find traces of the semiotic affecting and emblazoning the book upon the action. In *Errors*, Dromio of Ephesus, confronting his master, compares his beaten body to a marked page:

> If the skin were parchment, and the blows you gave were ink,
> Your own handwriting would tell you what I think.
>
> (iii. i. 13–14)

Although the body and the page remain conditionally apart, the pun on parchment and skin returns us to an almost essential analogue, wherein the body carries an inexorable record of its experience, which is distinct from the voice. What is written is translated in the very act of writing, representing not the author (Antipholus), but the book itself (Dromio). The page turns its subject outward against the pressure of the writing hand. Like the idea of the play, the idea of the book simulates its own metaphorical discourse, and discusses the image and the body of the actor through which it moves. The relationship between the book and the body is made up of many and various strands: recently, Douglas Bruster has examined the increasingly personal nature of print in the 1590s, locating satire, eroticism, and a developing awareness of 'authorship' in the relationship between the death of a writer and the popularity of their works.[12] Similarly, Georgia Brown has focused on how constructions of identity and authorship began to find expression in ideas of transgression, fragmentation, and deviation.[13] Yet, where the body of the author, the physicality of the text, or the individuality of the voice may begin to emerge in the interrogation of the dynamic between

[12] Douglas Bruster, *Shakespeare and the Question of Culture: Early Modern Literature and the Cultural Turn* (Basingstoke and New York: Palgrave Macmillan, 2003), 66–93.

[13] Georgia Brown, *Redefining Elizabethan Literature* (Cambridge: Cambridge University Press, 2004). Brown particularly focuses on Ovid and how, in both using and, as it were, abusing classical texts, writers of the late sixteenth century began to find their identities in the margins; deviating from paradigms, ornamenting prose, or challenging the relationship between rhetoric and representation.

words and matter, the transmission of books as love-tokens suggests a tangible relationship between lover and beloved played out in the physical donation and acceptance of the object. The figurative capacity of Shakespeare's books, however, is constantly emerging in the journey that a metaphor makes from 'cause to effect, effect to cause'.[14] According to Henry Peacham's *The Garden of Eloquence* (1577): 'Metaphor is [the] artificial translation of one word, from the proper signification, to another not proper, but yet nigh and like.'[15]

But why and in what way did the book become a suitable metaphor for the body and the soul, particularly as metaphor is predicated upon a 'nigh and like' relationship?[16] In *Romeo and Juliet* the book supports the rhetorical emblazoning of Paris; Lady Capulet instructs her daughter to 'Read o'er the volume of young Paris' face'

> And find delight writ there with beauty's pen:
> Examine every several lineament,
> And see how one another lends content:
> And what obscur'd in this fair volume lies,
> Find written in the margent of his eyes.
> This precious book of love, this unbound lover,
> To beautify him, only lacks a cover.
>
> (I. iii. 84–90)[17]

Lady Capulet's extended conceit plays upon the various conditions of the reader who becomes—by virtue of her observation, her interpretation, her engagement with the text, (the lineament, the margin, the pen)—the fulfilling element of the process of production. The book is made up of two entities, the leaves and the cover, which are reflected by two bodies

[14] Lechner, *Renaissance Concepts of the Commonplaces*, 128–9.

[15] Henry Peacham, *The Garden of Eloquence* (London: H. Jackson 1577), 4.

[16] In tracing the tropological origins and emergence of the book of the heart, Eric Jager locates a general transition of textual exegesis from scholarship to desire in the rise of vernacular love literature of the twelfth century. More particularly, however, he explains that 'from the early thirteenth century . . . lyric and romance began to portray the lover's heart also in expressly textual terms': Eric Jager, *The Book of The Heart* (Chicago and London: University of Chicago Press, 2000), 71. In support of this Jager cites *Roman de la Rose*, an 'allegorical dream-vision begun around 1230–35 by Guillaume de Lorris and completed some forty years later by Jean de Meun'. Jean's part of the poem, he explains, 'draws heavily on scholastic ideas and metaphors, and the book of the heart that it cites several times is clearly adapted from an academic model—often with deliberately comic effect' (p. 72).

[17] Because of the substantive variations in text, including both the Oxford and Norton editions working from Q1 and Q2, I have referred to the Folio text and modernized both spelling and typography.

that 'beautify' and bind through their union and consummation. Juliet is both the reader and the binding who, in reading Paris, completes the process of perfection, the 'precious book of love'. Here, the book specifically supports the conditions and consummation of love, because it provides a dynamic process of physical and cognitive engagement that is both sensual and sensible.

As Lady Capulet suggests, the semiotic of the book releases a figurative fabric of possession and consumption in which reading and reception simulate the harnessing of one body to another, augmented by the sense in which the woman's mind will reflect and accommodate the man's imperative. According to Edmund Tilney's *The Flower of Friendship*, for the wife, the face of a husband 'must be her daily looking glass, wherein she ought to be always prying, to see when he is merry, when sad, when content, and when discontent, whereto she always frame her countenance'.[18] The idea of the book offers an image of two bodies bound by the same conditions, in which the beloved may read 'the margent of his eyes', and, perhaps, 'frame her countenance' to that end. However, as well as the romantic or social bond, the book also supported an explicitly sexual metaphor. Whilst John Taylor, 'publishing a prostitute's character in 1622, justifies giving his "Booke the Title of a *Whore*" since a book, "like a *Whore* by day-light, or by Candle . . . is euer free for euery knaue to handle"', James Shirley, in *The Cardinal* (1641) has Antonio describe his companion's object of desire as:

> A pretty book of flesh and blood, and well
> Bound up, in fair letter too. Would I
> Had her with all the errata![19]

Towards the end of the sixteenth and early seventeenth centuries, the body and the book became further intertwined, sexually and secularly, through the iconic space of the female reading. Sasha Roberts explains: 'If men are shown to seduce *with* books, women are frequently represented as being seduced *by* books. Textual and sexual experience are assumed to be intimately linked in the body of the woman reader.'[20]

---

[18] As quoted in Frances E. Dolan (ed.), *William Shakespeare's 'The Taming of the Shrew': Texts and Contexts* (Boston and New York: Bedford Books of St Martin's Press, 1996), 30–1.

[19] As quoted by Gordon Williams, *Shakespeare, Sex, and the Print Revolution* (London and Atlantic Highlands, NJ: Athlone, 1996), 49.

[20] Sasha Roberts, 'Shakespeare "creepes into womens closets about bedtime": Women Reading in a Room of their Own', in Gordon McMullen (ed.), *Renaissance Configurations: Voices, Bodies, Spaces, 1580–1690* (Basingstoke and New York: Palgrave, 2001), 42.

The reception and popularity of *Venus and Adonis* (1594) saw Shakespeare become a synecdoche for the sexual female reading, so that, in 1641, John Johnson could claim:

There as also *Shakespeere*, who (as *Cupid* informed me) creepes into the womens closets about bedtime, and if it were not for some of the old out-of-date Grandames (who are set over the rest as their tutoresses) the young sparkish Girles would read *Shakespeere* day and night, so that they would open the booke or Tome, and the men with a Fescue in their hands should point to the Verse.[21]

The male here is imagined in terms of his dominant and privileged role as the phallic explicator of verse. Shakespeare, however, translates the book into the body through the vagaries of knowledge and desire, narrative and love: Lysander's 'love's stories written in love's richest book' (*Midsummer Night's Dream*, II. ii. 128), or Berowne's 'women's eyes', from which he 'derives' the 'doctrine': 'They are the books, the arts, the academes' (*Love's Labour's Lost*, IV. iii. 326). When the book enables this journey, it appears to map and re-map the relationship between the corporeal and the cognitive. When King John wonders if, on looking at his daughter, the Dauphin 'Can in this book of beauty read "I love"?' (II. i. 486), or when Lady Macbeth warns her husband: 'Your face, my thane, is a book where men / May read strange matters' (I. v. 61–2), or when Hector berates Achilles, 'O, like a book of sport thou'lt read me o'er' (*Troilus and Cressida*, IV. vii. 123), the book is explored, like the body, for traces of the artless heart and the honest soul. According to its representational potential, the semiotic of the book revolves on stage with an image of its reader, as Mistress Page complains: 'writ with blank space for different names' (*Merry Wives*, II. i. 66). Thomas Dekker, in *The Honest Whore*, capitalizes on such potential:

> I read
> Strange Comments in the margin of your lookes:
> Your cheeks of late are (like bad printed Bookes)
> So dimly charactered, I scarce can spell,
> One line of love in them.[22]

According to Julie Stone Peters, 'Actors could be "volumes" appearing larger than life in "larger print"', and 'the theatrical face (legible

---

[21] John Johnson, *The Academy of Love* (London: For H. Blundon, 1641), 99. Cf. Williams, *Shakespeare, Sex, and the Print Revolution*, 9, and Sasha Roberts, 'Shakespeare "creepes into women's closets about bedtime"', 45.

[22] Fredson Bowers (ed.), *The Dramatic Works of Thomas Dekker*, ii (Cambridge: Cambridge University Press, 1955), part 2, III. i. 127–31.

or otherwise) could be a page for the imprint of character'.[23] The relationship, here, between the actor and the book is predicated upon the ability of the book to perform, to image one thing and disclose another, to offer words or signs beyond the visible requisites of its presence, to be read or rejected, accepted, or undermined. The relationship between the actor and the book is dependent, like that of Juliet and Paris, upon the dialectic between reader and read, where the reader/audience may 'spell', 'print', 'read', and 'comment' on the text that interprets as it moves between character and performance.

The representational relationship between the book and the body is one of the various ways in which we become aware that the object is not a static symbol, but an image constantly shifting according to the demands of its mimetic space. The nature of the book—its material depth, prehistory, ideologies, aesthetic and intellectual differences, type, marginalia, binding, size, and content—asks us to engage with the processes by which we make meaning valuable. Reading is one of these processes. Alberto Manguel suggests that reading itself is a 'metaphoric vehicle', which 'in order to be understood must itself be recognized through metaphors'.[24] When we read, or misread—people, signs, places, bodies, books, things, selves, and memories—we become involved in an endless cycle of meaning which is organized not only by our learned cultural cognition, but by the contexts and expectations through which we move. Arthur Kinney, in his exploration of some of the objects on Shakespeare's stage, explains the way in which our minds appropriate, map, and accept the world around us:

The human organism interacts with the environment, both physically and culturally, and semiosis, the making of meaning, derives from both sets of information. The culture assigns particular meanings and sometimes particular values to objects it acknowledges, such as Richard II's mirror, and such significations may involve contemporary, embodied dispositions such as the late Tudor idea that mirrors of crystal would reflect the images before them. But such a trajectory of interaction—what Pierre Bourdieu conceived of as *habitas*—might also take historical meaning into account, such as the medieval sense of the mirror made of tin or steel that only imperfectly (arbitrarily or purposefully) revealed a true reflection.[25]

[23] Julie Stone Peters, *Theatre of the Book 1480–1880: Print, Text and Performance in Europe* (Oxford: Oxford University Press, 2000), 109, 111.
[24] Alberto Manguel, *A History of Reading* (London: Flamingo, 1997), 170.
[25] Arthur Kinney, *Shakespeare's Web: Networks of Meaning in Renaissance Drama* (London and New York: Routledge, 2004), p. xx.

As this extract reminds us, we are always reading, both forwards and backwards, to make our worlds representational. But when the book enters the playing place, we are forced to confront how we read, and how that act is being constantly interrupted and dislocated by its own metaphoric status. When Shakespeare asks us to 'hear with eyes', we are reminded that the book enters the playing space both to disrupt our 'reading' and disturb our senses. The landscape of the book, through which we discover both the material object and figurative language, reveals places in which ideas, practices, and processes associated with reading, printing, writing, or marking unfold as devolved sites of representation. Whereas the material presence of the book asks us to consider the nature of the prop, the symbolic space occupied by the object, and the physical relationship between the actor, his stage, and the volume, it also asks us to notice what sort of book we see and how, for example, Ovid's *Metamorphoses* or a book of hours, or a commonplace book, busies the theatrical space with sex, spirituality, or memory. The book, like the stage, is always in conversation with its parts.

## 'THE BOOK IN MANY'S EYES DOTH SHARE THE GLORY'

There are four areas of critical inquiry central to the background and justification of this project: the history of the book; the role and rise of the public theatre; Shakespeare's use of Ovid; and Shakespeare's reading, including his use of sources and intertextual material. Equally important are the intellectual, cultural, and political discourses that support the production and dissemination of the book: humanism, the Reformation, and particularly the translation of the Bible into English; vernacular writings and translations, including the essay, prose fiction, and conduct books; the commonplace book and the printed play. Separately, these lines of inquiry and productions have been well documented, and all have an important role, to a greater or lesser extent, in supporting the fabric of this argument. However, the particular aim of this project is to examine the performance of the book upon Shakespeare's stage. The institutional and cultural value of the theatre has long been established as informing and exposing the movements of early modern practices. More recently, the iconic, material, literal, and metaphorical vagaries of the book have been recognized as seminal within the development of early modern culture.[26] The purpose of *Shakespeare and the Idea of the Book* is to locate and examine the interaction of these media upon Shakespeare's stage. Julie Stone Peters's recent book, *The Theatre of the Book* (2000), is a significant contribution to the study of the book and the stage, in which she establishes that 'The study of the relationship between theatre and printing is . . . not a sideline in the history of communication but the paradigmatic instance of the interaction between text and performance.' However, her particular focus is on the book as play-book or script and the impact of publishing in enabling and establishing theatre. It is the book, she argues, that gave theatre 'an image of itself'. Likewise, David Scott Kastan's *Shakespeare and the Book* (2001) examines the status and role of publication, text, and authorship within the trajectory of Shakespeare's dramatic career and its afterlife. Though considerable contributions to both the history and evolution of the book and the stage, neither of these works concerns itself with harnessing the particular iconic and metaphorical book of Shakespeare's theatre.[27]

Incremental work on the history of the book has only recently found its place as an essential interdisciplinary space for both the intellectual and the anthropological discourse of early and modern culture. The

[26] Since the seminal work of W. W. Greg, D. F. McKenzie, R. McKerrow, A. W. Pollard, Roger Chartier, and H. S. Bennett, the history of the book has acquired an ever-increasing importance within both comparative and cultural studies. The body of work dedicated to the study and exposition of the impact and implications of the book is continually evolving. Currently, the most significant contributions to this discipline, ranging from the material production to the cultural and cognitive evolutions, include Lucien Febvre and Henri-Jean Martin, *The Coming of the Book: The Impact of Printing 1450–1800*, trans. David Gerad (London and New York: Verso, 1997); Anthony Grafton, *New Worlds, Ancient Texts: The Power of Tradition and the Shock of Discovery* (Cambridge, Mass., and London: The Belknap Press of Harvard University Press, 1995); idem, *Commerce with the Classics: Ancient Books and Renaissance Readers*; Jerome Lectures, 20 (Ann Arbor: University of Michigan Press, 1997); David R. Olson, *The World on Paper: The Conceptual and Cognitive Implications of Writing and Reading* (Cambridge: Cambridge University Press, 1994); D. R. Woolf, *Reading History in Early Modern England* (Cambridge: Cambridge University Press, 2000). For a broader anthology of the history of the book, see David Finkelstein and Alistair McCleery (eds.), *The Book History Reader* (London and New York: Routledge, 2002), which includes post-modernist essays on the sociological implications of literacy, authority, and authorship; and John Barnard, D. F. McKenzie, and Maureen Bell (eds.), *The Cambridge History of the Book in Britain*, iv: *1557–1695* (Cambridge: Cambridge University Press, 2002).

[27] Perhaps the three other most significant contributions to the specific area of this book are Robert S. Knapp, *Shakespeare: The Theatre and the Book* (Princeton: Princeton University Press, 1989); Jeffrey Knapp, *Shakespeare's Tribe: Church, Nation and Theatre in Renaissance England* (Chicago and London: University of Chicago Press, 2002); and Ann Righter, *Shakespeare and the Idea of the Play* (London: Chatto & Windus, 1962).

early modern period is of course central within this discourse, since it sees the inception of both the printing press and the public theatre, institutions which Peters describes as having 'grown up together'. The tremendous body of work that has contributed to this subject charts the chronological, anthropological, and topographical dissemination of the press: the humanist, religious, and political appropriation of printing, and the flow of technology, literacy, and polyphonic voices that began to flood northern Europe from the latter half of the sixteenth century. Jakob Ayrer's *Opus Thaeatricum* (1618) sums up the impact of the press: 'For any that disappear or are destroyed in one country or place are easily found again in countless other places, so that in human experience there is nothing more enduring and immortal than books.'[28] Elizabeth Eisenstein, crucially, brought the history of the book into its rightful context with her seminal volume *The Printing Press as an Agent of Change* (1979).[29] Eisenstein centralized the role of the printing press in the development of all aspects of late medieval and early modern culture. However, whilst foregrounding the press as the nexus where art, science, theology, politics, self, and state met, she also recognizes that, within such a melting-pot, no one aspect was exclusive of any other. Since her publication, scholars have variously re-deployed her arguments or tried to retrieve a more balanced view of the press within the early modern period. Adrian Johns, for example, argues strongly that science, and most particularly Tycho Brahe, enabled the transmission of crafts and cultures which then became epitomized in the exchange and ideology of the book.[30] Others have argued that the distinctions engendered by the manifestation of the book, both inherently and explicitly, between an oral and a literate culture wrongly distinguish two media that continued not only to operate concomitantly but remained synthesized and active.[31] William Slights argues, for example,

[28] As quoted by Peters, *Theatre of the Book*, 109.

[29] See also her more condensed work, Elizabeth L. Eisenstein, *The Printing Revolution in Early Modern Europe* (Cambridge: Cambridge University Press, 2000).

[30] Adrian Johns, *The Nature of the Book: Print and Knowledge in the Making* (Chicago and London: University of Chicago Press, 1998). Johns explains that 'Tycho has come to personify the role of print in transcending place and rendering natural knowledge universal. He has thus become emblematic of the transformation of local craft into global science' (p. 10).

[31] Adam Fox, *Oral and Literate Culture in England 1500–1700* (Oxford: Clarendon Press, 2000); Walter J. Ong, *Orality and Literacy: The Technologising of the Word* (London and New York: Routledge, 2000); Peters, *Theatre of the Book 1480–1880*; Janette Dillon, *Language and Stage in Medieval and Renaissance England* (Cambridge:

that printed marginalia were a graphic testimony to the continuing and reciprocal relationship between orality and literacy: 'the margins served both the silent lector and voluble lector, thus further collapsing any rigid distinction among oral, manuscript, and print transmission.'[32] Yet the contention seems to be whether the press and the book were instruments or effects of the profound social and epistemological transitions that took place in the early modern period.[33] The work of book and theatre historians, as well as Shakespeare scholars, is fundamental to the prehistory of this book, yet, as is frequently noted, these disciplines and approaches tend to remain separate. Lukas Erne's *Shakespeare as Literary Dramatist* is central to the shift that is beginning to take place, and to unite textual, historical, and critical scholarship. Erne's compelling argument sees Shakespeare as a writer for both the page and the stage, and has important implications for the broader questions of this book. But whereas Erne focuses on the status and discrepancies of extant texts and the conditions of theatre to expose Shakespeare as a writer and a dramatist, my concern is with the plays' representations of the book and not the authorial relationship between play-book and publication. Erne's thesis, however, also marks a shift in the kind of important scholarship that is addressing writing and playing simultaneously: Patrick Cheney's work on Shakespeare's sonnets, and his forthcoming work on drama, seeks to explore the ways in which Shakespeare consciously synthesizes the literary with the dramatic.[34] Although focusing on the 'language of authorship' through poetry, Cheney rightly claims that 'Shakespeare's poems and plays record a sustained conversation not merely on theatre but also on the art of poetry, and often the works conjoin a discourse of poetry and theatre in engaging and historically important ways.'[35] Similarly, a number of significant books are emerging on the relationship between the book and nationalism, the literary, social consciousness and

---

Cambridge University Press, 1998); and William W. E. Slights, *Managing Readers: Printed Marginalia in English Renaissance Books* (Ann Arbor: University of Michigan Press, 2001).

[32] Slights, *Managing Readers*, 7.

[33] The debate between the book as an agent and an effect of change is equally central to the religious upheavals that were both charted and constructed by the book. The literal and emotional proximity of Foxe's *Book of Acts and Monuments* to the vernacular Bible under Elizabeth I testifies to a singular and profoundly important instance of the book in practice as both instrument and effect.

[34] See Patrick Cheney, *Shakespeare, National Poet-Playwright* (Cambridge: Cambridge University Press, 2004), and his forthcoming sequel which will focus on the drama.

[35] Ibid. 10.

politics that seek to expose the status of the book in the evolution of cultural identity.[36] Many of these books are deeply suggestive as to the ways in which drama and the book become involved in cultural and personal revolutions, but to a greater extent they continue to separate these genres and platforms for the interrogation of wider materialism. The idea of 'new materialism',[37] however, is profoundly important in the ways in which it has opened up the literary and dramatic field to the vast significance of objects and their lives. *Subject and Object in Renaissance Culture* brought 'a sense of how objects have a hold on subjects as well as subjects on objects' to bear on questions of interpretation, understanding, and historicism.[38] More recently, Arthur Kinney's *Shakespeare's Web* draws us through the significance of objects, not just for their symbolic or cultural weight, but also for the ways in which they are part of, and dictate, the patterns by which we make meaning. Kinney's chapter on books perhaps comes closest to what this project aims to explore. Kinney offers a brilliant exposition of the mind's neural activity in making and receiving meaning, and uses this approach to focus on Hamlet's book within a linear narrative, in which meaning is contained by the cognitive patterns through which the sign operates. My approach, by contrast, is to explore the deeply unstable nature of Shakespeare's books, and to pursue the profound, violent, sceptical, secular, or devoted questions they raise within the context and drama of the bodies that hold, touch, speak, read, or destroy them. Shakespeare's books are unstable, protean, mimetic objects and ideas which have the capacity, above any other article on-stage, to challenge, replicate, and interrogate the limits and aspirations of the early modern theatre.

Central to the disruption of word and image were the seismic shifts that took place during the Reformation. The Reformers notoriously celebrated the printed vernacular word as a source of both power and change, and, in his Acts and Monuments, John Foxe famously sets the Pope against the press:

---

[36] See Marta Straznicky's *Privacy, Playreading, and Women's Closet Drama, 1550–1700* (Cambridge: Cambridge University Press, 2004); Susannah Brietz Monta's *Martyrdom and Literature in Early Modern England* (Cambridge: Cambridge University Press, 2005), Zachery Lesser's *Renaissance Drama and the Politics of Publication* (Cambridge: Cambridge University Press, 2004); and Philip Schwyzer's *Literature, Nationalism and Memory in Early Modern England and Wales* (Cambridge: Cambridge University Press, 2004).

[37] Hugh Grady, 'Shakespeare Studies, 2005: A Situated Overview', *Shakespeare* 1 & 2 (2005), 102–20.

[38] Margreta de Grazier, Maureen Quilligan, and Peter Stallybrass (eds.), *Subject and Object in Renaissance Culture* (Cambridge: Cambridge University Press, 1996).

The Lord began to work for His Church not with sword and target to subdue His exalted adversary, but with printing, writing and reading. How many presses there be in the world, so many block-houses there be against the high castle of St. Angelo, so that either the pope must abolish knowledge and printing or printing at length must root him out.[39]

Within a more secular context, Francis Bacon in *Novum Organum* celebrated 'printing, gunpowder, and the sea man's compass' as the 'three things [that] have changed the whole face and state of things throughout the world'.[40] In *2 Henry VI*, however, Shakespeare has Cade offer an anachronistic and more demotic view on the divisive nature of print and sovereign censorship:

Thou hast most traitorously corrupted the youth of the realm, in erecting a grammar school: and, whereas before, our fathers had no other books but the score and the tally, thou hast caused printing to be used, and contrary to the king, his crown, and dignity, thou hast built a paper-mill. (IV. vii. 27–31).[41]

Cade's comment gestures at the profound impact of the press on the peasant or illiterate class. Yet there is an awkward contention between the historically despotic Cade and the anti-hero of Shakespeare's play. The characterization of Cade is ambivalent, so that whilst we recognize the figure as self-aggrandizing and oppressive, the commonwealth of Shakespeare's Cade articulates many social and economic concerns of the latter sixteenth century, not least of all the socio-political conflict between the literate and illiterate classes. The demographics of literacy become fundamental to any examination of the role and impact of book production in any culture, which in turn creates a wealth of post-modernist discourse on the social distribution and stratification of power and authority.[42] As the word and the representation of signs

---

[39] As quoted by Eisenstein, *Printing Revolution in Early Modern Europe*, 151.

[40] Francis Bacon, *The Novum Organum of Sir Francis Bacon* (London: Thomas Lee, 1676), 17.

[41] This line reference is to the Norton edition, which uses the Folio as the control text; based on the Oxford edition, however, it also includes Q material. For ease of reference I have maintained the Norton's type but followed the text and punctuation of the Folio.

[42] Levels of literacy are notoriously difficult to calculate in this period, not only because of the absence of any information relating to the measurements or proportions of the reading public, but also because of the difficulty of determining what criteria to use. David Cressy claims that 'Only one type of literacy is directly measurable, the ability or inability to write a signature. . . . People who formed signatures are counted as literate; those who made marks in default are counted as illiterate': *Society and Culture in Early Modern England* (Aldershot and Burlington, Vt.: Ashgate Publishing Company, 2003), ii. 2.

came under increasing pressure from both iconoclasm and scepticism, Shakespeare's theatre began to interrogate the semiotic of the book. Yet, during the period that witnessed the rise of the Reformers and the shift from the iconic to the interpretative, the emblematic relationship between the book and literacy became increasingly complex. Referring to the teachings of the Ten Articles, Archbishop Lee, for example, allowed 'images' to 'be suffered only' as 'unlearned men's books', so that images became visual narratives, which the illiterate could 'read'. The book, then, was not a stable emblem of the learned, but an image which supported different versions of information, both visual and intellectual. But despite the notorious difficulty of calculating literacy in this period, and the different 'types' of literacy (writing, reading, or 'marking'), language, as Tiffany Stern explains, was a commodity:

First, plays provided a source of jests and anecdotes; they supplied the quips and one-liners that could be used to spice up conversation later: "so there be among them that will get jestes by heart, that have gathered a Common-place booke out of Plaies, that will not let a merriment slip, but they will trusse it up for their own provision, to serve their experience at some other time". . . . For those who could not read, the theatre was one of the few places that would offer the carefully honed and crafted language of love; already by 1598 Marston is horrified by "Luscus" who learns phrases of Shakespeare's *Romeo and Juliet* off by heart:

> Luscus what's playd to day? Faith now I now
> I set thy lips abroach, from whence doth flow
> Naught but pure Juliat and Romio.[43]

The theatre translates the book, as it were, in performance, offering its image as 'unlearned men's books' for both the literate and the illiterate to 'read'.

## 'BY THIS OUR BOOK IS DRAWN, WE'LL BUT SEAL'

Between the construction of the first public theatre in 1576 and the end of the sixteenth century, six theatres were opened in London.[44]

---

[43] Tiffany Stern, *Making Shakespeare: From Stage to Page* (London: Routledge, 2004), 20–1.

[44] James Burbage's 'Theatre', built in 1576, is usually recognized as the first purpose-built public theatre. However, scholars often count the Red Lion (1567), an inn renowned for its public performances, as the first theatre. The six theatres built between 1576 and 1600 include the Theatre (1576), the Curtain (1577), the Rose (1587), the

It is almost impossible to overestimate the impact and importance of the theatre during this period. Partly as a product of socio-political ceremony, partly as an evolution of medieval moralities and classical drama, partly as a transitional arena for the amalgamation of rhetoric and ribaldry, and partly as a response to, and reflection of, the aspirational and changing imperatives of humanism, the theatre became a powerful place of metamorphosis and potential. The stage was a nexus of the brilliant and the grotesque, of desires and delusions. The playhouse was a place to meet prostitutes, to bait bears, to see the revolutions of the times and the baseless fabric of this vision; it was both a 'conjuring glass' and 'a mirror up to nature'. John Pitcher best describes this hybrid stage as signalling the 'emergence of two histories, one of material objects and the market place . . . and the other of an eruption and opening in human consciousness'.[45] Pitcher's description itself exposes the theatre's fusion of the menial and the mesmeric, and, significantly, the commodification of representational pleasure. The phenomenon of theatre has been substantially and variously documented through its spatial and architectural nuances,[46] its iconoclastic and political evolution,[47] its subjective and social resonance,[48] its esoteric scope,[49] its practical, symbolic, and material conditions,[50] and the mechanics of the collaborative space.[51]

Within Elizabethan culture, the power and presence of the theatre suffuse both communal and private discourse. Pageants, festivals, and public and religious ceremonies consistently reflect and reinforce the

Swan (1595), the Globe (1599), and the Fortune (1600). Two children's companies were built *c*.1600 at indoor theatres in St Paul's and the Blackfriars. See Janette Dillon, *Theatre, Court, and City, 1595–1610: Drama and Social Space in London* (Cambridge: Cambridge University Press, 2000), 32–3.

[45] John Pitcher, 'Literature, the Playhouse and the Public', in Barnard *et al.* (eds.), *Cambridge History of the Book*, iv. 351.

[46] Stephen Orgel, *Imagining Shakespeare: A History of Texts and Visions* (Basingstoke and New York: Palgrave, 2003); Steven Mullaney, *The Place of the Stage: License, Play, and Power in Renaissance England* (Chicago: University of Chicago Press, 1988).

[47] Michael O'Connell, *The Idolatrous Eye: Iconoclasm and Theatre in Early Modern England* (New York and Oxford: Oxford University Press, 2000); J. Knapp, *Shakespeare's Tribe*.

[48] Katherine Eisaman Maus, *Inwardness and Theater in the English Renaissance* (Chicago and London: University of Chicago Press, 1995).

[49] Frances A. Yates, *The Art of Memory* (London: Pimlico, 1992); idem, *The Occult Philosophy of the Elizabethan Age* (London and New York: Routledge Classics, 2001).

[50] Stern, *Making Shakespeare*; Andrew Gurr, *The Shakespearean Stage 1574–1642*, 3rd edn. (Cambridge: Cambridge University Press, 2003).

[51] Margreta de Grazia and Peter Stallybrass, 'The Materiality of the Shakespearean Text', *Shakespeare Quarterly*, 44 (1993), 255–84.

dynamic between art and authority. The dialectic between the written and the performed or iconic word often provided the basis for spectacular public occasions. The procession of Elizabeth I through the streets of London the day before her coronation is perhaps the most famous and theatrical synthesis of icon and inscription. Children, dressed as various Virtues, visually supported the scene, as did Latin inscriptions which were pinned to parts of the scaffold and verbally translated into the vernacular,[52] and the apotheosis of the ceremony was marked by the offering of the Bible in English: 'But as soon as she had received the book, kissed it, and with both her hands held up the same, and so laid it upon her breast, with great thanks to the city therefore.'[53]

The relationship between print and theatre found another expression in the Puritan anti-theatrical tracts of declaimers like Stephen Gosson and Philip Stubbes. Through distribution of pamphlets, and the dialogic debates made possible through print, the moral role of theatre came into contention; and, as Touchstone exclaims to Jaques, almost everything and anything dialogic became facilitated by print, from treatises to conduct books: 'O sir, we quarrel in print, by the book, as you have books for good manners.'[54] For proponents like Thomas Heywood, however, the book became a medium for the defence of theatre, and by virtue of the page returned its readers to the stage.[55] The book was often

[52] The text was pinned to a tree: 'And upon the same withered tree were fixed certain tables, wherein were written proper sentences, expressing the causes of the decay of the commonweale.... And upon the same tree also, were fixed certain tables containing sentences which expressed the causes of the flourishing commonweale': James M. Osborn (ed.), *The Quenes Maisties Passage through the Citie of London to Westminster the Day before her Coronacion* (facsimile of the publication on 23 January 1559) (New Haven: Yale University Press, 1960), 47.

[53] Ibid. 48. It is also interesting to note the reciprocal relationship between pageant and print, since Bishop John Bale anticipates much of Elizabeth's procession in his play *King John*, as Janette Dillon notes: 'There is a structural affinity, too, between Bale's *King John*, and Elizabeth's coronation pageant: both present the monarch interacting with the figure of *Veritas*/Truth, and this interaction in turn seems to confirm the sincerity and authenticity of the monarch-performer': *Language and Stage in Medieval and Renaissance England*, 106. It is also no coincidence that Elizabeth's coronation 'script' is now known to be the work of Richard Mulcaster, one of the most significant contributors to Elizabethan humanism. The relationship between ceremony, stage, and the word is developed through *Richard II*, in Ch. 4.

[54] Equally, the 'War of the theatres' exposes the way in which the text and the stage became reciprocal sites for lively, public expression, and as the satiric exchanges took place on-stage, the Bishop's Ban of 1598 aimed to cauterize them from the page (see Bruster, *Shakespeare and the Question of Culture*, 67–8).

[55] Heywood capitalized on the metaphorical potential of the stage as world, wherein the spectator could recognize that 'All men have parts, and each man acts his own';

modelled upon the structural and representational devices of the theatre; the preface could simulate the prologue, and the author could appeal to the imaginative ears and eyes of his audience.[56] One sixteenth-century commentator explains that 'unlike poetry meant for reading, dramatic poetry "joins together with the mind . . . the image of things which are represented, and acts upon the senses as if it were the thing itself" '.[57] Similarly, the metaphorical potential of the symbolic consciousness found its way through the 'world' to both the book and the stage.[58]

Heywood concludes his paean to the didactic opportunities of the stage by claiming that 'He that denies then Theatres should be,/He may as well deny a whole world to me' (*An Apology for Actors*, A4ᵛ). The marginalia to this final couplet reads 'No Theatre No World'. Similarly, John Marston claimed of plays that 'the life of these things consists in their action'. There is, of course, a wealth of discourse on the evolving 'author' of the sixteenth century, probably epitomized in the figure of Ben Jonson, whose entrepreneurial drive to publication within the context of his masques for James I, marked him, unlike Thomas Nashe, for instance, as balancing a self-created marketable identity within the caprice of royal politics. The subject of 'authorship' as it evolved during this period has recently become more central to any discussion of the early modern theatre, particularly through the works of materialist critics such as Stallybrass, Hulme, Barker, and de Grazia, and post-structuralists like Keir Elam, Jonathan Goldberg, Malcolm Evans, and Catherine Belsey. The significance of collaboration in play writing has begun to deconstruct any Romantic or post-Romantic notion of the single privileged genius, as it has also centralized the physical properties and values of the mechanics of book and play production. Whilst I recognize the importance and integrity of redressing this balance within early modern discourse, I do not attempt to offer a Marxist or materialist account of the discernible and physical mechanics of the book and its production within Shakespeare's theatre. My discussion is strictly focused on the way in which Shakespeare uses the literal and figurative book on-stage, and I am unable to take this discussion into the Elizabethan marketplace for reasons of both space and clarity.

[56] Within this context, the relationship between the book and the stage is superbly chronicled by Julie Stone Peters, who explains the fluctuating relationship between the book and the stage in terms of their appeal to the senses. The Aristotelian privileging of the ear over the eye (the ear functions here as the internal voice of the reader and the eye as something potentially seduced by images and more vulnerable to deception) raises the veracious, cognitive, and imaginative value of the book above that of the theatre. However, the fluctuating dialectic between the structures of the theatre and those of the book provided the potential for manipulating and accommodating levels of representational perspective.

[57] Robortello, as quoted by Peters, *Theatre of the Book*, 108.

[58] Dante's *Divine Comedy* is perhaps the first allegorical and emotional fusion of the representational potential of the book. In *Paradiso*, Dante looks down from heaven on to the world: 'In its depth I saw that it contained, bound by love in one volume, that which is scattered in leaves through the universe, substances and accidents and their relations as it fused together in such a way that what I tell of is a simple light': Dante Alighieri, *The Divine Comedy: Paradiso*, trans. John D. Sinclair (Oxford and New York: Oxford University Press, 1939), canto XXXIII. Eric Auerbach's famous exegesis of the narratives and language of realism sees that in the *Commedia*, 'More accurately than antique literature was ever able to present it, we are given to seek, in the realm of timeless

Whilst the book could offer, at least until the representational crisis of the late sixteenth century, a tangible exposition of the known, the stage could simulate 'the actions a man might play' and 'the revolutions of the times'.[59] Such metaphorical potential runs through Shakespeare's use of the book of fate or life on-stage and the imaginative scope of the Globe theatre as the 'world's stage'. Jonson famously canonized such an image in his comment on the destruction of the Globe by fire in 1613: 'See the World's ruins.'[60] However, it was only after the secularization of the theatre that 'the image of the world as stage' could become a significant trope. Anne Righter, in *Shakespeare and the Idea of the Play*, focuses on the way in which the play-within-a-play and the metaphor of drama transmogrifies from Pythagoras's prosaic and cognitive metaphor of life to the self-conscious fusion of the practical and the possible on the Elizabethan stage.[61] The trope of the world as both book and theatre reinforces the representational potential and pleasure of such structures and ideas. The developing crisis in representation, the expanding fissure between text and experience, image and word, the re-evaluation of an inherent value system, and an epistemological drive toward expanding the limits of individual endeavour foregrounded both the book and the theatre, in all their socio-political vagaries, as representational paradigms for the self in motion.

being, the history of man's inner life and unfolding': *Mimesis: The Representation of Reality in Western Literature*, trans. Willard R. Trask (Princeton: Princeton University Press, 1974), 202.

[59] Robert S. Knapp, in *Shakespeare: The Theatre and the Book*, pursues the cognitive psychology of the self's confrontation with 'the moving image'. For Knapp, the theatre proposes a 'hypothesis', which activates our communication with the 'real': 'A hypothesis, we might say, is a Machiavellian strategy in our war upon the Real; it is the position from which we spring into dialogue with the Other—into that *hypokrisis* from which Greek theatre developed; it is the part we choose—as rationally as we know how—in the social and metaphysical action, the *mythos*, that we see developing. Push further and a hypothesis turns out to be a moving image offered by a hypocrite' (p. 140).

[60] As cited by Yates, *Art of Memory*, 350. Yates quotes Jonson in the context of Robert Fludd's Theatre of Memory, which, she claims, is, in both architectural detail and concept, probably based on designs similar to those of the second Globe theatre. In the light of this, the theatre is constructed as a stage upon which not fictions but resemblances and representations are placed. The theatre is the acute repository for the real rather than the fictitious: ' "All the World's a stage". Fludd teaches us to reconsider those familiar words' (p. 350).

[61] Righter, *Shakespeare and the Idea of the Play*, 65. Righter explains that the theatre and the play-as-world metaphor developed to enable ideas of illusion a powerful place within the realms of imagined and represented reality: 'This belief was fundamental to the new relationship of actors and audience, and to the effectiveness of the play metaphor upon which the relationship was based' (p. 74).

## 'ALL SAWS OF BOOKS, ALL FORMS, ALL PRESSURES PAST'

One of the first things that we notice about Shakespeare's books, both literal and figurative, is that they frequently have a linguistic function. Within the drama, the book scores graphic marks, whether rhetorical, demonstrative, or implied, which often confront the ideas and limits of the communicable. These semiotic functions lead us to question how the book creates effects, and to what extent its potential and performance impose upon the drama. Alongside such questions of presentation are questions of evolution, and in what ways Shakespeare imagines and experiences the idea of the book. We notice, for example, that Ovid's *Metamorphoses* appears in the hands of Shakespeare's heroines at only the beginning and end of his career, in *Titus Andronicus* and *Cymbeline*. Drafting the heroine's consciousness at acute moments of violence or fear, *Metamorphoses* seems to emerge at, or expose, the point at which theatre is unable to represent the space between body and meaning. However, despite the physical and imaginative potential of the book, it frequently appears at acute moments of representational impasse. On the one hand, Shakespeare's prolific use of the word 'book', its figurative scope and theatrical presence, suggest a lucidity and a performative potential; on the other, as a representational rubric, the book offers theatre 'an image of itself', which also transcends the structural and synthetic boundaries of the stage in its ability to shift between the icon and the metaphor, to conflate meaning, and to extend allusion. In terms of the material book, I have chosen plays that not only draw acutely upon the presence and 'dumb eloquence' of a text, but also dramatically trace the limits of the mimetic through the margins of history or the order of the written word. At the beginning of Shakespeare's career, in *Titus Andronicus*, we are confronted with the book as a physical object and an imaginative musical score; as we 'learn to read' and 'to hear with eyes', we become aware of the bookish hinterland through which many of the plays move. In the following chapter I focus on *Cymbeline* and *Titus Andronicus*, which I have chosen not only for their chronological significance but, more importantly, for the material authority and imaginative eloquence of their books. The dramatic role of the book on-stage—when its presence is affected and interpreted by the performance and the place—leads us to a developing awareness of both the independent motion and the theatrical depth of the object. Where Lavinia is forced through mutilation to read 'sad stories chanced in the times of old' for her own barbaric silence, and Titus is given a 'lively warrant', 'pattern and precedent' to 'perform' the narratives he once took comfort in, Imogen falls asleep next to the book that will become her nightmare. Even as the book may import contemporary discourses or ideological imperatives, it is often supported by the play's thematic hold over its content and the characters' responses and readings of its role. Unlike the play-within-a-play, the book is attached to, yet constantly eliding, an articulate image of itself. Even in its presence, the book questions and transfers the limits of its own authority. Even as a language, the configurations of the book are subject to interpretation; and even as an object, the book is an actor. Given the enormous interpretive potential of ideas of representation within drama, the book signifies an extraordinary synthesis of the subjective and objective in action.

We notice from plays like *Love's Labour's Lost* and *The Taming of the Shrew*, in which the book becomes enmeshed in practices of teaching and transformation, that the representational function of the metaphor is constantly fluctuating. I discuss *Love's Labour's* and *The Shrew* together in Chapter 3, because both plays engage the book, although very differently, in the pursuit of desire and the pretence of learning. Although relying on different traditions, both comedies point to a specific relationship between the body and the book, through which I explore how the semiotic has come to permit a sexual and textual tension to develop under the auspice of learning, and in what ways Shakespeare uses the body of the actor/character to pervert this dynamic. Yet in *Hamlet* and *Richard II*, plays that negotiate the effects and authority of performance, the book appears to defy the representational rites of theatre. Focusing on *Richard II*, the relationship between the book and ceremony is examined in Chapter 4. Through the figure of the king, the play's attention to story and history, and the tension between iconoclasm and ritual, the book challenges the requisites of theatre and confronts ideas of truth. Emerging from the spaces between Catholicism and Protestantism, Richard II's 'book of heaven' exploits the volatile power of presence in the image and the idea of authority. In Chapter 5 I explore Hamlet's relationship with memory, which begins in the Ghost's command from the cellarage, through the rejection of Wittenberg, to 'The Mousetrap', navigating the dialectic between words and image in the radical soul. The play's use of the book, as Hamlet rejects his past, enters 'sadly', or madly, reading, and Ophelia is prostituted to 'colour' her 'loneliness' with 'devotion's visage' and a Book of Hours, makes the book central to the drama's sceptical interrogation of the relationship between matter and truth.

Finally, through *The Tempest*, Chapter 6 will expose the ways in which the book has become complicit in the very processes that it appears to defy. The plays I have chosen to focus on engage the material and semiotic of the book in performance. The theatrical presence of the book begins to harness the drama to processes of signification: processes, I shall argue, that challenge the very foundations upon which they are built. In *The Tempest* we immediately notice the ubiquitous power of Prospero's books, yet upon what basis, through what indications and contra-indications, contingencies, prisms, and performances does the book achieve such a status? And how does such status enable us to explore and identify the potential of text in play, and in what capacity does such potential, text and performance, contribute to the hermeneutic scope of early modern media in motion? These are some of the question that Shakespeare's books propose.

Intertextual references, sources, and identities are symptomatic of the intellectual and ideological climate through which Shakespeare formulates an idea of the iconic, material, or metaphorical book. However, my purpose is not to examine sources, nor to trace pretexts, since not only is such work extant, but it also pursues a different end. Shakespeare's intellectual and educational integrity is central to his hermeneutical and dramaturgical choices, but the use of the book on Shakespeare's stage does not explicitly manifest as either an intertext or a source, though traces of those functions are always present. Ovid, and particularly his *Metamorphoses*, features significantly within Shakespeare's theatre, not only as a material object which facilitates the drama, but, perhaps, also as a commonplace book from which Shakespeare retrieves and organizes thoughts, paradigms, and images that accompany rather than invade the play.[62] Shakespeare's use of Ovid operates on various paratextual levels, which range from serving

---

[62] See Jonathan Bate, *Shakespeare and Ovid* (Oxford: Clarendon Press, 1994). Bate explores Shakespeare's 'imitation' of Ovid's writings, as well as his more emblematic association with processes of transformation and poetics, through the contingencies of sixteenth-century humanism. Exposing humanist ideas of 'affinity' and 'allusion', Bate signifies different levels of interaction between the text and the imagination: 'an allusion may signal a more far-reaching correspondence, but it may be merely incidental or ornamental; an affinity may be made apparent on the surface of the text, but it may operate at the level of the imagination' (p. 190).

a poetic allusion or classical pre-text to manifesting in support of, and in juxtaposition to, the ineffable. The dramatic use of Ovid is significant to Shakespeare's stage, since the book materializes as an identifiable text and in direct relationship to the drama. However, although we may claim some certainty as to the texts and pre-texts of Shakespeare's education—his reading of Ovid, Plautus, Plutarch, and Holinshed—and though we may trace references or allusions to Horace or Cicero, Chaucer or Greene, only Ovid appears in book form on-stage. Learning what we can of Shakespeare's reading and education is important within the context of analysing the textual and dramatic choices that he makes, but we can no more assume a direct relationship between his schooling and his dramatic books than we can between his lovers and his sonnets.[63]

The Elizabethan theatre presented a space of social fusion, of aspiration, of the impossible, desirable, plausible, damned, and delightful; it devised and accommodated the imagination alongside the brutal and the mundane. The book grew up under the auspices of Christian humanism and civic endeavour, as well as in the classroom, the inns of court, the courtly coteries, the ballads in the barber shop, the doggerel in the street, the pamphlets and publications of everyday interaction; and the plays, protests, processions, and politics that came through the press marking, erasing, and eliding the 'revolutions of the times'. As the printing-house and the book stalls of St Paul's churchyard flourished, so did London's public theatres, the performances at the inns, the pageants and festivals, the executions and trials, of a culture that was building an image of itself through fashioning and refashioning conditions of communication and representation. On Shakespeare's stage, the book and the theatre find a vantage-point through the conjuring glass that shows that 'there is a history in all men's lives' and that 'every red-nosed rhymester is an author; every drunken man's dreame is a booke'.[64]

---

[63] The most recent exposition of Shakespeare's education is Robert S. Miola, *Shakespeare's Reading* (Oxford: Oxford University Press, 2000); however, most books on Shakespeare's life include some description of his grammar school education. See also Robert Weimann, *Author's Pen and Actor's Voice: Playing and Writing in Shakespeare's Theatre* (Cambridge: Cambridge University Press, 2000), and Virgil K. Whitaker, *Shakespeare's Use of Learning: An Inquiry into the Growth of his Mind and Art* (San Marino, Calif.: The Huntingdon Library, 1969).

[64] W. Chappell, *Popular Music of the Olden Time: A Collection of Ancient Songs, Ballads, and Dance Tunes, Illustrative of the National Music of England*, i (London: Cramer, Beale, & Chappell, 1893). Chappell includes this quotation from *Martin Mar-sixtus* (1592), in reference to the large number of ballads that were printed in the reign of Elizabeth I.

# 2

# 'Sad stories chanced in the times of old': The Book in Performance in *Titus Andronicus* and *Cymbeline*

When Lavinia, without hands or a tongue, flies after her nephew in pursuit of his books, or Imogen's nurse, turning down the page of Philomel's rape, leaves her mistress to the nightmare of Iachimo's desires, Ovid's *Metamorphoses* enters the playing space with the dramatic impact of a fugitive. Appearing on-stage as a graphic thought or an allusive dream, the book asks the play to 'read the subtle shining secrecies' of 'what obscured in this fair volume lies'.[1] Within the sum of Shakespeare's drama a specific material book appears in only two plays, which mark the length of his career, *Titus Andronicus* and *Cymbeline*. In both plays it is Ovid's *Metamorphoses*, and the text is the rape of Philomel. Ostensibly *Metamorphoses* fulfils a similar function in both plays, tracing the shadows of the woman's plight in actuality or potential. The book appears at the moment when theatre comes into contact with its own limitations, when the stage seems incapable of supporting an audible silence; yet, as Posthumus says:

> Be what it is,
> The action of my life is like it, which
> I'll keep, if but for sympathy.[2]

Although *Titus Andronicus* is replete with allusions, Aaron making the first to *Metamorphoses* in his anticipation of the rape of Lavinia, the

---

[1] William Shakespeare, 'The Rape of Lucrece', in *The Narrative Poems*, ed. Maurice Evans (Harmondsworth: Penguin, 1989), 101; *Romeo and Juliet*, I. iii. 87.

[2] William Shakespeare, *Cymbeline*, ed. J. M. Nosworthy, The Arden Shakespeare, 3rd ser. (London: Thomas Learning, 2000), v. iv. 149–51. All subsequent references, unless otherwise stated, are to this edition. Any deviations from the Folio, including stage directions, will be noted.

idea of the book first materializes in the context of both sympathy and diversion. Helplessly observing his mutilated and mute daughter, Titus declares:

> Lavinia, go with me;
> I'll to thy closet and go read with thee
> Sad stories chanced in the times of old.
> Come, boy, and go read with me; thy sight is young,
> And thou shalt read when mine begin to dazzle.[3]

Titus leaves the stage, with Young Lucius and Lavinia, in search of stories to 'beguile' her 'sorrow'; the next scene opens with such books as they may have found thrown onto the stage as Lavinia frantically pursues her nephew for a volume of such 'sad stories chanced in the times of old'. Before we see the books, however, we are given a sense of how they may be read, and although Titus looks for comfort in art, Lavinia will reveal tragedy in experience. The terrible tension that *Titus* establishes between art and experience begins in attitudes toward reading. Once we become aware of how reading will shape the action of the play, the many textual allusions are heavy with the dialectic between nature and art or, as John Marston said, 'How Nature, Art, how Art, doth Nature spill'.[4]

The woods, as both Aaron and Titus's Ovid have emblazoned them, become repeatedly inscribed with renditions of the rape wherein the mouth is the blood-stained hole that is marked by, yet cannot tell, its story. In anticipation of the events that will unfold in the wood, Aaron declares: 'This is the day of doom for Bassianus, / His Philomel must lose her tongue today' (ii. ii. 42–3). Aaron's emphasis is on the present; 'the day' and 'today' that will witness Lavinia's and Bassianus's ordeal releases Philomel into the active history of their lives, as though she, like the wood 'Patterned by that the poet here describes', is 'By nature' condemned 'for murders and for rapes'. This wood, as it turns out to be 'patterned by the poet', is translated into the mutilated body of Lavinia, who, like a tree, has been 'lopped and hewed . . . Of her two branches, those sweet ornaments / Whose circling shadows kings have

---

[3] William Shakespeare, *Titus Andronicus*, ed. Jonathan Bate, The Arden Shakespeare, 3rd ser. (London: Thomas Learning, 2000), iii. ii. 82–6. All references, unless otherwise stated, are to this edition. Any deviations from the Folio, including stage directions, will be noted.

[4] John Marston, *The Scourge of Villainie*, ed. G. B. Harrison (Edinburgh: Edinburgh University Press, 1966), Satyre I, *Fronti nulla fidel*, 14.

sought to sleep in' (II. iii. 17–19). The artistic and natural fabric of the
paratextual world supports Lavinia, as it is understood to exist through
*Metamorphoses*. Lavinia appears to animate her own history through the
semiotic of the book. Even before Lavinia has discovered her language of
the book, however, her body invites inscription. Titus sees his daughter
as 'a map of woe, that doth talk in signs' (III. ii. 12), from which he will
learn a new language:

> I will learn thy thought.
> In thy dumb action will I be as perfect
> As begging hermits in their holy prayers.
> Thou shalt not sigh, nor hold thy stumps to heaven,
> Nor wink, nor nod, nor kneel, nor make a sign,
> But I of these will wrest an alphabet
> And by still practice learn to know thy meaning.
>
> (III. ii. 39–45)

This language is born out of the 'unspeakable', which, as Lynn Enterline
observes, is central to Ovid's exploration of both representation and
sexuality:

Captivated by the perils of speaking subjectivity—a peril that includes even
the gods—Ovid continually renders these dangers as erotic dramas. In his
hands, the abstract problems of language—its (often tenuous) role as a form of
mediation between mind and world and its power to produce something new
in the world rather than merely represent or describe it—assume a distinctly
sexual guise.[5]

Although Lavinia's body may be eroticized in her silence, it is desexual-
ized by her ordeal. Her body, her form, becomes a 'map of woe'. She
is a surface drawn through by her distress with lines and proportions
that in their physical relation to each other mark her as something to
be deciphered. Her 'signs' imagine the frantic gestures she makes in an
attempt to make herself audible—discernible—locating her ordeal and
its narrative within the body of her presence. Lavinia's body becomes
the book from which Titus will learn to read. Titus charts his process of
learning through imitation; he will 'learn' her 'thought', and from that
thought he will replicate the unspeakable language of its communication, rendering Lavinia readable as he determines to read her. Titus's
analogy to the 'begging' hermit's prayers represents his commitment to

---

[5] Lynn Enterline, *The Rhetoric of the Body from Ovid to Shakespeare* (Cambridge:
Cambridge University Press, 2000), 28.

Lavinia as one of silent devotion bound by a body and a text. Meaning begins to become enmeshed in a developing relationship between the gesture and the sign, which is rooted in the narrative of Lavinia's body. From Lavinia's 'sign' Titus will extrapolate meaning through constant ('still') practice and determine its alphabet. In this way, Titus turns his daughter's silence into the makings of a legible language—an 'alphabet'—through both translation and practice. Humanist ideas of learning—imitation, practice, translation—begin to inform Lavinia's presence on-stage even before her pedagogic relationship to Young Lucius is realized.[6] Since no one can hear Lavinia, reading becomes the central model of signification. The 'alphabet' that begins in Lavinia is put together by those around her, dramatically performing the relationship between reader and text, wherein marks and signs are translated through recognition into a common structure of information and response. Yet we are not asked to 'read' Lavinia in the conventional sense of interpreting the body on-stage, wherein movements, asides, intonation, or irony reveal dual presence, dissimulation or double meaning; rather, we observe Lavinia for the surface, familiar patterns of truth; we must learn, as it were, to read the art as nature. The basic gesture that precedes the knowing world must be transformed by that knowing world into its representational system of signage. Yet Marcus reminds us that this is a potentially arbitrary process when he says of Titus: 'He takes false shadows for true substances' (III. ii. 81). The dramatic presence of the book forces the stage to confront the space between the body and its voice, and the horror of what realism lies in silence.

In the scene that directly precedes the flight of Young Lucius on to the stage, carrying and then scattering his pile of school books, Marcus learns to communicate with Titus by recognizing the different thought processes that make up their realities. This scene depicts Titus, his hand severed, and his family, of whom Lavinia is tongueless and handless, trying to eat together.[7] During the meal a fly enters the room and sparks off in Titus a violent and emotional struggle between representation and recognition, meaning and action. Titus begins by accusing his brother of incessantly reminding him of their predicament: 'O handle not the theme, to talk of hands, / Lest we remember still that we have none' (III. ii. 29–30). Soon after, Titus repents and declares:

---

[6] The Folio's stage direction cites 'young Lucius', and the text refers to him as 'Boy'; for the sake of syntax I will refer to him as 'Young Lucius'.

[7] This scene was not included in the published play until the 1623 Folio.

> Fie, fie, how franticly I square my talk,
> As if we should forget we had no hands
> If Marcus did not name the word of hands.
>
> (III. ii. 31–3)

Titus recognizes that 'the word of hands' bears little or no relationship to his own reality because it no longer signifies simply that part of the body that has been severed from him and Lavinia.[8] The word 'hand' signifies nothing because it does not carry the narrative that supports and surrounds his physical and emotional sphere, and, more importantly, the word has no power to effect their reality. When Marcus kills the fly, Titus demands a justification, which exposes this cognitive shift. Marcus explains that he killed the fly because it was 'coal-black' like Aaron, and sharing a nominal quality with Aaron signifies sameness. Here the word 'black', unlike the word 'hand', acquires a real significance that supports the efficacy of the sign. One of the things this scene demonstrates on an intimate and domestic scale is the process of shared cognition as it is made communication. Marcus and Titus recognize their social processes of thought, and it is through this recognition, and not the sign itself, that they learn to communicate. Once Titus has discovered the book, and Marcus the language, a similar process is available to Lavinia. For Lavinia, her thoughts and signs become both constructed and recognized by the book. The book, Ovid's *Metamorphoses*, forms and reflects the social process of thought in context.

Within these terms, and indeed much of early modern discourse, the role of the book raises questions as to the relationship between Nature and Art. Central to the redeployment of the poetic and aesthetic is a decorous balance between reflecting a pre-existing plenitude and articulating that richness in a fluent and full way. Famously, Jonson's preface to the First Folio affords Shakespeare such a skill: 'For, though the *Poets* matter, Nature be, / His Art doth giue the fashion'.[9] The right relationship between Nature and Art accepts the sign as though it is destined to reflect and familiarize our processes of both thought and language. The arrival of *Metamorphoses* on-stage, and the subsequent

---

[8] The 'hand' has a particular significance in the context of the written word, since the maniscule, or hand with pointing finger, was used in both manuscript and book margins to highlight important passages and paragraph breaks.

[9] Jonson's comment is, of course, tempered by a glance at mortal imperfection, since he appears to want to remind readers that Shakespeare needed to labour for his art: 'And, that he, / Who casts to write a living line, must sweat'.

reactions to the book, signal Art as having become Nature, and it is the response to that Nature that makes a value of Art.

The fly-killing scene comes to a close as Titus suggests to his daughter: 'I'll to thy closet and go read with thee / Sad stories chanced in the times of old' (III. ii. 83–4). Here the book is located as a refuge and an activity in which history will assimilate their relationship and offer comfort. When Young Lucius drops his books and Lavinia frantically searches out pages of Ovid, Titus misinterprets her actions, believing his daughter to be looking for the kind of 'sad stories' he suggested they read together. At this point, Titus stands only on the cusp of understanding, since, despite having dedicated himself to learning the language of his daughter's dumbness, he still observes her within the context of a particular system of thought:

> Some book there is that she desires to see.
> Which is it, girl, of these? Open them, boy.
> [*to Lavinia*][10]
> But thou art deeper read and better skilled:
> Come and take choice of all my library,
> And so beguile thy sorrow till the heavens
> Reveal the damned contriver of this deed.
>
> (IV. i. 31–6)

Soon Titus will realize the appalling irony of the books that lie between them, but here the books and his library lie beyond the bounds of the expressible. The books do not, as yet, enter into the tragedy of their lives. Yet, for Lavinia—and for Young Lucius—they are the very *logos* of the tragedy itself. Despite her family's commitment to reading Lavinia, even emblematically confronted with the material essence of the very process that Titus had earlier described, Marcus cannot decipher her gestures toward the book: 'What means my niece Lavinia by these signs?' (IV. i. 8). Yet, despite failing to relate Lavinia to the book, Marcus construes his niece textually, reassuring Young Lucius of her love for him through a Roman exemplar of maternal pedagogy:

> Ah, boy, Cornelia never with more care
> Read to her sons than she hath read to thee
> Sweet poetry and Tully's *Orator*
> Canst thou not guess wherefore she plies thee thus?
>
> (IV. i. 12–15)

---

[10] Stage direction from the Oxford edition.

Although Marcus reassures Young Lucius through reading, it is also through reading that the boy fears Lavinia:

> And I have read that Hecuba of Troy
> Ran mad for sorrow. That made me to fear,
> Although, my lord, I know my noble aunt
> Loves me as dear as e'er my mother did,
> And would not but in fury fright my youth,
> Which made me down to throw my books and fly,
> Causeless perhaps.
>
> (IV. i. 20–6)

Young Lucius's fear translates his reading into experience, and the aunt, with whom he read, into the subject that he studied: Hecuba's madness is the cognition, and Lavinia is the image that made him 'down to throw my books and fly'. Young Lucius's comment, 'Causeless perhaps', amplifies both the irony and the drama of the book's presence on-stage. Had he not made the textual connection, he would not have dropped his books, and Lavinia might not have found *her* textual precedent. The 'stories chanced of old' that Titus had promised Lavinia to beguile her sorrow until the gods stepped in are not mere adjuncts to their tragedy but the very signs—or 'alphabet'—themselves.

Young Lucius's frantic entrance in flight from Lavinia would probably position the dropped books centre stage.[11] Learning and books are assimilated and thrown directly into the present world of experience. Young Lucius's analogy to Hecuba is, as he well knows, insufficient. The prosaic distance afforded by literary education cannot prepare him for, or contend with, the immediate world of experience, and strategically, at this point, the books lie between him and Lavinia. History and the book are an inadequate bridge between innocence and experience, art and life, imagination and reality. However, although the material volume fractures the platea, carving up the central playing space into areas of the speakable, the readable, and the silent, the book itself seems to support the language of familial relationships. Despite both its generic distance and difference, the book precipitates and recognizes a way back from trauma and miscommunication. Perhaps because, or in spite, of the book's emblematic nature, it presides theatrically over the social body and the dynamic mind. The book lies upon the stage between three generations of readers, all of whom are able to understand each other by

---

[11] This is noted in the Arden edition, p. 216 n. 3.

virtue of the stories they have read and the book that they see. Marcus offers us a history of Lavinia as pedagogue and, like Titus, synthesizes reading and care, books and familial integration. The book provides the way back to communication and the family bonds. During this scene only Ovid's *Metamorphoses* is nominally referred to on-stage. However, the presence of a selection of books is important. Despite the sinister allusions to Ovid's tale from the outset, the material presence of his work here is situated within the recursive dialectic between history and change.[12] The impact of the scene and the importance of the book are directed by the process of choice. If only *Metamorphoses* appeared on-stage, it would speciously position Lavinia as an allegorical figure playing out a recursive historical continuum in which each character on-stage would simply fulfil their role.[13] The books must afford Lavinia a choice, and once that choice has been made, we realize in hindsight that the idea of the book has haunted the drama, as both narrative and aesthetic, like Philomel's 'tedious sampler'. The story of Philomel surfaces within the play through varying degrees of subtlety. Titus, observing Lavinia's frantic attention to the books, asks Young Lucius, 'what book is that she tosseth so?'. When he replies, ''tis Ovid's *Metamorphosis*; / My mother gave it me,' Marcus then makes a connection based on emotion rather than intellect: 'For love of her that's gone, / Perhaps she culled it from among the rest' (IV. i. 43–4). Young Lucius's mother is, of course, Lavinia's sister, yet Marcus's 'her' does not explicitly alert us to the dramatic irony of the sibling relationship.[14] However, Marcus points us to a physical and emotional response to the book that ushers in

[12] Heather James, in her lucid examination of empire and allusion in *Titus*, sees the role of Ovid as most significantly tied not only to the radical dislocation of rhetoric and referent but also to the rejection of Virgil: referring to the infamous scene in which Marcus discovers the body of his niece in high-blown phrases, she writes: 'Marcus . . . inadvertently turns Lavinia's maimed body into an emblem of Virgil's contamination by Ovid. At no other point in this citation-heavy play, not even when he brings on stage a copy of *Metamorphoses* as a prop, does Shakespeare offer his playgoers a greater temptation to pick up Ovid's book and read': *Shakespeare's Troy: Drama, Politics and the Translation of Empire* (Cambridge and New York: Cambridge University Press, 1997), 62.

[13] James L. Calderwood, *Shakespearean Metadrama: The Argument of the Play in 'This Andronicus', 'Love's Labour's Lost', 'Romeo and Juliet', 'A Midsummer Night's Dream', and 'Richard II'* (Minneapolis: University of Minnesota Press, 1971), argues for an allegorical reading of *Titus Andronicus*, in which the play 'metadramatically presents us with a rape of language, with the mutilation that the poet's "tongue" suffers when forced to submit to the rude demands of theatre' (p. 29).

[14] Technically Young Lucius's mother is Lavinia's sister-in-law; however, in the semantics of Elizabethan relations she would be called her 'sister'.

the body of Lavinia's sister, as Procne was to Philomel. Despite the
title of the book, Lavinia's attention to it, and the sisterly relationship,
Marcus does not appear to notice the significance of what he observes.
Later, as Titus plans his revenge, he will return to the story of Procne,
but here *Metamorphoses* seems to emerge on the stage through different
constructions of representation that alert us to the constant negotiations
between the prop, the body, and the voice that the theatre seems to deny
as much as encourage. The idea that we may 'read' language, body, and
symbol points simultaneously to a world of clarity and confusion, for the
relations between such things are always in a state of crisis. The power
of the book's performance often lies in the characters' ignorance of its
significance and, particularly, their lack of awareness of how they read.

The presence of the book, its textual content, and the characters'
use and response to it, again return us to the complex synthesis of
life and art. Despite the shaping force of *Metamorphoses*, the ways
in which the characters treat the text shows the play to resist any
sense of predetermination. Although, after the revelation of Lavinia's
rape, Titus returns us to the wood he hunted in as 'Patterned by
that the poet here describes, / By nature made for murders and rapes'
(IV. i. 57–8), his and Marcus's failure, despite their intention, to
recognize Lavinia's performance (her signs and props, as it were), as
well as the profound irony of some of their observations, prevents the
play from becoming a paradigmatic response to Ovid's tale. Equally,
Titus's appropriation of Procne's revenge and Marcus's reorganization
of Philomel's 'tedious sampler', acknowledges the role of the tale in
informing their cognition rather than dictating their actions. The
play's constant attention to choice makes way for the emergence of
the individual in its fragmentation of the past. Talking of 'a new
literary consciousness' that was emerging in the 1590s, Georgia Brown
specifically locates deviation from classical texts as the sign not only
of individuality but also of transgression; using Thomas Nashe as an
example, she writes:

In the writing of Nashe and the perverse individuality of certain kinds of erotic
and historical writing, a different interpretation of invention finds expression,
one which promotes what is novel in a text and finds value in the ways in which
the text *diverges* from its predecessors and contemporaries. As a consequence,
newness carries associations of transgression.[15]

---

[15] Georgia Brown, *Redefining Elizabethan Literature* (Cambridge: Cambridge University Press, 2004), 45–6.

The complex value system that emerges through the synthesis of newness and transgression renders such individuality both progressive and threatening. As the various characters alight on their changes to the Ovidian text—Aaron's 'improvement' on the mutilation of Philomel, Marcus's translation of the sampler into the sand, and Titus's treatment of Tamora as 'worse' than Procne's—the book becomes an explosive cue for the reinterpretation of experience.

Although Lavinia resembles Philomel in her experience of being raped and mutilated, there is no theatrical sympathy, dramatic or textual, in the comparison. The sympathy that Titus had hoped to find when the book was a diversion, a 'pleasing tale', is quickly destroyed when the text becomes a reality. The book has a role as poetic or prosthetic, but when it crosses the line between life and art, it must be dismantled by the private voice. In this way, the book becomes a radical object of threat, which must be constantly checked by the long lens of history or the distant voice of story. Appealing to Saturnius for his knowledge of Virginius's murder of his violated daughter, Titus explains that the story provides 'A pattern, precedent, and lively warrant / For me, most wretched, to perform the like' (v. iii. 43–4). Titus moves the story of Virginius from the static to the permissive by way of the paradigmatic. The story gives Titus permission to move beyond the boundaries of his cultural reality.

Like the tale of Philomel, the story of Virginius is manifest within the drama as a 'pattern' or 'precedent' that corresponds to an effective language of shared communication. However, Titus observes such a story as a living testimony to, or sanction of, the murder he is about to commit of his daughter. The story of Virginius is reanimated by its pertinence to life, and the living itself is what happens when 'pattern', 'precedent', and experience meet in the 'lively warrant' of the reader. The appalling irony of Titus's language is that he uses it to sanction the death—not the life—of Lavinia, and there is a sense here that the play itself is simply another story, playing out its narrative alongside the recursive texts of Ovid and Livy.[16] In articulating the narratives,

---

[16] Grace Starry West, in, 'Going by the Book: Classical Allusions in Shakespeare's *Titus Andronicus*', *Studies in Philology*, 79 (1982), goes so far as to claim: 'Whether specifically alluding to an ancient poem or not, they all have the education—and the erudition—to speak as if they were characters in a beautiful book' (p. 71). However, her suggestion that the characters' education supports their eloquent narrative of barbarism is in contest with her later claim: 'As Marcus Andronicus' first speech to Lavinia shows, he is apparently incapable of having a thought that does not either immediately point

Titus gives the stories a place in his own world which acknowledges the
truth of his experience. Yet, where story ends and experience begins is
not always clear in the play. The ambiguous interplay of the animate
'lively' and the inanimate 'pattern', as well as recourse to the written at
times of action, and oratory at times of contemplation, does not make
it clear how the play distinguishes *imitatio* from *mimesis*. Paradoxically,
however, it is during the book's performance on-stage that we are given
a moment of clarity as to the ways in which text represents thought.
Although both Marcus and Young Lucius begin to think textually,
observing Lavinia within the context of Cornelia and Hecuba, neither
character initially makes the present connection between the book and
experience. However, once Lavinia has located the tale of Philomel and
'signed' her attachment to it, Marcus advances his niece towards her
own text:

> My Lord, look here; look here, Lavinia.
> *He writes his name with his staff,*
> *And guides it with feet and mouth.*[17]
> This sandy plot is plain. Guide, if thou canst,
> This after me. I here have writ my name
> Without the help of any hand at all.
> Cursed be that heart that forced us to this shift.
> Write thou, good niece, and here display at last
> What God will have discovered for revenge.
> Heaven guide thy pen to print thy sorrows plain,
> That we may know the traitors and the truth.
>
> (IV. i. 68–76)

The presence of the book on-stage provides a graphic recognition of
the ways in which written language can provide a 'lively warrant' for
modes of being. Yet at the same time the vision of the book reminds
us of the impossible plight of the body that lies between speaking and
writing. Marcus continues to deploy Lavinia through the written word,
'Without the help of any hand at all'; and as he marks the sand with
his mouth and staff, the natural and the textual world meet as a version

---

to some literary precedent or take its inspiration from an event made beautiful by
literature. . . . So Marcus looks at the pitiful Lavinia from a poetic distance, then speaks
to her and of her in a thoroughly literary way. His obsession with beautiful speech has
made him silly and ineffectual' (p. 73). It seems unlikely that 'beautiful speech' can
render someone 'silly and ineffectual', whilst at the same time supporting his or her
position as a character in 'a beautiful book'.

[17] Stage direction, Q1.

of the self in crisis. Some ten years later in *Hamlet*, Shakespeare will develop the relationship between Nature and Art under the conditions of extremity, but here, as 'Cursed be the heart that forced us to this shift', Marcus extends the presence of the book for Lavinia to reconcile her body to the plight of her heart. Although, as Enterline says, 'Rhetoric, in the story of Philomela's tongue and tapestry, means taking the idea of symbolic action very seriously. It means acknowledging that the body is both a bearer of meaning as well as a linguistic agent, a place where representation, materiality, and action collide';[18] but the body becomes such a bearer of meaning only under duress, and symbolic action is the action of the powerless. The representational power of the materiality of the book alongside the materiality of the body shows the inadequacy of the body to bear the meaning of silence. Equally, however, the scene in which Young Lucius flies across the stage dropping his books is the child's most significant role within the entire play, and there is a sense in which his body is simply a vehicle for the books, rather than the other way around.[19] Young Lucius is literally the bearer of meaning. In the light of this, we begin to see how the book performs, and how its material presence and voices of the past share the stage with the Andronici. What we learn from the book, however, is how to read and, above all, interpret the space, learned or improvised, between the body and the mind. Reading remains central to the dynamic between character and narrative throughout the play, so that as the poet patterned the woods, Chiron and Demetrius patterned Ovid, Lavinia patterns Marcus, and Titus will pattern Procne and Virginius. As the various characters imitate, translate, or transgress their texts or selves, the play suggests that there is some essential, even authentic, 'book' from which all such stories began. If such a book is Nature, if Ovid's woods are self-generating in their tragedy, if, as Marcus says, 'O, why should nature build so foul a den / Unless the god's delight in tragedies?' (iv. i. 59–60), then all action is recursive as it plays out meaning in the fabric of its existence. But again we return to the central humanist and humanizing imperative of *Titus*, which is choice. The characters find their own humanities, however dubious those humanities might be, in the pursuit of their chosen ends, and we might see the tragedy of *Titus Andronicus* in Titus's initial denial of free will in the sacrifice of

---

[18] Enterline, *Rhetoric of the Body*, 6.

[19] Young Lucius also appears in the 'fly-killing' scene and the play's close; in both instances he has only one, brief speech.

Tamora's son. Grace Starry West, however, sees the play's juxtaposition of 'education' and 'barbarism' as confounding the essence of humanism or the right moral virtues of teaching:

Shakespeare has his former schoolboys, Chiron and Demetrius, use Ovid as a manual for successful crime. They have learned from Tereus' mistake as reported by the source and have cut off their victim's hands in addition to her tongue. Their brutal understanding and its pitiful results certainly ought to make us pause, those of us at least who believe education and learning always make men better, more civilized, and, ultimately, wise. These Goths are as civilised and as humane as Roman letters can make them. Yet their learning does not lead to wisdom; it only enables them to add refinement to their barbarism.[20]

Although Starry West maintains that 'Shakespeare's characters do learn from Ovid's book; but they learn how to be evil, not good', she sees education as providing the ability to 'refine' barbarism rather than exclude it. Yet the book in *Titus*, including its allusions, materializes the cognitive process between thinking and acting, and in allowing meaning to surface from silence, horror, and tragedy recalls the body to its basic human rights. How those human rights are exercised is not the province of the book alone, because the book is not essential or authentic, but in constant conversation with the bodies that surround it. The play's references to textual narratives acknowledge the efficacy of a shared cognition and the power of the interpretive will. Aaron's anticipation of the rape—'Philomel must lose her tongue today' (II. ii. 43)—or Titus's banquet reflect the play's events within the context of a linear narrative that is under constant disruption by its 'readers'. The book is dramatically effective, since it acknowledges the processes which normally take place on the margins of the discernible; through materializing thinking, silence, and translation, the presence of the book and its narrative show us how 'reading' is always taking place on the periphery of experience. When Aaron guides Tamora's sons to the rape of Lavinia, he describes the decorum of the wood:

> The emperor's court is like the house of Fame,
> The palace full of tongues, of eyes and ears;
> The woods are ruthless, dreadful, deaf and dull:
> There speak and strike, brave boys, and take your turns.
>
> (I. i. 626–9)

---

[20] West, 'Going by the Book', 72.

The woods shade the boys 'from heaven's eye', and, in contrast to the court, keep their secret. If Aaron devises Lavinia's ordeal from his reading of Ovid, Chiron and Demetrius learn from Aaron, who in 'improving' on the poet with the device of severing Lavinia's hands, translates his reading into the text of Lavinia's experience. Equally, it is only in hindsight that Titus recognizes these woods as made for 'murders and for rapes', 'patterned' by 'the poet', where they had once been made for hunting and were 'green' with the promise of love for Tamora and Aaron. If, as Starry West believes, education precipitates the tragedies, it also redresses them. The moment when Lavinia finds Ovid's book amongst Young Lucius's pile is a moment of profound dramatic relief, since the textual allusions that have hitherto supported the play are physically manifest as a source for change. The book is an outlet for human suffering because, irrespective of voice or tense, it brings both order and expression to trauma and revenge. Whether it is the dumbness of mutilation, or 'grief' 'like an oven stopped', *Metamorphoses* re-engages the characters in an effective awareness of their own condition; how far the book dictates that condition is dependent upon how we are guided through their processes of reading.

Yet how far the graphic text supports the endurance of human history is to some extent complicated by the very nature of Ovid's text in representing change and the metamorphic or even metaphorical relationship between story and event. On the one hand, the written word is manifest as the prehistory of experience, whether Lavinia may 'beguile' her 'sorrow' in 'sad stories chanced in the times of old' or tell her story in the tragic tale of Philomel. On the other, the written word enables transformation, locating the names of the rapists or outlining the 'complot' of their nemesis. The distinction between the book and the written word is that the book provides the dramatic moment of anagnorisis, representing 'story' as a point of mutual cognition beyond the requisites of speech or time, and exposing 'reading' as the cognitive process through which we bear meaning into our lives. Although Titus had suggested that the book might play this role, until Lavinia makes contact with *Metamorphoses*, he had not acknowledged the 'lively warrant' of its text.

When Tamora and her two sons, disguised as Revenge, Rapine, and Murder, seek Titus, they find him in his study, bearing 'papers':

> Who doth molest my contemplation?
> Is it your trick to make me ope the door,

> That so my sad decrees may fly away
> And all my study be to no effect?
> You are deceived, for what I mean to do
> See here in bloody lines I have set down,
> And what is written shall be executed.
>
> (v. ii. 9–15)

Titus's 'bloody lines', set down as he studies in contemplation, probably turn out to be the designs for his vengeful banquet, and, as such, come back into contact with *Metamorphoses*: 'For worse than Philomel you used my daughter, / So worse than Progne I will be revenged' (v. ii. 194–5). Titus, like Aaron, improves on art in devising something 'worse' than the book had set down. In extending the boundaries of Ovid's tale, Titus reclaims the text as his own as he writes the 'bloody lines' and determines that 'what is written shall be executed'. Yet the allusion to Ovid's tale engages the audience with theories of reading; we understand Titus's action in terms of revenge, but, perhaps more significantly, we hear him respond to the narrative as potential for action. Perhaps Titus has come so much to believe in the power of the written word to inform history that not only shall what is written be executed but who is written shall be executed too. In simply writing the denouement to Lavinia's tragic tale, Titus goes some way to fulfilling, or 'decreeing', its substance.

Titus appears to develop this belief in the written word after Lavinia's performance with the book; seeing Lavinia's revelation in the sand, he exclaims that 'The angry northern wind'

> Will blow these sands like Sibyl's leaves abroad,
> And where's our lesson then?
>
> (IV. i. 105–6)

Titus needs to transform the ephemeral lines upon the sand into something graphic and indelible:

> Let alone,
> And come, I will go get a leaf of brass
> And with a gad of steel will write these words,
> And lay it by.
>
> (IV. i. 101–4)

Whereas reading provided the window into Lavinia's story, Titus understands inscription as an expression of effective reality—something that, like his 'bloody lines', will render the 'lesson' permanent. However, despite the proliferation of the written in *Titus*, within the play-world the characters' assume an intimate, isolated, or merely allusive relationship to their written material. When Titus encourages his daughter to explore Ovid's text: 'Give signs, sweet girl—for here are none but friends—' (IV. i. 61), he does so within the private context of intimate relations, or when Aaron refers to the terrible dark wood in which Tamora's sons will attack Lavinia, all is shielded 'from heaven's eye', including the allusion. When Titus sends Chiron and Demetrius 'a verse on Horace', Aaron mordantly observes:[21]

> The old man hath found their guilt,
> And sends them weapons wrapped about with lines
> That wound beyond their feeling to the quick.
>
> (IV. ii. 26–8)

As Titus protected his 'bloody lines' from the eyes of his visitors, or sent his missives to the gods, 'Sweet scrolls to fly about the streets of Rome' (IV. iv. 16), text and textual allusions do not fully acknowledge a consensual awareness of the play-world until the play's final scene, and, even here, Saturninus responds with some confusion as to Titus's point.

Titus extracts his own history from that of Procne and Virginius. He sets his world against the written word, for 'more than that tongue that more hath more expressed', and, in doing so, such books become the 'eloquence and dumb presagers of . . . [his] speaking breast' (Sonnet 23). Titus has responded to the rape of Lavinia with a quotation from the same play through which Demetrius had anticipated it.[22] The text, whether Ovidian or Senecan, remains the locus for the characters in this scene, but as with his response to the fly and Aaron, Titus must learn how to be effective amidst 'false shadows . . . [and] true substances' (III. ii. 81). Before Titus engages with Lavinia and the book, he denies the telling of tales, through a textual allusion, which reflect life: 'Ah, wherefore dost thou urge the name of hands / To bid Aeneas tell the tale twice o'er / How Troy was burnt and he made miserable?' (III. ii. 26–8). Titus makes a distinction between 'Sad stories chanced in the times of old', 'some pleasing tale', and those which 'handle . . . the theme' (III. ii. 84, 47, 29), rejecting the last for reminding him of his life.

---

[21] Stage direction: *aside*, Johnson.

[22] Demetrius, in his anticipation of the act in I. i. 635, quotes from *Hippolytus*; Titus 'reacts to the discovery of it with a quotation from the same play': Bate, Arden Shakespeare, p. 216 nn. 81–2.

When the book surfaces, however, to 'wrest an alphabet' from the speechless Lavinia, to order a pattern for the chaos of their condition, or to anticipate resolution and justify revenge, the written word and its precedent offer an effective means of relief that does not teach the Romans evil but recognizes their experience of it. In *The Rape of Lucrece*, Tarquin tells us that 'Thoughts are but dreams till their effects be tried' (l. 353),[23] and in this way, books are just 'thoughts' until they represent a 'lively warrant' for life. *Titus Andronicus* is replete with ideas of learning, yet ultimately what the play engages in are processes of reading and misreading. In redeploying and imaging the book, the play performs ways in which we assimilate the written when it comes into contest with the real. However, to some extent, recourse to quotation or textual parallel is conventional in tragedy. In Thomas Kyd's *The Spanish Tragedy*, Hieronimo, grief-stricken and desperate for the revenge of his son's murder, enters reading a book. The book is Seneca's *Agamemnon*, and during his frantic soliloquy he quotes, in Latin, justifications and inspirations to enact his bloody revenge. The point of Hieronimo's book is that it turns him away from Christian patience and trust in divine vengeance to active personal revenge. Hieronimo appears not to have sought the book for this purpose, but alights on its precepts accidentally, even though he holds it in his hand. Previously, Hieronimo had expressed the agony of silence forced upon him in his quest for justice:

> I find the place impregnable; and they
> Resist my woes, and give my words no way.
>
> (III. vii. 17–18)[24]

The book inspires him to revenge and releases him from silence because it recognizes a version of giving his words a 'way' without resistance.

Yet, as Hieronimo finds revenge in the Old Testament, Titus infanticide in Livy, and Lavinia's ordeal is pre-empted by Ovid, we realize the profound limitations of the texts themselves. In recognizing the lively warrant of history, we also become aware of its inadequacies. Francis Bacon, in his approach to the intellectual development of the self, advises a rational objectivity in relation to either books or experience, in order to properly understand and interact with the world.

[23] Shakespeare, *Narrative Poems*; all references are to this edition.

[24] Thomas Kyd, *The Spanish Tragedy*, ed. J. R. Mulryne (London: A. & C. Black, 1989).

Neither can the experience of one man's life furnish examples and precedents for the events of another man's life: for as it happeneth sometimes that the grandchild or other descendent resembleth the ancestor more than the son; so many times occurrences of present times may sort better with ancient examples than those of the later or immediate times.[25]

And equally 'ancient examples' may resemble experience, but they cannot respond to it. 'Examples', 'ancient', or of 'the later or immediate times', furnish the reader with a network of communication through which he or she can move. This 'network of communication', as Vološinov claims, humanizes, 'since one cannot exist outside the network(s) of communication and remain human'.[26] The book re-presents networks of communication when the human is compromised. Lavinia, through her mutilation and rape, is rendered socially and culturally inhuman; bound by a society in which revenge can, to some extent, imitate justice, she can neither communicate her ordeal nor kill herself. The book proffers its pages as a 'network of communication' wherein those choices—revenge or suicide—can be restored. Predicated on humanism, the book humanizes; yet not in terms of signifying sapience, but rather as a way to transform silence, through the shared voice of literature, into the sound of something familiar and therefore sympathetic. In *Cymbeline*, the 'sympathy' that Posthumus observes in Jupiter's tablet might be expanded in terms of 'a (real or supposed) affinity between certain things, by virtue of which they are similarly or correspondingly affected by the same influence'.[27] The 'same influence' may recognize Warwick's injunction to Henry IV that 'There is a history in all men's lives', and the nature of the book to reflect experience, story, or even a version of the self, as Montaigne declares, 'my book and I go hand in hand together, and keep one apace', acknowledges a corresponding force between reading and being.[28] Yet, where, as in *Titus*, the text is realized in transgressing the material and perverting the reader, in *Cymbeline* constructions of reading are normalized through the triumph of life over art. Despite existing on the hinterland of their dramatic realization, both books, Imogen's *Metamorphoses* and Jupiter's tablet,

[25] Brian Vickers (ed.), *Francis Bacon: A Critical Edition of the Major Works* (Oxford and New York: Oxford University Press, 1996), 128.

[26] James R. Siemon, *Word against Word: Shakespearean Utterance* (Amherst, Mass., and Boston: University of Massachusetts Press A 2002), 25.

[27] *OED*, 1.a.

[28] Michel de Montaigne, *Essays*, trans. J. M. Cohen (Harmondsworth: Penguin, 1983), 237.

mark decisive turning-points—crudely, from comedy to tragedy, and from tragedy to comedy—in the play's action.

One of the first things we may notice about Shakespeare's books on-stage is that they often appear in the hands of women.[29] Imogen and Lavinia are Shakespeare's most significant 'readers', yet the book also appears strategically in the hands of Bianca (*The Shrew*) and Ophelia (*Hamlet*). Both Lavinia and Imogen read Ovid's *Metamorphoses* at critical moments in the play's action. Yet, whilst *Titus Andronicus* may explore action through the perversion of reading, *Cymbeline* looks behind the book in its exploration of the relationship between art and the imagination. In the context of Imogen's scene, the book and its textual allusions function simultaneously as a record of Iachimo's thoughts, a gesture of Imogen's vulnerability, and a prop in the construction of a bedroom scene. The dual ability of the book to appear as both poignant and ephemeral extends the dramatic space beyond the materiality of the stage and into the realms of the psychological. In contrast to *Titus*, where we notice the book's role in disrupting the unified reader, in *Cymbeline* both Imogen's and Posthumus's books appear at moments of intense privacy or isolation; strange intruders, Iachimo or the Leonati ghosts, however, complicate the relationship between the book and isolation.

We are taken into Imogen's bedroom through the wager between Posthumus and Iachimo that sets her virtue at the price of a bracelet. Iachimo's duplicitous means of gaining access to her privacy creates a dual sense of reality wherein we move from one perspective to another in the material and emotional construction of the scene. The scene begins as Imogen 'enter[s]' 'in her bed'. She has been reading for 'three hours' and, as it is 'almost midnight', asks her lady, Helen, to 'fold down the leaf where I have left'. Imogen asks for the taper to remain alight and falls asleep. Within the first few lines of the scene Imogen has been caught between her own story, her reading, and that of Iachimo, who narrates the action. However, at this point, we become aware of Imogen's plight only through the allusions of Iachimo's whispers. As Imogen falls asleep, Iachimo emerges from the trunk. At this moment we know only that Imogen has been reading a 'book', and it is Iachimo who immediately, and yet intertextually, takes up the narrative by way of 'Our Tarquin'. A

---

[29] The main exceptions to this are Hamlet and Henry VI, and exclude certain ambivalent references to *The Book of Common Prayer* which may or may not be put into the hands of various characters according to the director's discretion. References to 'reading' also occur in relation to the characters of Richard III, Brutus, Benedict, and Ulysses.

little later we will discover that, since Imogen was reading *Metamorphoses* and that the leaf is turned down at the tale of Philomel, she and Iachimo are 'reading' similar narratives within different 'books'. Yet, significantly, the book lies beside the sleeping body of Imogen, imaginatively and dramatically suspending her history within the pages of Iachimo's active dreams and her passive nightmare. For Iachimo, however, the parallel tale of Tarquin and Lucrece emanates from an independent desire which appears to emerge almost unconsciously.

As Iachimo surfaces from the trunk, he observes how 'Our Tarquin thus / Did softly press the rushes' (II. ii. 12–13), noticing Tarquin in the hushed fall of his own feet.[30] Or, a little later in his speech, when Iachimo sees the incriminating mole on Imogen's breast and declares: 'this secret / Will force him think I have pick'd the lock, and ta'en / The treasure of her honour' (II. ii. 40–2), he finds a similar analogy to Tarquin's extended assault in his approach to Lucrece's bedchamber, where 'his guilty hand plucked up the latch' (l. 358). The seething mass of Tarquin's desire, ambition, and determination that sets *The Rape of Lucrece* to a heart rhythm is condensed to a mere allusion, ironically lost through the single perspective of Iachimo, who, failing to harness the potential of his own references or Imogen's reading, very nearly lets the entire drama of this scene slip through his speech. Yet, as Jonathan Culler puts it, 'intertextuality is less a name for a work's relation to particular prior texts than an assertion of a work's participation in a discursive space and its relation to the codes which are potential formalisations of that space'.[31] The dramatic dynamic between Lucrece and Philomel ushers constructions of reading onto the stage that destabilize such formal divisions between genre and form. When Iachimo first meets Imogen, we find traces of Shakespeare's Tarquin in his response. Attempting to discern the nature of 'admiration' through the 'eye', 'judgement', or the 'appetite', Iachimo declares:

> Sluttery, to such neat excellence oppos'd,
> Should make desire vomit emptiness,
> Not so allur'd to feed.
>
> (I. vii. 44–6)

---

[30] Stanley Wells and Gary Taylor see the trunk in this scene as 'supply[ing] a potent visual image of his [Iachimo's] ascent from and descent into "hell" '. Stanley Wells and Gary Taylor, with John Jowett and William Montgomery (eds.), *William Shakespeare: A Textual Companion* (Oxford: Clarendon Press, 1987), p. 605.

[31] As cited by Brown, *Redefining Elizabethan Literature*, 36.

Whilst after the rape of Lucrece we are told:

> Drunken Desire must vomit his receipt
> Ere he can see his own abomination.
>
> (ll. 703–4)

Rather than demarcate the boundaries between the mind and the body or the stage and the page, Iachimo's language penetrates the scene with a sense of *déjà vu*, as though the immediate action is in constant conversation with its prehistory. Although Iachimo appears to transfer his desire for Imogen onto an apocryphal tale of Posthumus's lust, and although he assaults her virtue only symbolically in the removal of the bracelet, the allusive glances to Tereus and Tarquin are suggestive of an attack that is construed in reading. In *The Rape of Lucrece* the language of the book or text is often manifest as a gloss for sexual innocence or experience; noting the following verse, John Kerrigan writes: 'If Tarquin misreads, Lucrece fails to interpret. Innocence makes her illiterate, incapable of discerning Sextus' intent':[32]

> But she that never coped with stranger eyes
> Could pick no meaning from their parling looks,
> Nor read the subtle shining secrecies
> Writ in the glassy margents of such books.
>
> (ll. 99–102)

Later, however, Lucrece understands her rape as illuminated and written for all, even the illiterate, to read:

> The light will show charactered in my brow
> The story of sweet chastity's decay,
> The impious breach of holy wedlock vow;
> Yea, the illiterate that know not how
> To cipher what is writ in learnèd books
> Will quote my loathsome trespass in my looks.
>
> (ll. 807–12)

Even as she could not read, Lucrece will be read, and the book draws both the innocent and the abused into its semantic field. Imogen's sleeping body lies within this discursive space, which the book promotes, signifying experience or 'learning' in its most perverse sense.

---

[32] John Kerrigan, 'Keats and Lucrece', *Shakespeare Survey*, 41 (1989), 107.

Imogen's direction to the book before she sleeps may enable the allusive fabric of Iachimo's thoughts to emerge, and those thoughts, though they may be 'but dreams till their effects be tried' (l. 353), hang about the presence of the book with profound dramatic potential. The dynamic between the written and the dramatic word is to some extent amplified in the juxtaposition of 'forms'; whilst Imogen's book appears in material form on-stage, Iachimo's 'text', the tale of *The Rape of Lucrece*, decorates, through ecphrasis, the texture of the room. The way Lucrece's hair plays about her pillow as she breathes and Tarquin's 'drumming heart' and 'flaming torch' heighten the visual drama of Shakespeare's poem; we are told how Tarquin, having entered Lucrece's bedchamber with 'new ambition bred', responds: 'What could he see but mightily he noted? / What did he note but strongly he desired?' (ll. 414–15). Seeing, noting, and desiring become symbiotic activities, and noting, Tarquin's capture and retention of certain images, forms the compulsive link between perception and action. The external, visual image and the internal, mental image are supported by the word 'note' as if the eye and imagination respond to a single linear narrative. 'Note', however, carries a double meaning here, suggesting both record and distinguishing feature; Iachimo traces the word though both meanings:

> But my design.
> To note the chamber: I will write all down:
> Such, and such pictures: there the window, such
> Th' adornment of her bed; the arras, figures,
> Why, such, and such; and the contents o' th' story.
> Ah, but some natural notes about her body
> Above ten thousand meaner moveables
> Would testify, t'enrich mine inventory.
>
> (II. ii. 23–30)

Discussing the relationship between language and the body in Ovid's Metamorphoses, Enterline focuses on the word *Nota*:

On her tapestry, Philomela weaves a set of purple "notae," a noun that, as Marder observes, suggests several divergent yet crucial meanings. *Nota* may signify a written character—a mark of writing used to represent "a sound, letter, or word". It may signify the "vestige" or "trace" of something, like a footprint. It may also designate a mark or a stigma or disgrace particularly an identifying brand on the body. . . . Artist of her own trauma, Philomela sits down to translate something—an event, a body—that cannot be translated:

rape is an unspeakable sound; the medium of its communication, a "barbaric" loom; the "notes" that represent it, neither letter, mark, nor physical imprint.[33]

The 'natural notes' on Imogen's body and the 'notes' that Iachimo takes of the scene are translated by the reading material near at hand. Passive, even beautiful, Imogen's mole becomes a 'stigma' through the text of Iachimo's intent. Yet in Golding's translation 'nota' becomes 'letter':

> A warpe of white upon a frame of Thracia she did pin,
> And weaved purple letters in betweene it, which bewraid
> The wicked deede of Tereus.
>
> (vi. 736–8)

The dialectic between the 'note' and the 'letter' construes the body as a text to be both marked and read, or stigmatized and misread. Later, in response to the letters that Pisanio gave her establishing the assignation at Milford Haven, Imogen declares, 'To write, and read / Be henceforth treacherous' (IV. ii. 316–17). Against the normalized context of bedtime reading, the idea of the book threatens to disrupt meaning and destroy the female body.

Iachimo's semantic shift adumbrates one of the ways in which this scene asks us to register the dynamic between the visual and the written. 'The contents of th' story' could be the story he will tell Posthumus, the tale of the tapestry he later mentions, the visual narrative he will construct from the contents of the room, or Imogen's book and Ovid's *Metamorphoses*. Although Iachimo does not create a particularly detailed picture, the juxtapositions of writing, note, story, and body, alongside his own allusion to Tarquin, explores his experience through a synthesis of text and image that opens the dramatic space to the inference of Imogen's reading:

> She hath been reading late,
> The tale of Tereus, here the leaf's turn'd down
> Where Philomel gave up. I have enough.
>
> (II. ii. 44–6)

Yet just before Iachimo picks up Imogen's book, which of course he must do to notice both the contents and the folded leaf, he suddenly decides:

---

[33] Enterline, *Rhetoric of the Body*, 4–5.

No more: to what end?
Why should I write this down, that's riveted,
Screw'd to my memory?

(II. ii. 42–4)

Having seen the 'voucher' of Imogen's mole, Iachimo rejects the written
in favour of his memory, taking the 'note' of her body as the central
loci of his mnemonic storehouse. His observation of *Metamorphoses* is
the last observation he makes, and since he has gleaned enough—'No
more: to what end?'—it appears to play no part in the configuration of
Iachimo's picture or mental story. Although he must at least handle the
book to discover its turned-down page, and must read at least some part
of it to register 'the tale of Tereus', his reference seems both in passing
and dismissive. Yet 'the tale of Tereus', like that of Tarquin, is central to
the dramatic potential of the scene as it ushers in the reader to contend
with the voices and shadows that lie between the body of Imogen and
the mind of Iachimo.

In the symbolic construction of good and evil, light and dark often
become signifiers of a moral fabric. In *Lucrece*, the darkness contained by
closed eyes supports the innocence of not seeing, and, in not seeing, the
eyes are closed to the presence of evil. When Tarquin enters Lucrece's
chamber, her virtue shines through the dark of her shrouded room:

Even so, the curtain drawn, his eyes begun
To wink, being blinded with a greater light.
Whether it is that she reflects so bright
That dazzleth them, or else some shame supposed,
But blind they are, and keep themselves enclosed.

(ll. 374–8)

As Tarquin is briefly 'blinded' by Lucrece, he is kept from the sin of his
own desires as well as the vision that inspires them:

O, had they in that darksome prison died,
That they had seen the period of their ill!
.     .     .     .     .     .     .
But they must ope, this blessèd league to kill;
And holy-thoughted Lucrece to their sight
Must sell her joy, her life, her world's delight.

(ll. 379–80, 383–5)

Contrary to our expectations, darkness provides the moral relief from
sin, since sin is predicated on seeing. The gloaming of Imogen's

bedchamber suspends her narrative between the light and dark of Iachimo's presence, just as Imogen's closed eyes—if only Tarquin's had remained so—protect her from the violation of his presence. As the light dawns, 'Swift, swift, you dragons of the night, that dawning / May bare the raven's eye!' (II. ii. 48–9), Imogen has been dramatically suspended between four narratives, her own and Iachimo's, and Tereus's and Tarquin's, which have dressed the room in 'notes' and pages, books, and allusions. This scene marks a turning-point in the play, which we might crudely construe as from 'comedy' to 'tragedy'; releasing Imogen into a world of dissimulation, murder, violence, and exile predicated on misreading: 'To write, and read / Be henceforth treacherous' (IV. ii. 316–17). But whereas in *Titus* the written becomes the perverted prehistory of personal action, in *Cymbeline* written words are often displaced, ineffective, overwritten, or merely forgotten. Pisanio does not carry out Posthumus's injunction to murder his wife, and Imogen wakes up next to the headless body of Cloten, believing herself to have been betrayed by her friend. The book in Imogen's bedchamber adumbrates the possible and articulates the imagination; it neither foretells nor concludes, since it remains a passive accessory to the scene. Despite having read for three hours, Imogen never actually reaches the terrible moment of Philomel's violation, and despite Iachimo's careful rendition of the room, his artful mnemonics, loci, and attention to detail, he never mentions the book again. *Metamorphoses* amplified and contextualized the recesses of Iachimo's fantasy, but played no narrative or physical role in the evolution of their ultimate realities. Neither character takes up the book; whilst Imogen puts it down, Iachimo merely observes its presence. Since Iachimo communicates his desire through Tarquin rather than Tereus, and since Imogen is unaware of the threat to her, the book plays its part for the audience, teaching us to read the subtle secrecies of Iachimo's presence. The book is the sign to which the dramatic depth of the scene is referred but not realized. For the moment that it was on-stage, the book took Iachimo's language into the level of Imogen's dreams. Once he leaves, such dreams and such pages dissolve into thin air. Much like the play-within-a-play, the presence of the book serves to expose and image the processes through which we identify the real. The heavy shadows of *Metamorphoses* and the tale of Philomel signify what did not happen to Imogen, rather than what did. However, despite Iachimo's departure at the notice of 'where Philomel gave up', the tale is not over; the imaginative assault on Imogen almost reaches its experiential conclusion in Cloten's intention to rape her dressed as Posthumus: 'With that suit upon my back, will I ravish her' (III. v. 138–9). Cloten is of course apprehended and murdered by an irate Guiderius before he can get to Imogen, but the threat to her virtue and life, posed by the allusions to *Lucrece* and the visible presence of *Metamorphoses*, does not disappear with the close of the scene or its 'books'. Rather, Iachimo unleashes a devastating narrative that gathers momentum toward profound consequences, until Posthumus, imprisoned and sentenced to death, falls asleep, and, like his wife, wakes up next to a book.

When all seems lost to Posthumus—he has been captured and fettered, awaiting death, wrongfully ordered the murder of his wife, and lost his faithful servant—he is brought on to the stage between two gaolers. Shortly after their departure, Posthumus sleeps, during which time the ghosts of his dead family appear. At first Posthumus wakes from his dream/vision to find 'nothing' (v. iv. 129), yet reflecting on that nothing he realizes that in such a dream he is blessed:

> But, alas, I swerve:
> Many dream not to find, neither deserve,
> And yet are steep'd in favours; so am I,
> That have this golden chance, and know not why.
>
> (v. iv. 129–32)

Posthumus knows it was more than a dream—'What fairies haunt this ground?'—and in turning from 'nothing' to 'this golden chance', he sees the book:[34]

> A book? O rare one,
> Be not, as is our fangled world, a garment
> Nobler than it covers.
>
> (v. iv. 133–5)

---

[34] The inscription that Jupiter lays on Posthumus's breast is in fact only a short paragraph, and later Posthumus refers to it as a 'label'; thus in strictly semantic terms it is not a 'book' (given that a book is a 'collection of sheets of paper fastened together'). It does, however, have a 'cover', which suggests something more than a single sheet. My inquiry is based upon Shakespeare's use of the word 'book' and how and when that word is manifest in reference to a material object. Since Posthumus initially recognizes Jupiter's tablet as 'a book', I have taken the word to signify something more than a sheet of paper. I suggest that the idea of the book is employed since it signifies something greater, more inscrutable, or even more recondite in the arms of Jupiter than a single sheet. Equally, a 'tablet' might conjure an image of something in stone, marble, or even metal, but as Posthumus carries it about him for the rest of the play, we must assume that it is reasonably, and discretely, portable.

His observation of the book marks the turning-point from the dream to the present, as well as being a vestige of the 'reality' of both; the book bridges the space between those two states and physically testifies to a relationship between them. The language of Posthumus's response directs our attention to ways in which the book might appear; in order for Posthumus to express the hope that this book, unlike 'our fangled world', may be as good as it seems, we may assume the book to be visually exciting. The attention to 'fangled', 'garment', and 'cover' suggests a material quality of some decoration. On the other hand, it may be the sheer presence of the book and the arresting circumstances through which it appears that lead Posthumus to approach it with a mixture of suspicion and excitement. However the book is theatrically presented, it harbours a dramatic significance in its very essence. Like Imogen's book, however, not only does it accompany Posthumus's sleep; it also remains in the hinterland of his proper awareness. He, like Shakespeare's Lucrece, is figuratively illiterate, yet whereas Lucrece's illiteracy is attached to her innocence, Posthumus's illiteracy is a product of his ignorance. As Posthumus reads, he also fails to read, returning to the quality of the dream for its support of irrational construction: ''Tis still a dream: or else such stuff as madmen / Tongue, and brain not' (v. iv. 146–7). Yet Posthumus is right to find refuge in his dream, and its sense in senselessness, for it is at this point and during this scene that the book signifies anagnorisis.

Posthumus's use of the word 'rare', combined with the strange synthesis of dream and vision, recalls 'Bottom's dream'. When, in *A Midsummer Night's Dream*, Bottom wakes from the caresses of a drugged Titania, he declares: 'I have had a most rare vision. I have had a dream past the wit of man to say what dream it was' (IV. i. 203–4). Bottom cannot understand his dream or vision, and, like Posthumus's, his experience both is and is not. Whilst Jupiter's tablet and the ghosts' verse adumbrate things past and things to come, Bottom's rare vision signifies the play-world's subversion of sensory reality, which, although it is ultimately rejected, foregrounds the play's attention to perception. Both uses of the word 'rare' seem to signal a sensory distortion, but one that needs to be taken seriously. Bottom's admission that he can neither understand nor describe his experience suggests both his acceptance and the significance of what has occurred: 'The eye of man hath not heard, the ear of man hath not seen, man's hand is not able to taste, his tongue to conceive, nor his heart to report what my dream was' (IV. i. 204–7). Although a moment of comedy, Bottom's synaesthesia also reflects the interference of the fairy or cosmic world, as the faculties of man are disturbed by unearthly intervention. The kind of madness that Bottom describes as he wrenches our senses from their proper place is similar to Posthumus's appraisal of his own experience having read Jupiter's book:

> 'Tis still a dream: or else such stuff as madmen
> Tongue, and brain not: either both, or nothing,
> Or senseless speaking, or a speaking such
> As sense cannot untie. Be what it is,
> The action of my life is like it, which I'll keep,
> If but for sympathy.
>
>                                                    (v. iv. 146–51)

Jupiter's text, although indecipherable to Posthumus, offers a possible narrative of resolution with which the audience is already familiar; we know that the 'lopped branches' of Cymbeline in the shape of Guiderius and Arviragus have survived, and that the 'lion's whelp', Posthumus, shall embrace Imogen, the 'tender air'. Posthumus, however, finds no meaning in the words themselves, but only in their strange configuration, and even though more 'like a dream than an assurance', he finds the book sympathetic, since in impression it resembles the 'action' of his life. Yet Posthumus takes this book and its 'sympathy' as a valediction, since he believes he is about to die. Whereas for the audience Jupiter's book provides a vision of relief and resolution, for Posthumus it is simply a talisman that affords him some comfort in a 'sense' he 'cannot untie'.

Like Lavinia's *Metamorphoses*, Posthumus's book is a way back into the play-world; yet, unlike Lavinia, Posthumus cannot appropriate the text for its potential relief. The significance of the book is echoed ironically in the language of the gaoler. Since Posthumus had decided to 'keep' the book 'if but for sympathy', he is presumably holding it in some way (although his 'shanks and wrists' are 'fetter'd') when the gaoler, talking of death, the great acquitter, says: 'Your neck, sir, is pen, book, and counters; so the acquittance follows' (v. iv. 170–2). Although both the language and the sentiment are those of book-keeping or accounting, the gaoler's attention to sleep ('but a man that were to sleep your sleep' (v. iv. 175)) and the pertinence of the book are deeply ironic in the context of Posthumus's awakening from the dream of his life with the book of resolution.

The tablet that Jupiter lays upon his breast determines and communicates the narrative of Posthumus's fortune and future. Posthumus calls it a book, and it comes to signify, in both Jupiter's imperative and Posthumus's analogy, the past, present, and future text of his being:

> This tablet lay upon his breast, wherein
> Our pleasure his full fortune doth confine.
>
> (v. iv. 109–10)

However, although we may have some idea as to the meaning of Jupiter's text, it is not until the end of the play and the work of the soothsayer that the information is dramatically decoded. As it stands, the contents of the book can be harnessed only abstractly, wherein the idea and not the word is meaningful. Yet the idea or abstraction of the book is not Jupiter's point. Posthumus's blatant misapprehension exposes the ways in which the book can operate within the confines of the drama. In both scenes with a book there is anamorphic potential: whilst for Imogen the book lies beside her sleeping body as a narrative from which she reads, for the audience the book emblazons her sleeping body with 'the contents o' th' story'; equally, whilst the book lies upon Posthumus's breast as a response to his dreams and a configuration of his future, for him it is an emblem of confusion with which he identifies impressionistically in order to die. In both cases the book responds to the body of the reader and the power of reading, or misreading, to express the inexpressible and sign the dramatic turning-points in the play's action: the book maps the ways in which both imagination and interpretation determine the choices we make. What begins to emerge from Shakespeare's use of the book in both these plays is how it may occupy a psychological space beyond the immediate requisites of the scene.

One of the central bookish tropes in both *Titus Andronicus* and *Cymbeline* is the relationship between the written and the gods. Both plays invoke the presence of the book within the context of justice and divine intervention. *Titus* is more ambivalent, since the play traces a loss of faith in a theistic world. Titus began by waiting for 'the heavens to reveal the damned contriver' of Lavinia's ordeal, and Marcus imagined the hand of God in Lavinia's sandy scrawl:

> Write thou good niece, and here display at last
> What God will have discovered for revenge.
>
> (iv. i. 73–4)

Yet, as the play develops, and Titus has 'not a god left unsolicited', he takes upon himself the act of 'mortal revenge' through the 'lively warrant' of the book. Whereas Titus initially sees *Metamorphoses* only as an observer of Lavinia's pleas to heaven, lying beside her as she 'lifts' 'up her arms in sequence thus', and offers his library 'to beguile' her 'sorrow' until the heavens act, Posthumus's book is a direct gift from Jupiter, 'wherein / Our pleasure his full fortune doth confine' (IV. i. 37, 35). It is unlikely that either of the plays suggests a directly iconic relationship between the book and heavenly interaction, since both plays trace their allusions through the fugitive; however, the proximity of the book to miscommunication and injustice adumbrates a potential form of relief when conventional networks have failed. Although *Cymbeline* is set in pre-Christian Rome and invokes pagan gods, the apparition of Jupiter, 'upon his eagle back'd' holding a book (IV. iv. 109–10), is reminiscent of an Anglican lectern, carved in the shape of a spread eagle and supporting a Bible. Classically, Jupiter represents anger and warfare, and he unenthusiastically arrives in Posthumus's dream. His 'godly' presence is reluctant, and his oblation of the book appears as a substitution for any real engagement with Posthumus's predicament. The book then remains with Posthumus as a token of his potential relief. The three books that appear in both these plays require, and are dramatically dependent on, interpretation and the 'reader'. Posthumus identifies himself as such in terms of (de)construction; turning the book over to the soothsayer, he declares: 'Let him show / His skill in the construction' (V. v. 434–5). The book is then 'read', as a performance and a process, by the soothsayer, who construes the inscription as a construction itself:

> Thou, Leonatus, art the lion's whelp,
> The fit and apt construction of thy name,
> Being Leo-natus, doth impart so much.
>
>                    (V. v. 444–6)

The soothsayer validates Posthumus's sympathetic response to the book as a 'fit and apt construction' of his identity. From Posthumus's confusion ('sense in hardness') comes the language of restoration, which facilitates the resurrection of shared realities towards the restoration of community. The book marks the culmination of justice, as it is drawn from the heavens and laid with a 'most heavy hand':

> The fingers of the powers above do tune
> The harmony of this peace.
>
>                    (V. v. 467–8)

Shakespeare's use of the material book in these plays, its theatrical presence, devolved 'readers', and semiotic scope, suggest the ways in which the book could accommodate and precipitate what Bakhtin would call the 'utterance'. In other words, the visible and dramatic book on-stage negotiates our awareness of other voices within the play and how those voices—whether they originate in Ovid or Philomel, Tarquin or Tereus, Jupiter or the soothsayer—enable other voices and signs to appear and determine our ways of seeing. In imaging the book and the characters' responses to the book in their various contexts of high trauma, silence, fear, threat, or confusion, we are drawn into the polyphonic sounds of the written word. In positioning the book on-stage, Shakespeare appears to extend theatre's inquiry into representation through the vagaries of the reading mind and the oppressed body. The books do not serve as metaphors or allegories of life. Instead, much like the audience's experience of watching the play, they expose us to the ways in which we interpolate the voices, justify the fantasies, or make sense of the senselessness of our realities. And when the material book lies on-stage it casts shadows, out of which voices of dissent emerge, bodies are dismantled, and memories are compromised.

# 3

# 'The lunatic, the lover, and the poet': Teaching, Perversion, and Subversion in *The Taming of the Shrew* and *Love's Labour's Lost*

Written within about two or three years of each other, *The Taming of the Shrew* and *Love's Labour's Lost* are Shakespeare's only comedies to explore the pursuit of love through the semiotic of the book, its institution (the school), and its ideology (humanism). To begin with, in both plays, the book is introduced through its particular relationship to the institute of learning. However, almost immediately, the imperatives of the play-world begin to destabilize the idea of the book and its pedagogic context. In *The Shrew*, Lucentio's school for lovers and Petruchio's 'taming school' evolve as powerful, yet ambiguous methods of achieving the same end. Both lovers wager their intentions through performance and *imitatio* in a city famed for its university and a play-world intent on a marriage of profit and delight. Equally, in *Love's Labour's Lost* the nature of the Academe authorizes a peculiar image of the book, which opens the play in an attempt to define and herald the potential of the 'book men'. Yet, quite quickly, such aspiration leads the men into a labyrinth of language in which they become lost in their search for meaning. In examining *The Taming of the Shrew* and *Love's Labour's Lost* together, I will explore the ways in which representations of love are scrutinized through the book and, more particularly, how a language of the book emerges in the dynamic between the lover and the beloved which seeks to both fetishize and contain the body of the woman. Whilst in *The Shrew* we may identify a dialogue between teaching and taming 'under the name of perfect love', in *Love's Labour's* we become aware of a more sophisticated semantic field in which the book provides an imaginative and ideological landscape for the evolution of a potential self. Ostensibly, *The Shrew* and *Love's Labour's* share a bookish topography of love and learning; they also share a slightly ambiguous ending in suspended resolution, as well as navigating an unresolved scepticism in the relationships between men and women. Yet, even within the few years that separate these plays, the book has shifted from an erotic object to a deficient form.

## 'FAITH, HE IS GONE UNTO THE TAMING-SCHOOL.' 'THE TAMING SCHOOL! WHAT, IS THERE SUCH A PLACE?'

George Gascoigne's 1575 translation of Ariosto's comedy *I Suppositi* (*Supposes*) offers a loose model for the plot of Bianca and Lucentio in Shakespeare's *The Taming of the Shrew*. Here Polynesta, our Bianca equivalent, explains to her confused nurse that she does not love Dulipo (because he is not in fact Dulipo), to whom the nurse had thought she was betrothed:

The man whom to this day you have supposed to be Dulipo (as I say) Erostrato, a gentleman that came from Sicilia to studies in this city, and even at his first arrival met me, and of such vehement force were the passions he suffered that immediately he cast aside both long gown and books, and determined on me only to apply his study.[1]

Erostrato, on falling in love, directly exchanges his books for his beloved, and is determined 'to apply his study' only on Polynesta. Erostrato, unlike Lucentio, throws off his books to woo his beloved; but, like Lucentio, he approaches his desire with the alacrity and eloquence of a scholar. Whereas one lover may 'cast aside' his books and another 'offer' them, the book and the book of the heart surface as lucid and symbolic objects of exchange.

When, in *The Taming of the Shrew*, Lucentio falls in love with Bianca, he exchanges his individual pursuit of 'ingenious studies' for the role and appearance of a schoolmaster. Armed with 'small books of Greek and Latin', Lucentio takes up his position, and, as Hortensio warns us to 'Stand by and mark the manner of his teaching', he declares:

---

[1] Geo[rge] Gascoigne, *Supposes and Jocasta*, two plays translated from the Italian, the first by Geo. Gascoigne, the second by Geo. Gascoigne and F. Kinwelmersh, 1575, ed. John W. Cunliffe (Boston and London: D. C. Heath and Co., 1906), i. i. 109–18. I have modernized the spelling.

Luc. Now, mistress, profit you in what you read?
Bian. What, master, read you? First resolve me that.
Luc. I read that I profess, the Art to Love.
Bian. And may you prove, sir, master of your art.
Luc. While you, sweet dear, prove mistress of my heart.

(iv. ii. 6–10)[2]

This scene marks the apotheosis of Lucentio's seduction of Bianca, and the performance and tension of this interaction depend upon processes of reading and misreading. Whilst Lucentio aligns himself with the erotic implications of Ovid's poem, Bianca resists the animate body of Lucentio's text by consciously deflecting his meaning back to the static book. Lucentio initiates the dialogue according to the emblematic and hermeneutic potential of the lover's 'book'. Such hermeneutic potential emerges through the book's presentation of a symbiosis between text and reader. The image of the book and the particulars of *The Art to Love* are connected and supported by reading and the body's textual and sexual relationship to profit and delight. Attitudes to reading—to unfold, to discover, to appropriate, apprehend, devour, and delight—are actions and ideas that support both the reading of a book and the desiring of a lover. Yet, as Alberto Manguel explains, reading itself is dependent upon a larger metaphoric network:

To say that we read—the world, a book, a body—is not enough. The metaphor of reading solicits in turn another metaphor, demands to be explained in images that lie outside the reader's library and yet within the reader's body, so that the function of reading is associated with our other essential bodily functions. Reading . . . serves as a metaphoric vehicle, but in order to be understood must itself be recognized through metaphors.[3]

The idea of reading thrusts the book into a figurative relationship with the body, creating a discursive space for the body and the book to emerge through synecdoche and metonym as corresponding parts in search of a whole. The cognitive field of recognition and understanding to which Manguel refers, Arthur Kinney exposes as the central cerebral process through which our brain apprehends and organizes its reality:

---

[2] William Shakespeare, *The Taming of the Shrew*, ed. Robert B. Heilman (London: The New English Library Limited, 1966). All further references, unless otherwise stated, are to this edition. This edition is based on the Folio, deviating only in emending F's incomplete act divisions and various 'unclear or erroneous speech assignments'.

[3] Alberto Manguel, *A History of Reading* (London: Flamingo, 1997), 170.

And the brain operates not by independent stimuli, such as observations or aphorisms set down in the notebook in one's hand, mind, or memory, but only by making patterns of such observations and aphorisms that are firmly entrenched by neural reinforcement and at the same time always subject to change.[4]

Understanding is therefore always dependent upon networks of meaning, patterns that exist through both cultural and natural signs. The flexibility of these patterns is determined by experience and external factors which the mind accommodates at the same time as it processes familiar or uncanny material. The book for Lucentio provides both a material article for, and a figurative advance into, a language of reciprocation. 'Reading', as the cognitive process which supports the physical and metaphysical response between image and expression, connects the body of Lucentio to his metaphor, which in turn draws in and upon the body of Bianca through the potential of the book in hand. Whereas Chapter 2 explored the relationship between the body and the book in violence and extremity in *Titus Andronicus*, here the female body comes into contact with its pages, not through the 'unspeakable' or 'barbaric', but through another kind of silence, the suppressed language of the erotic and the fetishistic. As *Titus* imported Ovid to confront the aesthetic relationship between horror and language paralysed in a body's enforced silence, *The Shrew* delivers *The Art to Love* and the *Heroides* to expose the erotic space between reading and confessing, fantasy and imitation. Through *The Art to Love* Lucentio traces, not letters and text with which either to decipher his beloved or to determine his eloquence, but wants, passions, and feelings. The idea of the book is a metonym for Bianca's body, the 'reading' of which remains in the hands and mind of Lucentio. Despite the often conventional tropological use of Ovid, the dialogue between Bianca and Lucentio is supported by the idea of the book, rather than the text itself. Ovid does not interpolate between the lovers; his work simply signifies the concept of female desire, the idea of reading, and the titular promise which Lucentio proposes as his will and his intention. The book, here, is dependent upon a wider network of reading which draws on figurative notions of interpretation and interaction and humanist contingents of imitation and effect. What Bianca must 'learn' is that in giving himself to 'The Art to Love', Lucentio absorbs and fetishizes the textual and sexual female. That this

---

[4] Arthur F. Kinney, *Shakespeare's Web: Networks of Meaning in Renaissance Drama* (London and New York: Routledge, 2004), p. xiv.

idea of the woman is generated and sustained by the classroom further endorses the speaking silence of 'maiden sobriety' with which Lucentio initially fell in love.

Whilst Katherina's shrewishness makes her undesirable, Bianca's beauty is characterized by Lucentio's desire for her 'silence'. Lucentio's love originates in a synthesis of eye and ear:

> But in the other's silence do I see
> Maid's mild behaviour and sobriety.
>
> (I. i. 70–1)

Lucentio's love for Bianca begins in seeing her 'silence', from which he extrapolates perfection, construed as the feminine values of mildness and sobriety. The word 'other' is central to Bianca's attractiveness, since it is in her 'otherness' that silence becomes physical enough to rival the bodily presence of the shrew. Joel Fineman, discussing the 'substantial nature' of Bianca's silence and the 'often overlooked' distinction between speech and silence in the play, declares:

This opposition, speech versus silence, is important, but even more important is the fact that it is developed in the play through the more inclusive opposition here suggested by the metaphorical way in which Lucentio "sees" Bianca's "silence". For Bianca does in fact speak quite often in the play—she is not literally mute—but the play describes this speech, as it does Bianca, with a set of images and motifs, figures of speech, that give both to Bianca and to her speaking a specific phenomenality which is understood to be *equivalent* to silence. This quality, almost a physical materiality, can be generally summarized—indeed, generically summarized—in terms of an essential visibility: that is to say, Bianca and her language both are silent because the two of them are something to be *seen*.[5]

But what endorses this visible silence in a woman who is obviously not so? Bianca is characterized almost entirely in opposition to Kate; her beauty and virtue emerge from the kind of silence that must be 'material' to compete with noisy physicality. The book and the classroom conspire to support much of this material silence.

In line with humanist assumptions, the book and its material underpinned the evolution of the educated female as much as the male. Perhaps the two most crucial distinctions between the education of the

---

[5] Joel Fineman, *The Subjectivity Effect in Western Literary Tradition: Essays toward the Release of Shakespeare's Will* (Cambridge, Mass., and London: October Books, 1991), 130.

male and the female, however, were, first, that the male was directed toward social pride and intellectual responsibility, and the female toward a silent, pious, and domestic attitude; and secondly, whereas the male fashioned himself alongside fabulous and historical warriors, knights, patricians, sages, and heroes, the female largely learned through antithesis the penalties of transgression and the rewards of virtue. Bianca's 'silence' throws Katherina's behaviour into relief, and the image and body of Bianca, at least initially, become a paradigm of how female education should *look*. Against Katherina, Bianca is constantly reaffirming the righteousness of the women's education. Katherina becomes the transgressive symbol whereby women could be threatened—bestial, noisy, excluded, and, above all, alone. The role of the book in the fashioning of the female mind was distinctly tied to the ideological containment of her body.[6] Juan Luis Vives's occlusion of Ovid's *Art to Love* in his *Instruction of a Christian Woman* augments the male celebration of pious and restricted education alongside chastity and verbal and bodily restraint. The importance of mimesis in humanist learning was largely predicated upon a faith in the developed moral and intellectual integrity of the individual. Women, however, were not credited with such discernment or control, so their education needed careful handling, particularly when 'The assumption was that individuals could be brought to internalise paradigms of exemplary masculinity or femininity by reading a book or copying an aphorism'.[7] The relationship here between male imperative and female imitation is similarly played out in the main plot of Katherina and Petruchio. Petruchio's teaching of Kate, unlike Lucentio's seduction of Bianca, is distinctly not 'by the book', and such a juxtaposition of these two ideas of teaching and loving is brought into sharp relief in Petruchio's travesty of a marriage ceremony, during which he throws *The Book of Common Prayer* to the ground and 'cuffs' the priest.[8] However, both men offer their object of desire an example through which they aim to achieve satisfaction:

---

[6] See William C. Carroll, 'The Virgin Not: Language and Sexuality in Shakespeare', *Shakespeare Survey*, 46 (1993), 107–19; Eve Rachele Saunders, *Gender and Literacy on Stage in Early Modern England* (Cambridge: Cambridge University Press, 1998); Suzanne W. Hull, *Chaste, Silent and Obedient: English Books for Women 1475–1640* (San Marino, Calif.: Huntingdon Library, 1982); and Clare Sponsler, *Drama and Resistance: Bodies, Goods, and Theatricality in late Medieval England* (Minneapolis and London: University of Minnesota Press, 1997).

[7] Saunders, *Gender and Literacy*, 2.

[8] Although the play is not set in Protestant England, I recognize *The Book of Common Prayer* in the marriage ceremony, as would any member of an Elizabethan audience.

whereas Bianca may be located in the schoolroom and the pretexts of desire, Kate is situated outside institutional decorum and practice in demotic ballads and folklore. Kate is forced, almost homoeopathically, to internalize her suitor's behaviour in order to reject it and be received back into the kind of structure (of sobriety and silence) that Bianca, at least initially, represents.

Vives directly and persistently equates good learning with chastity, so that, for his women, right knowledge is commensurate with purity. As chastity is the corollary of decorum and diligence, Vives strikes out against the 'perjury, deceits, murder, slaughter, [and] destruction love has caused', citing Helen of Troy as a flagrant example. However, it is Eve who epitomizes the sin of her sex, when Adam 'for the love of Eve lost and castaway mankind'. Thomas Salter's *The Mirror of Modesty* (1579), is similarly concerned with the education of the female:

> I would not have a maiden altogether forbidden, or restrained from reading, for so muche as the same is not onely profitable to wise and vertuous women, but also a riche and precious Jewel, but I would have her if she reade, to reade no other bookes but such as be written by godlie Fathers, to our instruction and soules health, and not suche lascivious Songes, filthie Ballades, and undecent bookes as be most commonly now a daies sette to sale.[9]

Vives, like Salter, emphasizes the interrelationship between learning and sanctity, which seeks to contain women within the boundaries of prescribed information and authority.[10]

> For it neither becometh woman to rule a school, nor to live amongst men, or speak abroad, and shake of[f] her demureness and honesty, either all together, or else a great part; which if she be good, it were better to be at home within and unknown to other folks, and in company to hold her tongue demurely, and let few see her, and none at all to hear her.[11]

Here again the relationship between seeing and hearing is central to the presence of the 'good' woman; Vives's woman is only to be seen in silence.

---

[9] As quoted in Saunders, *Gender and Literacy*, 8.

[10] This view was largely hypothetical, and does not represent the actuality of the female relationship to learning; rather, it imagines a fantasy that both the mind and the body of a woman can be controlled and maintained by her education. However, although women were not in practice 'silenced' by marriage, the proportion of reading-only literacy amongst women testifies to their restraint in public. Equally, that such opinions were circulated by leading (and, in Vives's case, royal) humanists reflects a very real anxiety as to the place and potential of the female voice.

[11] Foster Watson (ed.), *Vives and the Renascence of Women* (London: Edward Arnold, 1912), 55.

Vives articulates the overarching masculine fear of the public female voice, which is expressed in many sixteenth-century conduct books as a kind of, if not literal, promiscuity. Vives sanctions his argument with reference to the Apostles: 'And unto his disciple, Timothy, he [Paul] writeth on this wise: "Let a woman learn in silence with all subjection." But I give no licence to a woman to be a teacher, nor to have authority of the man, but to be in silence.'[12]

The decorous silence prescribed in conduct books, however, also functions figuratively as it signifies the importance of the controlled female body:[13]

Open female mouths—whether giving vent to gusty laughs, wide yawns, or unrestrained speech—carry a double threat, as late medieval court cases make clear. They breach corporeal boundaries, making the woman's body dangerously open, while also disrupting social relations by launching the dangerously open body into the social realm. For this reason, advice aimed at closing the female subject, one that is less of a threat to the masculinist social order.[14]

Silence is conspicuously problematic in many of Shakespeare's heroines, notably, of course, Cordelia, Isabella, and Hermione, but in *The Taming of the Shrew* conceptual and nominal silence is manifest in relation to both physical beauty and language. The sisters are physically emblazoned through their behaviour, so that whilst Bianca is 'maiden', 'mild', and 'gentle', Katherina, for most of the play, is referred to in devilish and brutish terms. Such a process of characterization enables Katherina's transformation to be realized in both physical and social terms at the end of the play. Although Katherina is initially described as beautiful, she quickly becomes blazoned by her shrewishness, and only her ultimate docile performance restores her beauty, so that in Petruchio's exclamation, 'now there's a wench, come kiss me Kate', we see Kate as the new object of desire and Bianca as the petulant other.

---

[12] Foster Watson (ed.), *Vives and the Renascence Education of Women*, 56.

[13] The relationship between the body and the book was not, of course, confined to the female reader: 'The many paintings and engravings of Renaissance figures holding books, their fingers marking a page, suggest what [Roger] Dranton calls the "corporeal element in reading" opens into the history of the body and the self as well as of the book': Kevin Sharpe, *Reading Revolutions: The Politics of Reading in Early Modern England* (New Haven and London: Yale University Press, 2000), 46. However, the graphic relationship of the book to the body was usually emblematized in terms of physical male dominance and female sexuality. Whilst many images depicted men holding books with their fingers inserted into the pages, women were shown holding the book to their crotch, hidden in their skirts or reading in bed.

[14] Sponsler, *Drama and Resistance*, 63.

The materiality of silence within the context of female education is endorsed and emblematized by the idea of the book. The teaching of Bianca is immediately and consistently associated with the book. Gremio's presentation of Lucentio to Baptista is played through a humorous irony at the expense of both scholarship and Bianca's education:

> I promised to inquire carefully
> About a schoolmaster for the fair Bianca,
> And, by good fortune, I have lighted well
> On this young man—for learning and behaviour
> Fit for her turn, well read in poetry
> And other books, good ones I warrant ye.

(I. ii. 165–70)

We know that Gremio has neither inquired nor inquired carefully, but in asserting so, he establishes the sincerity of Baptista's request. Yet Gremio's attitude to Bianca's education is immediately what we might call sentimental. Nominally he refers only to 'poetry', thereby eschewing at least five of the seven liberal arts, and such other books as there might be are simply 'good ones', and although 'good books' refers particularly to the classics, Gremio's is a studied vagueness.[15] The books, the text, even the tutor himself, are defined according to the imperative. Although the books may exist, although the tutor may appear (as Cambio indeed does), and although the majority of the play-world may observe Cambio in earnest, the name of the book at this point is in fact nothing more than a metonym. For Katherina, however, the book is absent. Our only pedagogic experience of Kate is in the context of music, and one she immediately destroys. We do not see Katherina in the schoolroom, we see only the disgruntled Hortensio, who has had a lute broken over his head. This, like the book, is emblematic, since music functions on-stage within its own network of meaning; through the commonly held notion of the 'music of the spheres' or the 'music of men', music reflected the state of things, so that, as Tiffany Stern says, 'The broken or mutilated instruments seemed to be employed at times when "harmony" has been in some way shattered'.[16] Where Katherina's 'frets' symbolize her shrewishness, Bianca's books support

---

[15] Since Baptista also employs a musician in Hortensio, we might assume that Bianca and Katherina's education is intended to include grammar, rhetoric, and music.

[16] Tiffany Stern, *Making Shakespeare: From Stage to Page* (London: Routledge, 2004), 109.

her silence. The idea of the book creates a space for Lucentio to enter into a reciprocal contract with Bianca, and, once the role of the book has been established, the context becomes 'All books of love'. Here too, we might notice the relationship between love and story—whilst Tarquin tries to seduce Lucrece with 'stories to her ears [of] her husband's fame' (l. 106), or Lady Capulet's blazoning of Paris 'that in gold clasps locks in the golden story' (I. iii. 94), or *A Midsummer Night's Dream*'s presentation of 'love's stories written in love's richest book' (II. ii. 128), or even Othello's seductive 'witchcraft' in the telling of his story: 'if I had a friend that loved her, / I should but teach him how to tell my story' (I. iii. 163–4), love, and represented, or ecphrastic love, is bound to the reading body of desire.

Lucentio's attitude to Bianca is ironically anticipated by Gremio, who, in the hope of winning Baptista's approval, decides 'by any means [to] light on a fit man to teach her [Bianca] that wherein she delights' (I. i. 110–11). The notion of 'delight' proposed by Horace and frequently redeployed by humanists and coterie writers—most famously, Sidney—here establishes a playful dynamic between the head and the heart at the hands of the male. Although the phrase was rooted in a scholastic commitment to mix the intellectual with the pleasurable, and thereby embrace the full potential and reward of knowledge, Thomas Thomas's use of 'affection' and 'desire' in his definition of *studios* suggests a semantic synthesis of the academic head and the desiring heart. Thomas expounds the term as 'desirouslie, . . . with diligence and affection . . . with taking pleasure and delight'.[17] Affection is also commonly used in this period to mean or suggest sympathy, and not only does sympathy acknowledge the exclusion of antipathies, it also implies a harmonious reciprocity. The readiness with which the scholar can 'apply his study' to the beloved suggests the ways in which the language of the book could also become the language of the heart.

Much of Lucentio's attitude toward study and the book emerges in his conversation with Tranio, in which he declares himself to be a rather ambivalent scholar. Lucentio explains that he has arrived in Padua (famous for its university and dissemination of Aristotelian discourse) to embark on 'A course of learning and ingenious studies', so that he may 'deck his fortune with his virtuous deeds' (I. i. 9, 16). This rather sketchy attitude to scholarship is taken up by Tranio, who wryly

---

[17] All early modern dictionary definitions can be found at <www.chass.utoronto.ca/english/emed/emedd. html>.

responds by warning his master not to commit to learning at the expense of pleasure: 'No profit grows where is no pleasure ta'en' (i. i. 39). Specifically, Tranio asks him not to 'so devote to Aristotle's checks / As Ovid be an outcast quite abjured' (i. i. 32–3). Both of Tranio's statements anticipate Lucentio's language of seduction played out in Bianca's schoolroom. The reference to Ovid wittily glances at *The Art to Love* in warning Lucentio against his own restraint as well as the poet's own exile. Similarly, Tranio's echo of Horace's statement, 'Omne tulit punctum qui miscuit utile dulci', anticipates Lucentio's pleasurable reading of Bianca: 'Now, mistress, profit you in what you read?' (iv. ii. 6). Tranio concludes his speech with the advice, 'In brief, sir, study what you most affect' (i. i. 40), upon the utterance of which Bianca enters.[18] Both the comedy and the creative value are largely dependent upon our awareness of the adaptability of the book to the beloved (an adaptability that has more convoluted dramatic resonance in *Love's Labour's Lost*), and the kind of 'pleasure' that Tranio refers to celebrates sex over scholarship. The readiness with which sex can be translated from learning and the book given in exchange for the body exposes the discursive field through which the book moves as it takes in the hand that holds or writes, the eyes that read or desire, the mind that imitates or absorbs, rejects or glosses, and the body that opens or closes.

When Lucentio translates himself and Tranio into two of Ovid's 'sisters': 'As Anna to the Queen of Carthage was, / Tranio, I burn, I pine, I perish, Tranio' (i. i. 154–5), he amplifies and augments the relationship between woman, desire, and book. As love turns Lucentio to his female textual precedent, his heart becomes 'fleshily' realized in the very visceral conditions of burning, pining, and perishing. Lucentio's 'teaching' of Bianca is anticipated not only in his own scholarship but also in the pre-texts through which he imagines her. Sex and text become almost inextricably linked to the relationship between a man and a woman. The teaching and taming of both women in this play is based upon the 'book': Bianca is taught the extent of Lucentio's desire through lines and layers of Ovid, whereas Katherina is tamed through the books that do not appear in the classroom. Her taming is supported by books of hawking as well as ballads and pamphlets in the fabliau tradition, of which the anonymous 1550 verse tale *A Merry jest of a Shrewde and Curst Wyfe, Lapped in Morrelles skin, for*

<hr />

18 SD] F.

*Her Good Behaviour* is a notorious example.[19] Petruchio, unlike his counterpart Lucentio, never brings such books on to the stage, but the teaching and taming that direct the play bring the relationship between the book and courtship into sharp relief.[20] As Petruchio hurls 'priest and book' to the ground, we become aware of the book's performative potential (be it appropriated or rejected) in the pursuit of love.

Lucentio offers Bianca a text which he hopes she will refer back to him: ' "*Simoi*", I am Lucentio, "*hic est*", son unto Vincentio of Pisa, "*Sigeia tellus*", disguised thus to get your love' (III. i. 31–3). Yet here the 'real' text of Ovid's *Heroides* plays an ambiguous role, since on the one hand the Latin exercise simply enables Lucentio's romantic interpolations to emerge through the conditions of the schoolroom but, on the other, Lucentio's witty displacement of gender roles, which sees his Penelope pleading for Bianca's Ulysses, endorses a travesty of the gender dynamics he appears to be exploiting. Whereas the book had initially enabled a contact and an exchange, an ellipsis in the 'text' is now created and translated into individual intention and desire. The structure of teaching and the transmission of texts provide a pre-text for both imitation and expression. Lucentio's articulation of his desire through his own translation harnesses and imposes upon Bianca a precedent for her response. The precepts of the grammar school are reconditioned by the requisites of desire. Lucentio interposes his Latin lines in response to Bianca's request to 'Construe them'. Bianca's request seems to imply both her knowledge and her acquiescence in Lucentio's presentation of *Heroides* as a palimpsest. The construction she asks for recognizes the activity of the text as complicit with that of the lover, whilst at the same time retaining the verisimilitude of the tutorial. But even though the book of the heart here becomes the book *construed* as the heart, Ovid's text continues to sustain and support the dynamics of the scene as Bianca maintains the textual dialogue and replies:

---

[19] Despite Petruchio's taming of Katherina like an animal, his methods are, to some extent, humanist; he bases his methods on observation, imitation, and repetition.

[20] Although Petruchio tames his shrew without any specific recourse to scholarly or romantic text, he initially identifies possible classical pre-texts for his case: 'Be she as foul as was Florentius' love, / As old as Sibyl, and as curst and shrewd / As Socrates' Xanthippe' (I. ii. 68–70). The plight and patience of Socrates were frequently redeployed in humanist texts, including Erasmus's colloquy, Robert Snawsel's *A Looking Glass for Married Folks* (1610), and Matthew Hopkins's *A Juniper Lecture*, as well as *A Homily of the State of Matrimony* (1623).

Now let me see if I can construe it. *Hic ibat Simois*, I know you not, *hic est Sigeia tellus*, I trust you not, *Hic steterat Priami*, take heed he hear us not, *regia*, presume not, *celsa senis*, despair not. (III. i. 40–3)

The dialogue between Bianca and Lucentio is constructed through the text, and by virtue of that text the couple 'read' each other, partly through the material book that is held between them, and partly through the figurative potential that such practices of reading assume. The idea of reading augments the necessary intimacy and privacy of their interaction and, since Hortensio must not hear them, the text of Ovid shelters the 'silent' text of their selves. In this way, their reading of each other is covered by the book. Bianca does not construe Ovid; she construes Lucentio, and his 'text' becomes the lesson. However, the choice of text is neither arbitrary nor without significance. The heroines of *Heroides* are imagined through their letters to absent lovers, and we might recognize a similar synthesis in the process of composition, desire, and identity as is apparent in the use of *The Art to Love*.

Although expressions of sexual desire did not obviously accommodate the language of the book until the thirteenth century, 'One of its most important ancient sources was Ovid'.[21] As the sheer eroticism of Ovid's poem, *The Art to Love*, may have contributed to his banishment and the poet spending the rest of his days in exile, the performance of the text re-creates a space for the imaginative relationship between desire and suppression.[22] However, the erotic nature of the text was not confined simply to explicit description but to an evocative synthesis of sexuality and writing. Ovid 'had used writing symbolism in sexually suggestive ways, as with the confidante carrying a love-letter "concealed by a broad band on her warm bosom," or even a secret message written directly on her body'.[23] In this way, the written material itself becomes implicated in sexual contact and fantasy, and the idea of Ovid supports an image of how the language of desire moves within and without the pages of text. Contrary to *Metamorphoses* and Philomela's 'purple letters', and the translation of sexual into

---

[21] Here the notion of sexual desire needs to be separated from love, since spiritual and religious love have significantly informed the semiotic of the book in its emotional and corporeal relationship to the expressive subject.

[22] Although it is often claimed that the Emperor Augustus exiled Ovid on the basis of his love poetry, it is not settled.

[23] Eric Jager, *The Book of The Heart* (Chicago and London: University of Chicago Press, 2000), 66.

textual wounding, the female body becomes a site of exploration, of interpretation, and of discovery as hidden desires and suppressed texts meet in the whispers of the lovers. Georgia Brown, however, posits the use of Ovid as a significant inflection toward guilt and wantonness:

Ovid's compendious epic suggested ways in which competing values could be brought together to challenge existing conceptions of literature, and his luxuriant wantonness challenged the simplicity of conventional moral judgements based on the denial of sensual experience, by insinuating a connection between poetic creativity and sexual desire which made literary morality a chimerical goal and eventually freed literature from the necessity to be didactic.[24]

Referring to the title of Ovid's poem alone is enough to establish a witty transition from the scholar to the lover, and, yet, rather than function intertextually, the book provides a hinterland through which desire can move from the material to the physical. Once Lucentio has brought *The Art to Love* to bear upon his situation, he is able to open up a discursive space that enables the voices of the lovers as well as those of the text to explore the book of the body: 'Now, mistress, profit you in what you read?' (IV. ii. 6). Within the context of love, the reading further exposes the importance of mutuality, since both the pursuit of love and the pursuit of knowledge require the presence of another. Whereas the pages and content of a book translate the absent or textualized 'author', loving demands an imagined or objectified beloved—either way, neither state can exist in isolation. The presence of the book between the lovers initiates a pretext for the fulfilment, or at least acknowledgement, of two roles. The metaphor of 'reading' sustains the book, as the idea of Ovid harnesses the lovers. The subtle transition from Ovid's *The Art to Love* to the reading and dialogue of the lovers shifts the focus from the possible text of the poem to the exposition of their selves. Much of this dynamic is dependent upon the 'isolated' or secretive position of the lovers, and the nature of the book's content re-affirms the clandestine space they occupy on stage. Vives explains that such a book was expelled from the woman's curriculum. Shortly after asserting that 'As for a woman, she hath no charge to see to, but her honesty and chastity', Vives declares, 'Therefore in my mind no man was ever banished more rightfully than was Ovid, at leastwise, if he was banished for writing the Craft of

[24] Georgia Brown, *Redefining Elizabethan Literature* (Cambridge: Cambridge University Press, 2004), 41.

Love.'[25] Similarly Stephen Gosson, in *The School of Abuse*, accuses Ovid of lasciviousness: 'In Rome when Playes or Pageants are showne, Ouid chargeth his Pilgrims, to creepe close to the Saintes, whome they serve, and shewe their double diligence to lift the gentlewomans roabes from the ground.'[26] Thomas Lodge, however, in his 'Reply', railing at Gosson for failing to have rightfully 'breath[ed] out the sweete promises to the good, the curses to the bade', states: 'These be the songes of Sion, these be those rebukes which you oughte to add to Abuses; recouer the body, for it is sore, the appe[n]dices thereof will easily be reformed, if that we ar at a staye.'[27] Here Lodge synthesizes the body and the book through both the author and the title; Gosson's ignorance has abused his Abuses, and his Abuses has abused him until all are 'sore'. The relationship between the book and the body is ever present, yet it appears to find its full expression in the sexuality of the woman.

'Pornography', meaning to write the whore, became bound up in the nature of reading. The term itself is ambiguous, and seems to emerge not in the intention but in the effect; Richard Braithwait, in *A Survey of History: Or, A Nursery for Gentry* (1638), explains the male reader of 'Stories of Love':

when they fall upon any passage that complies with the lightnesse of their fancy, so highly affect it, as nothing more delights them, than to discourse of such ayry pleasures, as present themselves in a cursorie manner to their deluded conceits. These are altogether of Stories of Love; where every line workes such moving impressions in their unsteady fancies: as they reduce every period of Loves discourse, to a Sceane of Action; wherein they wish themselves Prime-actors, to close in a personall re-greet, with so light and sensuall a Relation.[28]

Reading was itself the sexualizing process that marked, through role-play, fantasy and imagination, touch and fetish, the content of the book. Lucentio appropriates lines from the *Heroides* though which he acts out his love for Bianca 'with so light and sensuall a Relation'. In a scene from *A Mad World My Masters* (1608), Middleton comically

---

[25] Foster Watson (ed.), 'J. L. Vives: Instruction of a Christian Woman, Translated into English by Richard Hyrde in 1540', in *Vives and the Renascence Education of Women*, 34, 34–5.

[26] Stephen Gosson, *The Schoole of Abuse, 1579* (Menston, Yorkshire: Scholar Press, 1972), Cᵛ. I have modernized the typography.

[27] Thomas Lodge, *A Defence of Poetry, Music, and Stage-Plays* (London: The Shakespeare Society, 1853), 17.

[28] Sigs. Tᵛ⁻ᵛ. This is taken from an unpublished paper by Katherine Craik, 'Reading Renaissance Pornography', 2005.

exposes the ambivalently erotic nature of how woman and text are used to impress chastity through fear and example. Middleton's hero, Master Harebrain, having become consumed with jealousy and sexual insecurity, employs a courtesan (Lady Gullman) disguised as a 'pure virgin' to read piety to his 'erring' wife. The iconic use of devotional works was not unusual, since such books supported the cultural and educational strictures upon women; Middleton, however, through a juxtaposition of convention and duplicity exposes the fragile relationship between husband, wife, and book. Having enlisted Lady Gullman, Master Harebrain directs this 'pure virgin' to his wife, explaining:

I have convey'd away all her wanton pamphlets, as *Hero and Leander, Venus and Adonis*: oh, two luscious mary-bone pies for a young married wife! Here, here, prithee take the *Resolution*, and read her a little. . . . Terrify her, terrify her; go, read to her the horrible punishments for itching wantonness, the pains allotted for adultery; tell her her thoughts, her very dreams are unanswerable.[29]

The book in question, *A Book of Christian Exercise Appertaining to Resolution,* a popular and widely used book, never achieves any stable or iconic meaning on-stage, since, as soon as Harebrain leaves the women to their book, Lady Gullman counsels Mistress Harebrain in the art of deception and pleasure:

> If he chance to steal upon you, let him find
> Some book lie open 'gainst an unchaste mind,
> And coted Scriptures, tho' for your own pleasure,
> You read some stirring pamphlet, and convey it
> Under your skirt, the fittest place to lay it.

(i. ii. 90–4)

Yet, rather than neglect the books (erotic or devotional), Lady Gullman simply advises the use of one to cover up the other.[30] This ambiguous use of the book is equally exposed in the history and practice of marginalia and annotation: William Slights, discussing the

[29] Thomas Middleton, *A Mad World, My Masters*, in Gāmini Salgādo (ed.), *Four Jacobean City Comedies* (Harmondsworth: Penguin, 1975), i. ii. 45–8, 53–5. Within the context of this chapter, there is some degree of irony that Shakespeare's *Venus and Adonis* is specifically mentioned as a banished text, while it makes frequent appearances as an explicit and a popular book; according to John Johnson, as I quoted in the Introduction, the popularity and content of *Venus* almost made Shakespeare a synecdoche for sexuality: 'Shakespeere . . . who creepes into women's closets about bedtime'.

[30] It is plausible that this is the 'book of devotion' that Polonius places in the hands of his daughter to entrap Hamlet; the ambiguously sexual use of this text on-stage further amplifies Hamlet's almost erotic disgust at Ophelia reading. See Ch. 5 below.

extent to which marginalia directed, fashioned, and even created the reading experience, explains: 'The religious counsel offered in a volume such as the immensely popular *Book of Christian Exercise* could equally well serve opposing factions if it were properly reedited and reannotated.'[31]

Master Harebrain's attempts at annotating and editing his wife stem from the book, but are gloriously undermined by the body of the reader(s). Reading appears as an exercise in which the woman and her thoughts are localized and managed, and although the male may be a proponent of the book, the reading of it is harnessed and managed by the female body. The ambivalent figure of the prostitute/virgin amplifies the already sexualized encounter with the book, and her teaching of Mistress Harebrain to conceal her 'stirring pamphlets' blatantly places devotional material above the skirt and 'other' material below. What remains central, however, is the woman's skirt or genitals in relation to the book. Although the book may serve on one level as the male interrogation of female presence, on the other, it both represents and enables female sexuality. Whereas we have seen how humanists like Vives and Salter expose women to certain types of education to manage her fallen mind, for Middleton and other writers of the period, the book supported sex. In John Taylor's *The Practical Part of Love* (1660) he 'describes the chief item in the pornographic library of "Loves Academy" as "a Book that had no Title, and therefore I cannot tell its name; I was almost as much pleased with looking on its outside, as on its inside . . . I could not find that it had above two leaves in it" '.[32] As Gordon Williams explains, Taylor 'has in mind a figure which became common currency following its use in Marlowe's *Ovid* (1580s), where the lover declares that even if he sees his lady "ope the two-leav'd book" to a rival, he will trust her words of innocence "more than mine eyes" '.[33] Middleton amplifies the ambiguous relationship between woman and book in his synthesis of sexuality and chastity. For Harebrain the book will condemn his wife's 'thoughts and her very dreams', yet, for the audience, such condemnation is rerouted by the body of the reader to the humiliation of the 'teacher'. Thus the bodies of the readers always precede the performance of the book, and it is within this context that

---

[31] William W. E. Slights, *Managing Readers: Printed Marginalia in English Renaissance Books* (Ann Arbor: University of Michigan Press, 2001), 15.

[32] Gordon Williams, *Shakespeare, Sex, and the Print Revolution* (London and Atlantic Highlands, NJ: Athlone, 1996), 49.

[33] Ibid.

Lucentio introduces how he is reading (as he acts and desires) before what he is reading (*The Art to Love* and Bianca).

Gremio, synthesizing sexuality and 'teaching', registers the material and aesthetic significance of the book:

> Hark you, sir, I'll have them very fairly bound—
> All books of love, see that at any hand,
> And see you read no other lectures to her.

> (I. ii. 145–7)

Here the image and aspect of the book transcends any specific textual imperative; the beauty of the object—its 'fair' binding, amorous content, and material and visual monopoly—identifies the relationship between woman and book as pleasing referential property, and may well be the kind of 'Stories of Love' to which Braithwait later refers. The book of love will, hopes Gremio, offer a precedent and a pre-text for Bianca's response. Equally, in the presentation of 'this small packet of Greek and Latin books' to Bianca's father, a set of codes is established which take symbolic precedent over the scholar himself. The performance through which Gremio and Tranio present Lucentio is played out through a series of ideas, which find their apogee in the donation of the books. Whilst Gremio establishes Lucentio's academic history (in comparison to the equally spurious Hortensio), 'this young scholar that hath been long studying at Rheims—as cunning in Greek, Latin, and other languages, as the other in music and mathematics' (II. i. 79–82), Tranio offers 'this small packet of Greek and Latin books' to seal the contract and facilitate the exchange. Almost as soon as Baptista holds the books in his hands, he directs Lucentio to his daughter: 'take . . . the set of books. / You shall see your pupils presently' (II. i. 106–7). But although both tutors are sent to both pupils, it is only Bianca's teaching that we witness. The books, therefore, despite being Greek and Latin, have only ever been books of love and destined for Bianca. Initially, the books ritualize and mark an exchange of authority from the father to the lover. Such an exchange is introduced by the figure of the tutor who, in the case of Lucentio, creates a nexus between the authority of the teacher and that of the husband. The father's bestowing of his daughter to her husband is anticipated in the transaction with the books. And, importantly, Tranio, who has become 'Lucentio', is now fatherless ('supposed Lucentio / Must get a father, called supposed Vincentio' (II. i. 400–1)), as is Cambio, since he is merely an impostor fashioned for a part. When Lucentio becomes the tutor to Bianca, he is 'fatherless', and therefore is himself both the patriarch and the pedagogue. Directly after Lucentio has left for Bianca with his books, Petruchio enters and establishes his material position in relation to marrying Katherina. The idea of exchange—of offering and receiving—is augmented under the terms of marriage. In this way, the book becomes the receptacle for the uneasy relationship between institutional containment and subversive fantasy.

The woman, text, and lust are implicitly and explicitly imagined in writing and reading. Although a stable idea of the female reading is somewhat complicated by a controversial history of devotion and desire, Lucentio directly transfers his appetite and ambition to Bianca, as he also uses the work of Ovid as a pre-text of eloquence. The processes of expression and response made available by the book are amplified in the play's exposure of teaching practices. Equally, the nature of the woman's body is dramatically supported by the idea of the book, the silent, discernible, yet physical text idealizes and exposes the fantasy of the contained female. Authors and intertextual references open up this space for the readmission of the male, and it is within this context that it is no surprise how far Katherina's submission speech is intertextually supported by *A Homily of the State of Matrimony*. The particular books in *The Shrew* enable the characters to bring a version of communicable love into being whilst maintaining the presence of the body as a token of male desire. In *Love's Labour's Lost*, on the other hand, the book takes centre stage to become the place in which art and love vie for a language of truth beyond the space of the body.

## 'THAT UNLETTERED, SMALL-KNOWING SOUL'

*Love's Labour's Lost* opens with the king's declaration that he and his attendant lords shall study: for three years they will eschew all other desires and imperatives. Their court 'shall be a little academe', and 'still and contemplative in living art', they will cheat 'cormorant devouring time' in attendant fame and recognition. Navarre presents his lords with an oath, which requires them to devote themselves to learning at the expense of all else, particularly women, and it is at this point that the 'book-men' consider what it is to learn and what it means to study.

BEROWNE.[34] What is the end of study, let me know?
KING. Why, that to know which else we should not know.
BEROWNE. Things hid and barred, you mean, from common sense.
KING. Ay, that is study's god-like recompense.
BEROWNE. Come on, then, I will swear to study so
    To know the thing I am forbid to know,
    As thus: to study where I may well dine
    When I to feast expressly am forbid.

(I. i. 55–62)[35]

The language of feasting, prohibition, concealment, sanctity, and fealty
glances at the opening speech of Marlowe's *Doctor Faustus*, and sets an
ambiguous tone of righteous aspiration and dangerous aggrandizement.
Berowne's later reference to 'angel knowledge' (I. i. 113) is hinted at here
as something more than the 'Schoole Diuinitie' or the 'contemplatory
knowledge of God, angels, and soules of men', which underpinned
the academic study of metaphysics.[36] Conventionally, the language of
appetite is usually associated with transgression rather than asceticism,
since the latter is normally accompanied by a bodily restraint, whereas
the former's combination of satiation and sapience images Eve's fatal
pursuit of knowledge and food in Paradise. However, this consumerism
comes to rest in Moth's satiric observation that 'scraps' have been
'stolen' from 'the great feast of language' (v. i. 34–5), which casts a
very human shadow over divine potential. Yet Berowne's navigation
of the senses in his understanding of Navarre's request anticipates the
significance of sex in scholarship. However, desire and knowledge did
not automatically signify sex. In medieval scholasticism the physical
body became sanctified in its pursuit of the absolute and faithful
heart, a trope which continued into the seventeenth century. George
Whither, in his book of emblems, depicts an image in which 'desire'
signifies the love of the faithful and learned: displaying 'A smoking
and winged heart sit[ing] on an open book', the motto reads 'The

[34] The Norton edition, largely using the Quarto text of 1598, prints 'Berowne' as
'Biron', however, in line with the rest of this book, I have maintained the 1623 Folio
orthography.

[35] All references are to the Norton edition. Although most modern editions of *Love's
Labour's Lost*, including the Norton Shakespeare, follow the Quarto of 1598, they also
include the Folio scene divisions and the, still contentious, replacement of Catherine by
Rosalind in Berowne's first exchange with her. Here I follow Norton with the exception
of 'Berowne' for 'Biron'.

[36] See Bullokar's definition of 'Intelligence' and 'Metaphysickes' (1616), at the Early
Modern English Dictionary Database.

Heart of him that is upright, in Heavenly-knowledge, takes delight', whilst the epigram explains: 'The book represents wisdom; the winged heart, desire for knowledge; the smoke those perturbations within man until he understands heavenly wisdom.'[37] Yet Navarre's displacement of women, the appetite with which the men chew over their commitment, and the contest between forms of gratification foreground the sensual body and the cerebral book.[38] At this point, however, Navarre seems only to observe the importance of the female in her exclusion 'on pain of losing her tongue', and Berowne is, as yet, unaware of the potential power and performance of his synthesis. Much of this dialectic between love and scholarship, as in *The Shrew*, is informed by Ovid's *The Art to Love*; yet whereas, in *The Shrew*, Ovid exposes a particular and erotic semiotic in the art of seduction, here, although not nominally referred to, it shadows the development of the play.

The opening dialogue between Navarre and Berowne circumnavigates various themes that the play will later confront and expand; together they adumbrate the commonplace humanist trinity—passion, action, contemplation—as well as the dispute, experienced by every conscientious courtier, between reason and passion, and, not least of all, the dialectic between self-knowledge and knowledge. What links these ideas, exploits their ambiguities, and exposes the 'great feast of language' at the outset are the words 'study' and 'book'. 'To study' is either an individual, even private, act of meditation or a more social, didactic act of intellectual and mnemonic endeavour. However, the idea of study we find elsewhere in Shakespeare, in *Hamlet* or *Titus*, for example, with its powerful and profound ability to propel the subject through recesses of thought and private places has no semblance here. Rather, as Thomas observes, and I quoted earlier, *studios* is an activity that involves desire and affection, which, even within the initial Academe, is translated by the men into something more whimsical and exclusive. The language of desire haunts the cognitive process that engages the mind in a quest to obtain or reflect, imagine or represent, a language of 'knowing', be it condemned or consumed. However, the play offers three different confrontations with a broader idea of knowing and learning through the

[37] See Huston Diehl, *An Index of Icons in English Emblem Books 1500–1700* (Norman, Okla., and London: University of Oklahoma Press, 1986).

[38] Within the context of the emblem, it might be tempting to read Armado's later disparaging reference to the 'sweet smoke of rhetoric' (particularly if we relate Moth's 'cannon', from where this smoke came, to the phallic pen) as pointing to the kind of rejection of 'heavenly wisdom' for temporal pleasure that underpins the play.

semiotic of the book. The king and his lords present one perspective, which is directly set up in opposition to the Princess and her ladies, who accommodate another, and the third is the exposition of specific modes of education expressed by Holofernes, Nathaniel, and Armado. Unlike in *The Shrew*, none of these encounters with the book is explored for instant dramatic gratification; rather, they extend the *idea* of the book into a hinterland of knowing and longing that seeks to authorize the self.

Berowne's difficulty in accepting the king's proposition is expressed though his inability to reconcile himself to a reasonable definition of 'study'. Initially, the word conjures an empty, or at least confounded, prospect, which he then perceives as an elite exercise harbouring its own rewards—'Study knows that which yet it doth not know' (I. i. 68)—until at last he comes to an impasse:

> Study is like the heavens' glorious sun,
> That will not be deep searched with saucy looks.
> Small have continual ever plodders won
> Save base authority from others' books.

> (I. i. 84–7)

Conceptually, the play toys with both Christian and Platonic ideas of knowledge, salvation, and election. Whilst the Academe itself, Navarre's esoteric aspirations, and a male-orientated quest for Truth can be associated with Plato, notions of love/charity, metaphysics, and semantics are rooted in Christianity and, more specifically, Protestantism. Berowne disengages himself from, and mystifies, 'study' through manipulating its heavenly allusions in Christ/Cosmos (sun/son) and aspiration and ineffability ('will not be searched'). Equally, in 'continual plodders' and 'base authority' he treats methodical scholarship pejoratively. Yet, ultimately, Berowne turns 'study' from an activity to a thing and, as a thing in itself, it supports an inherent value and signification, which works to contain the word and exonerate him from any active part in its performance. By manipulating study into an abstract position, Berowne is able to dispense with its allusions, and formulate the power of the word to orientate its own end without becoming involved in that process. The idea that the word is responsible for its own reality is central to the play's exploration of how love becomes love, and 'representations' (written, spoken, performed, and fabricated) are central to that exploration. Just before this pronouncement Berowne had declaimed:

> Why, all delights are vain, but that most vain
> Which, with pain purchased, doth inherit pain;

As painfully to pore upon a book
To seek the light of truth while truth the while
Doth falsely blind the eyesight of his look.

(I. i. 72–6)

Referring to the kind of stoicism that came under similar fire in humanist discourse, Berowne dismisses the act of learning as 'painfully to pore upon a book'. Berowne casts a distinctly temporal and transitory shadow over the exercise in which Navarre had hoped to find immortality. The end and the act are self-defeating and unrewarding, since the 'truth' of scholarship only dims the light and blinds the eye. The metrically assertive 'look' overrides the 'book' and reorientates the book's journey through the senses, which becomes more sophisticated and more subtle as the play develops.[39] Whereas, here, the book impinges on the eye to overshadow the figurative text of grace or truth, later Navarre's eye becomes the book in which Boyet reads the 'still rhetoric' of his love for the Princess. Such 'still rhetoric' is reminiscent of the eloquence of Sonnet 23's books, which become the 'dumb presagers' of the poet's breast. The figurative potential in the discourse on study allows us to see the ways in which the semiotic of the book can create a poetic typography of the body and the mind. Whilst the Princess separates the word from the ornament, since beauty 'needs not the painted flourish' of 'praise', but is 'bought by the judgement of the eye', Boyet observes a talking silence in the expression of Navarre's 'face's margin': 'But to speak that in words which his eye hath disclosed / I have only made a mouth of his eye / By adding a tongue' (II. i. 250–2). Boyet inscribes the space or 'still rhetoric' that lies between the body and the word. Conventionally the book often supports the metaphor of reading or discerning a person's feelings/disposition by their face. Although, famously, Duncan disputes such a skill in *Macbeth* ('There's no art to find the mind's construction in the face' (I. iv. 11–12) ), Shakespeare, in love, often uses the book as a leap through silence. We have already seen how Lucentio 'sees' Bianca's maiden sobriety in her silence, and reads her body in response to Ovid. Yet, in *Love's Labour's*, the women's resistance to the 'word' is explored through their rejection of the 'painted flourish' of poetry, which finally leads them to refer their lovers to the kind of solitariness that the

[39] It is worth noting this relationship between 'look' and 'book' within the context of the textual discrepancy of Sonnet 23. How far we may observe a synthesis between books and looks is deeply suggestive about the relationship between an actor and his part, the book and the stage.

bookmen could not initially sustain. The violent distrust of the 'painted flourish' sets the women apart from any real communication with the 'maggot ostentation' (v. ii. 409) of Navarre's court, and is based upon an evaluation of the representational relationship between truth and art. The ethical ambivalence of the 'painted word' resonates throughout *Hamlet*, and the 'smart lash' that Claudius's cheek conscience receives equally centralizes the betrayal of language by art. Ultimately, however, the women conclude their lovers' declarations by understanding them to be 'At courtship, pleasant jest, and courtesy', thereby negating not only the oaths that the men had taken to abjure such courtship, but the language of courtly love. As Berowne laments, their 'sport' does not end like 'an old play', and what 'comedy' there is emerges as insincere and untenable. Only the sign that emerges as the truest expression of itself has value, and love, prey to the vicissitudes of self-interest, must find more than the beloved to talk about.[40]

The intensity with which the bookmen set up their Academe—their particular ideas of knowledge, what it means to them to aspire and achieve such learning, and the language through which they dispute this commitment—adumbrates a space within the play that will function negatively or deficiently. According to Georgia Brown, however, such notions of negativity were central to the emergence of newness and writing in the 1590s. Bearing this in mind, she asks us to

redraw our model of the Elizabethan literary system, to renegotiate our understanding of the relation between amateur and professional, triviality and seriousness, novelty and tradition, public and private, and to revise our understanding . . . of the role played by forms of negativity and deficiency in effecting cultural change.[41]

The role of negativity and deficiency is one that is acutely explored through the 'literary' in *Love's Labour's*. From the idea of study, the men wrest a self-conscious fabric of language, which is set next to, and against, the pretentious and pedantic dictates of Armado and Holofernes. In its organized written form, love runs covertly alongside the 'sweet smoke of rhetoric' into 'maggot ostentation', and in both strains they remain deficient. For both Armado and Berowne, for instance, the book and its

---

[40] In these terms, it is music that emerges as the purest form of art or representation, since it manifests as the absolute expression of itself and cannot be represented, as itself, in either words or images. Silence too, as it can be neither represented nor described, perhaps comes closest to our purest mode of human expression.

[41] Brown, *Redefining Elizabethan Literature*, 55.

study create a space out of which the men creep to secretly write their love. The peculiarities of space within Shakespeare's plays have often been noted for their dramatic effect; the forest of Arden in *As You Like It*, the island in *The Tempest*, the heath in *King Lear*, or the wood in *A Midsummer Night's Dream* all work to impose counterintuitive pressures on the characters, and Anne Barton has shown how the park, the court, and the 'play' affect different tides of illusion and artificiality in *Love's Labour's*.[42] Albeit unwittingly, the bookmen create negative structures through which they move in the hope of change. Barton claims that the Academe is organized precisely within the conditions of its own failure:

> The paradox of the Academe and the reason why its failure is not only understandable but absolutely necessary lie in the fact that this elaborate scheme which intends to enhance life and extend it through Fame and even beyond the boundaries of the grave would in reality, if successfully carried out, result in the limitation of life and, ultimately, in its complete denial.[43]

The necessity of this failure, however, supposes that in opposition to the Academe lies the potential of success. What the men aspire to, and most particularly Navarre, is the production of their own meaning, their own selves that, on the exclusion of women, will exist in the book. The 'great feast of language', which the play parodies, initially imagines the idea of the book as the esoteric, even elliptical, storehouse out of which all prospects of celebration and self-knowledge emerge. The relationship between woman and book, unlike in *The Shrew*, however, is mutually exclusive; whereas the latter promises immortality, the former betrays the all too human fallibility of desire.

Conventionally, the book or writing was often a symbol of how the self could express immortality or fame, and Geoffrey Whitney celebrates this idea in an emblem of a ruined building alongside a pile of books on a table, which bears the motto 'Scripta manent' and the epigram: 'Writing lasts when all other monuments decay in time.'[44] Navarre's commitment to study reveals his desire for both recognition and a feeling for something that lies beyond his park gates. Navarre creates

---

[42] See Bobbyann Roesen (Anne Barton), 'Love's Labour's Lost', in Felicia Hardison Londré (ed.), *Love's Labour's Lost: Critical Essays* (New York and London: Routledge, 2001), 125–44.

[43] Ibid. 127.

[44] Diehl, *An Index of Icons in English Emblem Books*, 33. In the nineteenth century, Victor Hugo, in *The Hunchback of Notre Dame*, similarly iconicized this image, when the priest, seeing from his study window the shadow cast by the cathedral, looks down at his books and says 'This will kill that.'

his own 'building' out of the book, which defines the boundaries of his court in excluding women and transcending earthly delights.[45] The desire to transcend and move beyond the intellectual confines of the court is often explored in the men's physical shifts within the play. As the Princess and her ladies are installed on the periphery of the palace, the men begin to travel towards them as they each individually step outside their sworn place and declaim their love. From their nebulous Academe they bring with them a belief in the force and efficacy of language, but, crucially, one that can be translated into temporal gain. However, the play only charts a potential which is ultimately never fulfilled, and in the women's deferral of their lovers for a period of isolation or evolution, they are in some respects returned to the 'trial' or 'war against affections' with which the play began. Even though Berowne is the Academe's fiercest detractor, it is he who is set the most specifically linguistic task of conversing with 'groaning wretches' and the 'speechless sick'. Although the Princess declares she is not one 'to teach a teacher', that is precisely what the women set out to do.

To some extent, and as Barton suggests, the men's rebellion against the constraints of the Academe demonstrates a shift from knowing to being, and this shift is performed through a recognition of the compatibility—rather than exclusivity—of these terms. As Gremio advised Lucentio, and as many diverse writers of the period, including Montaigne, Francis Bacon, Robert Burton, and Roger Ascham, recognized, knowledge must be accompanied, indeed augmented, by experience. The lovers' recourse to text, to the sonnet, the written page, 'numbers', and prose, situates the development of their love alongside their attention to the exploration of language. As Navarre and his lords develop that sense of self-consciousness through the text (rhyme, prose, extempore, line, and type) of love-poetry, they attach themselves to an evolving history of love and letters. However, as Brown suggests, discussing the literary transition from essential text to author, this self-conscious production of meaning can render texts, and here even the authors themselves, opaque:

---

[45] In excluding women, and thereby procreation, Navarre focuses his entire desire for immortality on the written and reputed idea of his self. The contest of the represented self between the marked page and the imprinted child not only informs the language of love (as when Viola warns Olivia: 'Lady, you are the cruell'st she alive / If you will lead these graces to the grave / And leave the world no copy' (*Twelfth Night*, I. v. 211–13)), but significantly informs the language and structure of the sonnets.

The production of meaning from the point of view of both author and reader is rendered self-conscious, and the text becomes an opaque medium, rather than the transparent incarnation of pre-existent Truth, as language and style turn back on themselves and explore their own origins, history and conventions.[46]

Emerging through their own ideas of 'books' and 'writing', the men reproduce this 'old-fashioned' truth in their love-letters. Unable to handle origins, history, or conventions, the lovers' words resort to opaque essentiality that is immediately made redundant by the more prescient women, who are themselves the bringers of a fluidity that works against conventional form.

*Love's Labour's Lost* has been often described as Shakespeare's most language-orientated play; in other words, it self-consciously navigates and explores structures of meaning, ideas of discourse, and the language of language.[47] Within this matrix, meaning and the idea of meaning are attached to various themes and places within the play. Nathaniel, for example, examines the 'word' and the teaching of philology for its contradictions and illogical constructions. Yet, once the men have secretly abandoned their abjuration of women, they turn their ambition to describing their love. The Princess and her ladies, in their rejection of love as 'courtesy', deferral of consummation, and insistence on a truth beyond appearance, expose a deeper desire for signification than the play has hitherto seemed capable of supplying. Having wrested their aspiration and awareness from the book of study, the men apply themselves to writing, where they might have read. As the play began, tracing what it would mean to study, so the bookmen evolve through what it would mean to love, and how to mean it.

The transition of the book from humanist article to female metaphor is determined by Berowne to release him, not only from the oath but also from the self-reliance of Stoical living. The educational directives

---

[46] Brown, *Redefining Elizabethan Literature*, 45.

[47] Keir Elam, in *Shakespeare's Universe of Discourse: Language-Games in the Comedies* (Cambridge: Cambridge University Press, 1984), makes a distinction between 'language' and 'discourse'; in terms of Elizabethan English, he explains that the former specifically refers to different tongues, Latin, French, Spanish, etc., and the latter refers to 'language in *use*'. Elam's emphasis on the 'pure self-activity of the word' (quoting Cassirer) understands Shakespeare's use of the word as a dynamic and autonomous instrument that exchanges kinetic energy and meaning within a system of 'self-advertising' response and representation. I have, however, maintained the modern understanding of both 'discourse' and 'language' in order to avoid any confusion within New Historicist or post-structuralist terminology and for consistency within the book as a whole.

of the Academe are consciously self-reflexive, and life, for Berowne at least, is about reciprocity. The expressive, effective text of written desire seems to appear to the bookmen as a blessed and tangible relief from the nebulous idea of 'Things hid and barred' from 'common sense'. The written word, offered in poetic verse or sonnet, is a consistent trope throughout the play, appearing as a performance of the presence of the word itself. Whilst the women often comment on, and occasionally mock, the nature and efficacy of rhyme, the men plunge at it to affect their desire. Armado, desiring a Muse to aid his seduction of Jaquenetta, declares: 'Assist me, some extemporal god of rhyme, for I am sure I shall turn sonnet. Devise wit, write pen, for I am for whole volumes, in folio' (I. ii. 162–4).

Armado is a figure of fun both within and without the play-world, and we might draw parallels with a number of Renaissance writers who looked to 'some extemporal god of rhyme' to conjure their pen, not least of all Sidney in his opening lines to *Astrophil and Stella*.[48] Although the king mocks Armado, he in fact articulates a version of the behaviour of the bookmen; 'turning sonnet' is turning the beloved into a sonnet, and in so doing, this practice aims to identify and appropriate the thing it describes. However, the women's reaction aims to expose this belief in referential love as both naïve and superficial. The idea that the book can somehow embody its inscription is carried over from the original idea of the Academe and translated into the texts of love. The written text provides an expressive link between the physical and metaphysical conditions of truth in meaning. Both scholarship and love must emerge as processes through which we may travel to seek truth and reflection: both depend upon a reciprocal relationship with the object, be it the book or the beloved, and neither scholarship nor love can exist inherently or in isolation. The women reduce the men's search for signification to mere graphic configurations of words, referring the men's need for reflection back to them, and their own sentience to truth as beyond the margins of pre-text. Whilst the women recognize and reject an embodied sign of love, the men persist in offering their love in verse, as though the text itself has become the embodiment of something more than its medium. The women devote their disparagement not to

[48] There are other instances where the play draws images similar to those in *Astrophil and Stella*, most particularly the rendering of fair as black. For a discussion of Sidney in relation to *Love's Labour's Lost*, see H. R. Woudhuysen's introduction to the Arden edition, 3rd ser. (Walton-on-Thames: Thomas Nelson, 1998), 2–6, 11–14.

the peculiarities of love, but to its construction in writing. Receiving the king's letter, the Princess declares:

> Nothing but this?—yes, as much love in rhyme
> As would be crammed up in a sheet of paper
> Writ o'both sides of the leaf, margin and all,
> That he was fain to seal on Cupid's name.
>
> (v ii. 6–9)

Like Armado's rapacious attitude to 'some extemporal god of rhyme', the king's lack of linguistic restraint breaches poetic decorum, and amplitude takes precedence over intimacy: form and quantity become a synecdoche for love. Yet, at the same time, the childlike lack of restraint, the crammed page, and homage to an abstraction of love in Cupid and rhyme denote the king's inexperience in both emotion and expression, inexperience that Boyet has already noticed in the busy silence and still rhetoric of the king's eye. The intellectual naïvety of Navarre and his lords was initially suggested by their inability to harness or express the studious standards to which they would commit themselves; as the play develops, however, the women expose a similar naïvety that sets words before expression. Dramatically, the women govern the audience, since we have only their responses to the love-letters, rather than the letters themselves. Such little faith is placed in the words that the women turn on the materiality of the page. Rosaline laconically observes that Berowne's verses 'hath drawn my picture in his letter':

> PRINCESS. Anything like?
> ROSALINE. Much in the letters, nothing in the praise.
> PRINCESS. Beauteous as ink—a good conclusion.
> CATHERINE. Fair as a text B in a copy-book.
>
> (v. ii. 39–42)

The women, attending to the graphology, pun on Rosaline's ethnicity, likening her to the colour of ink,[49] and it is only in this empirical

---

[49] It is not entirely clear whether Rosaline has dark hair and eyes or dark skin. There are a number of references to her as 'dark' within the play, and it is clear that her colouring is discordant with the synchronic ideas of courtly beauty. However, the poetic trope of configuring or copying the beloved's beauty in black ink or lettering is not uncommon: Sidney uses it to great effect in both *Arcadia* and *Astrophil and Stella*. It is Stella's 'beamy black' beauty that the poet 'copies' on to the page: 'When Nature made her chief work, / Stella's eyes / In colour black, why wrapt she beams so bright? / Would she in beamy black, like painter wise, / Frame daintiest lustre, mixt of shades and light?' (7. 1–4).

way that Berowne has captured an image of his love. The women
are compelled to make a tendentious leap to discover a semblance of
themselves, and, in this case, it is localized not in the ritual of verse but
in the visible marks upon the page. Catherine, drawing upon the image
of a schoolroom exercise, likens Berowne's composition to translation
or repetition, 'text B' being only a version or image of the original (A),
and not the thing itself. Even in image, figurative or ironic, Berowne has
managed only to capture a copy of a copy in an attempt to configure his
beloved. The women's attitudes to these missives set them by the written
page as living marginalia. Slights argues that 'the printed marginalia
did more than any other material feature of book production in the
period to determine, from book to book, the nature of the reading
experience'.[50] The women *are* our reading experience; they point, like
maniscules (holding the page in their hands), to what we must read,
hear, and see; they tell us the colour of the ink and the layout of the
page. The powerful image of the ink as copy of the beloved, but not
the love, has an equally arresting counterpart in the play's frequent
reference to the 'snow-white pen'. As I have already suggested, the
relationship between the book and the body had tremendous figurative
potential, and whereas in *The Shrew* we witness Lucentio's creation of
intimacy in the interpretation and eroticism of Ovid and Bianca, in
*Love's Labour's* the relationship between the corporeal and the textual
is ambiguously and, at times unsettlingly, sexualized. Later, in *Othello*,
the hero explicitly terms Desdemona's virginity as an unmarked page
now defaced by her adultery: 'Was this fair paper, this most goodly
book, / Made to write whore upon?' (IV. ii. 73–4). In 'goodly', Othello
conflates good (pure, chaste) with godly, directly imaging the virtuous
female with Christian education and her body with the Bible. In this

---

Shakespeare, similarly, drew analogies between the dark colouring of his beloved with
the ink through which they were marked in verse: 'What is in the brain that ink may
character, / Which hath not figured to thee true spirit?' (Sonnet 108). The championing
of black as the new blonde ('Then will I swear beauty herself is black, / And all they foul
that they complexion lack') is not exclusive to Shakespeare and Sidney, and, as Stephen
Booth points out, 'the self-consciously heretical practice of praising dark hair and dark
eyes was an established part of the tradition it violated'. In the context of *Love's Labour's
Lost*, Rosaline's 'blackness' has often been the subject of critical contention, since it is
not clear whether it refers to specific features or her ethnicity. Elements of her darkness
come under attack from other characters in the play, which has led some critics to
interpret Shakespeare's portrayal of her as 'alien' or 'other'. However, my interest is in
the relationship between writing and meaning, ink and aesthetics.

[50] Slights, *Managing Readers*, 3.

condemnation, Othello stains his wife's body with sin and the scourge of another man's mark, making and inscribing her a whore. Here, however, the trope is completely reversed, since the body is not the book, but the ink, and fair is not beautiful, but black, and the page is not white, but the pen, and we read not the text, but the margins.

Further confounding the conventional trope of love-poetry, the Princess robustly rejects the bookmen 'to the death'; even accepting the possible quibble on orgasm, her stubborn determination in these terms darkly anticipates the play's awkward, and unsuccessful, navigation of love and death. Turning away from the letters and the love, the Princess announces:

> No, to the death we will not move a foot,
> Nor to their penned speech render we no grace,
> But while 'tis spoke each turn away her face.
>
> (v. ii. 145–7)

It is tempting to infer from the Princess's reference to 'foot' that she is punning on the metrical foot and pronouncing that they will not return the affections with similar, rhythmic, copies of love.[51] The women's view that the men are merely playing at courtesy in copy may be exacerbated by the spaces in which they receive their rhymes. Since the bookmen operate within the symbolic structure of precedent and sonnet, and since they try to trade inherent meanings across words, distance, and estrangement in the park, which houses the Princess and her ladies, they lack the supporting correlative of court. The passage of the book from court to nature (park or forest) emerges rather differently in *As You Like It*, where the Duke, exiled and outcast, claims of his new environment that he 'will find books in the running brooks, sermons in stones and good in everything'. The Duke's comment ennobles him; we see him as a man of Christian hope and intellectual faith. But equally, as Alison Thorne says, such an attitude recalls his courtly aspect: 'The sense of books makes nature comprehensible. It also makes it comfortable, by restoring a courtly sensibility.'[52] Yet in *Love's Labour's* the bookmen conspicuously and consciously step outside their 'court space' and their Academe; the spaces of the court and the park are incompatible, which

---

[51] Shakespeare puns on 'foot' as metrical rhythm and body part in *As You Like It*, when Rosalind says of Orlando's love-poetry: 'the feet were lame, and could not bear themselves without the verse, and therefore stood lamely on the verse' (III. ii. 155–7).

[52] Quoted in Kinney, *Shakespeare's Web*, 58.

is why the women are lodged there and why the men can love there. Visually on-stage, the men are presented obliquely, for they are being observed; the stage space is not symmetrical, even if they were to stand platea or locus, we are forced to see them at an angle according to the position of their observers. The space they carve out for love—because of the imperatives of their world and Academe, because the Princess and her women reside in the park and cannot enter the court—is theatrically radical. Unlike the Duke's Arden, this space is not supposed to carry cultural and social signs within it; nor is it supposed to import them. For love, in this play, and the writing of love are challenges to the organized space of court, park, and stage. Contrary to *As You Like It*, *Love's Labour's* does not use the written word to 'restore courtly sensibility' but to bypass it. For these moments, the stage space is uninhabitable—the speaker should not be there, nor should his observer.

The nature of the uninhabitable or the deficient paves the men's journey from book to beloved. The charade in which the men fail to recognize their true lovers on the basis of their dress makes a spectacle of the women's fears. The women's distrust of the men's relationship to language is symbolically amplified in the male attachment to the fripperies or 'silken taffeta phrases', as it were, of appearance. Berowne's later description of language within the flattering fabric of ostentation goes some way to augment the play's exposure of words as surrogate intimacy. The charade of the Muscovites allegorizes the play's treatment of static and inanimate signs. The unfortunate entrapment brought about by the women is effected as they each adopt a token of the others' dress. During the Muscovite performance, the disguised 'book men' try to court the women, and, unbeknown to them, prostrate themselves before the wrong lady; Longueville, hoping for some capitulation, says, 'Let's part the word', to which Catherine responds, 'No, I'll not be your half' (v. ii. 249). Putting aside the sexual innuendoes, the dialogue suggests a particular understanding of the word within the play's search for signification. Richard Mulcaster's *Elementarie* (1582), a standard humanist text, explains how the noun performs its meaning: 'What a cunning thing it is to give right names, and how necessarie it is, to know their forces, which alredie given, bycause the word being knowen, which implyeth the propertie the thyng is half known, whose propertie is emplyed.'[53]

---

[53] As quoted by William C. Carroll, *The Great Feast of Language in 'Love's Labour's Lost'* (Princeton: Princeton University Press, 1976), 13.

The 'force' and purpose of the word is that it inherently contains half of what it represents, so that, if we 'part the word', half shall be the thing itself, and half the activity of the signified idea. Longueville's attempt to 'part the word' appears to act or 'employ' love in conjunction with its inherent signification. Longueville's attention to the word surfaces as part of the bookmen's belief in the authority of language to release inherent meaning. Locating the word in its parts signals Longueville's perception of himself as an appendix to the performing sign, and suggests a profound faith in the authority of language to determine his reality. Equally, Catherine's devolved relationship, wherein she has the capacity, in reciprocating his love, to re-form the word, glances at the more 'earthly delights' of Platonic Image and Form. Representing half of Longueville's objective and meaning, Catherine has the ability to harness the word and contain the 'force' of the word between them. Longueville's skittish approach to seduction situates his relationship to his beloved within a powerful and evolving discourse on love and language. His playful parting of the word indicates a much more serious and problematic area in the play, where all meaning is subject to disruption once it stands apart from the speaker and the subject. Yet the prevailing understanding of language in early modern hermeneutics imagines the word as a contained and reflective mirror of the perceived and empirical world; the process of naming and referencing works both adorns and augments a reasonable structure of engagement and response. Poetry, as we are frequently reminded in its arcane inspirations or intellectual apologies, elaborates on the known and knowing world through association, attachment, and sensory imagination. The location of language in the mirror-mind is symptomatic of the harmonic relationship between man and his world that simultaneously defines and designs him: for the bookmen the union of lover and beloved has become the language of naming.[54] Yet, in this, the men make no distinction between love rendered meaningful in the pre-texts of poetry and love rendered communicable in contact with the beloved. The language of love becomes a contentious site of meaning as it floats freely in the unspecified space of deficiency and disenchantment.

[54] See above. For Carroll, the act and implications of 'naming' are central to the play. The emphasis on the propriety and impropriety of naming arises not only from his argument for the centrality of language, but also from a pre- and post-lapsarian dialectic between essential and corrupt language which, for Ann Barton, is expressed in the contention between reality and illusion: Roesen, 'Love's Labour's Lost'.

In one respect, the dialogue between Catherine and Longueville is symptomatic of the discourse-dance through which the characters emerge, choosing or rejecting properties and rhythms of the word. In another respect, Catherine's response is indicative of a wider, more sceptical concept of marriage, which, like education, determines the behaviour of the woman according to her reflective response to her husband.[55] John Case, in his *Thesaurus Oeconomiae* (1597), addresses various questions concerning the moral responsibilities and social dynamics incumbent upon the married couple. Case values love highly as a condition of marriage and, in determining the language of affection between couples, argues for a degree of flexible subjectivity. The language of love cannot and should not be tried on empirical or existential grounds, and 'affection' is therefore deemed to be exempt from finite rules of representation. Case focuses our understanding on a relationship between representation and love that finds no absolute relief in naming:

> Finally to say that the father is more like God is to confuse finite with infinite, and words with reality: there is no comparison between God and man, and though in name the father may seem more to resemble God as begetter and cause, the similitude in name only is no cause for greater affection, since love is seen in the truth of affection, not in the shadow of a name.[56]

For Case, language—particularly the language of love—is only a shadow of the feeling it expresses, since not only are feelings metaphysical, but language is only an idea of the 'truth' searched for in words but supported by emotion or action. Emotional truth, and faith in that truth, as it is, and in order for it to remain so, is always at a distance from semantics. This apparently romantic view of love is qualified by Case as he advocates temperate and reasonable conduct in marriage:

---

[55] Robert S. Knapp, in his essay ' "Is it appropriate for a man to fear his wife?": John Case on Marriage', *English Literary Renaissance*, 28 (1998), 387–415, charts the language and ceremony of marriage within the concept of community. One of Case's concerns is the role and value attached to truth or illusion in the language and dynamics of conjugal living; for example, does it matter if your wife is not the most beautiful woman in the world if you, as her husband, believe her to be? What are the social and cultural consequences of truths and illusions supported by perception? Interestingly, in the context of this chapter, Case understands the relationship between man and wife as similar to Sidney's understanding of the functions and benefits of poetry. Knapp suggests: 'By explicitly associating his understanding of the relationship between man and wife with Sidney's account of the function of ideal, poetic images, he lets us see something of the way in which "Petrarchan" literary thought could have ethical, psychological, and spiritual effects within marriage' (p. 402).

[56] Ibid. 398.

And as he insists in the *quaestiones*, this is neither idolatry nor intellectual error: the husband admires his wife rather than adores her; he does not make a god or idol of her, but rather the mirror and consolation of his life; this judgement is necessarily a matter of affection and opinion, not of knowledge and intellect.[57]

The distinction between knowledge and affection is central to the trajectory of the play. Navarre and his lords began their search for knowledge heavily informed by feeling—whether it was the desire for something beyond their status or the abjuration of physical pleasure—in rejection or pursuit, but their desire leads them into an awkward and ambiguous synthesis of affection and intellect. As Case suggests, only in registering the limits of opinion and intellect can a harmony of love and knowledge be sustained. Once the bookmen step outside the boundaries of their prescribed knowledge—the court, the oath, the clothes—they lose the support of a sympathetic reality. And it is this absence of sympathetic support that translates their love into 'jest' or 'courtesy'. However, this is not to say that the women merely misunderstand them, for the bookmen have much to learn, and when Berowne returns us to the book at the end of the play, we realize that the men have simply transferred their idolatry from the book to the beloved, hence their various trials at the close. This understanding of language and love is, as yet, too sophisticated for Longueville, and, unlike Case, his separation of love from knowledge is not based upon perceptive approaches to truth. Whilst Case deems affection to be ineffable and exempt from absolute definition or objective correlatives, Longueville supposes love to be as prescriptive as learning, but subject to a different discipline and an alternative text. The lovers' rather desultory relationship to either language or love is summed up in Rosaline's comment on their performance: 'Ah, they were all in lamentable cases. / The King was weeping-ripe for a good word' (v. ii. 273–4).

The play on the general absence of 'a good word', either in approval from the women or affection from the men, suggests the seminal difference that such a word would have made. Indeed, the very proliferation of puns situates the word as a significant part of the infrastructure of the play;[58] but the 'good word' that the king could not provide was the harmonic signification of moment and meaning, word and self.

[57] Ibid. 409.
[58] For an insightful and provocative look at the role of the pun in creating and releasing meaning, particularly in relation to sexuality and gender definition, see Carroll, 'The Virgin Not'.

Of course, the women are largely culpable for this destabilization of language, since it is through their transference of identities that the men fail to overcome the obstacle of objectification. Yet the women's role in exposing processes and failures of translation illuminates our faith in naming to affect reality. In contrast, the bookmen's deference to the letters of love highlights their inexperience, and emerges as a particular and public aspect of their humiliation. The hopeless lovers are forced into obliquity through the eyes of each other as well as the audience. Believing themselves to be alone they fall upon the opportunity to declaim:

> BEROWNE. By heaven, I do love, and it hath taught me to rhyme and be melancholy, and here [*showing a paper*] is part of my rhyme, and here [*touching his breast*] my melancholy.
> LONGUEVILLE. I fear these stubborn lines lack power to move.
>     O sweet Maria, empress of my love,
>     These numbers I will tear, and write in prose.
> DUMAIN. This will I send [an ode], and something else more plain,
>     That shall express my true love's fasting pain.
>
> (IV. iii. 10–13, 50–2, 117–18)

As Berowne demonstrably performs a relationship between his heart and his text on-stage, we see how (*showing a paper, touching his breast*), when the written word comes into contact with feeling, a dialogue between thought and action emerges. In a need to animate their silenced selves, the men move beyond the imaginative (and here, public) presence of the book to the idea of poesy, wherein convention and form appear to determine the space between isolated emotion and reflexive being. As each lover steps forward with his own idea of love, he exposes 'rhyme', 'lines,' 'numbers', 'prose', and 'odes' as free-floating signs of intimacy. For the lovers, verse pattern as ritual or pre-text operates in a similar way to the schoolbook primer, as a copybook on which to impress and initiate their selves. In this way rhyme, metre, and form seem to embody the very idea of poetry, and poetry seems to embody the very idea of love.

The response of the three lords to their desire and writing denotes three different, but all parodied, ideas of the transaction between language and feeling. Berowne makes a metonym out of rhyme and love, and therefore the former will always mean the latter. Longueville feels hampered by the boundaries of verse, and turns to prose in the hope of a more liberal range of meaning. And Dumaine, perhaps most interestingly, caught by an awareness of the limits of language to represent the self, sends his beloved two alternative missives of desire, an ode and 'something else more plain'. All three men feel confident that, whatever their particular method, the generic constructs of 'poesy' will write and represent their inner feelings. The possibility of the private self or individual consciousness in language, as isolated from either imagination or experience, is subject to doubt. As the play navigates the two most profound human emotions of love and grief, we begin to wonder whether the ability to access and respond to the self in language will always remain in translation.[59] Yet neither love nor grief fulfils itself in *Love's Labour's Lost*, since both states are deferred or suspended. Love and grief have alternately and separately reorganized intentions and hopes; but neither state provides an entirely satisfactory fabric on which to inscribe the evolution of the subjective self.

The play's presentation of learning runs in different directions: what we might call the potential and the pedantic. The sub-plot of the schoolmaster and his team runs rather obliquely alongside the main play; in terms of love, it crudely harnesses and amplifies the basic boytriestogetgirlthroughloveandlanguage theme. In terms of learning, however, it brilliantly confronts the conceptual and strategic marks of discourse, parodying the pedant, the prescriptivist, and the grammarian, whilst simultaneously presenting language as the most exceptional and essential of arts.[60] Whilst the Princess and Rosaline discuss the configurations of graphology and what Walter Ong would call 'the word-in-space', Nathaniel, Armado, and Holofernes attend to the nature and problem of elocution and decorum.[61] The men's attitude and attention to language, in the rites of translation and iteration, are straightforward parodies of the humanist schoolmaster and the popular

---

[59] It is the character of Mercadé who epitomizes both love and loss: he enters the play at a critical moment, in terms of the resolution of desire, with news of the King's death.

[60] Although it is important to remember that the characters of Armardo, Holofernes, and Nathaniel, to some extent, are representative of the initial imperatives of humanism. Such precise and thoughtful attention to language, its form, technicalities, and movements, are seminal points in evaluating the nature of 'translation' and how words move through 'historical distance'.

[61] Although Ong describes the printed word as particularly spatially orientated according to its mechanical production: 'Texts are thing-like, immobilized in visual space, subject to what [Jack] Goody calls "backward scanning".' Equally, the nature of the written word apparently declares its authenticity in visual presence: 'orality relegates meaning largely to context whereas writing concentrates meaning in language itself': Walter J. Ong, *Orality and Literacy: The Technologising of the Word* (London and New York: Routledge, 2000), 99–100, 106, 122.

primary texts of philologists such as Lily, Mulcaster, and Perkins. The satire is explored in this relationship between 'teacher' and text, learning and language. Nathaniel, like his companions, seeks precision in excess, hyperbole, and zeugma; attempting to explain the ineptitude of Dull, he suggests: 'Sir, he hath never fed of the dainties that are bred in a book. He hath not eat paper, as it were, he hath not drunk ink. His intellect is not replenished, he is only an animal, only sensible in the duller parts.' (IV. ii. 21–3).

Language in *Love's Labour's Lost* is in search of language, and the book, according to Nathaniel, is the iconic map of that journey. Before Berowne develops his sophistic argument centralizing the figurative status of the book, Nathaniel deconstructs it metaphorically to exemplify the ignorant, or starved, Dull. Nathaniel strips the sum of the book into its component parts to imaginatively re-form them as a process of ingestion that the animal, in its primitive and uncivilized world, is condemned to live without. The feasting or eating of knowledge by way of the book is the original premiss from which Navarre set out, and here Nathaniel attempts to represent that 'scholarly' claim literally. His only way of expanding or developing the role of the book within the ideological self is to articulate a literal transaction between material and metaphor in an effort to reassure himself of the *feeling* of learning. Nathaniel registers his superiority through his elaborate use of the figurative book; extending his image through the corporeal appetite and physical condition, he sustains his ego in semantics. The ease with which Nathaniel accommodates the transition of the book from icon to metaphor is an important part of his definition of self: using the book as a formative sign he creates for himself and his colleagues 'a little academe', or he tries to. Commenting on Armado's amorous letter to Jaquenetta, Nathaniel claims that:

> Study his bias leaves, and makes his book thine eyes,
> Where all those pleasures live that art would comprehend.

(IV. ii. 102–3)

Unlike the bookmen, Nathaniel is able to create a sustainable bookish surface because it is entirely self-referential, and here, also unlike Navarre and his lords, he can synthesize love and learning without losing his integrity. Nathaniel neither steps outside, nor denies, the linguistic and intellectual imperatives by which he exists, so that he is always within the space and moment of his own semantic field. Nathaniel's ability to articulate his subject through a bookish hinterland marks him as one who has 'fed of the dainties that are bred in a book', 'eat[en] paper', and 'drunk ink'. In referencing a sustainable relationship between world and book, Nathaniel comments:

> NATHANIEL. . . . . for society, saith the text, is the happiness of life.
> HOLOFERNES. And certes the text most infallibly concludes it.
>
> (IV. ii. 147–8)

Irrespective of the sentiment, Holofernes returns the authority to the text, since, even though such happiness lies with society, the truth of the judgement lies with the written word. It seems impossible for either Holofernes or Nathaniel to separate themselves from the ideology and edicts of text, and together they perpetuate a synchronic system of bookish supremacy. The word of the book or the text fixes meaning, establishes authority, recognizes the speaker, and determines experience. As Berowne works toward his anagnorisis, his recognition and redefinition of aspiration and affection, he prepares an oath:

> Where is a book,
> That I may swear beauty doth beauty lack
> If that she learn not of her eye to look?
> No face is fair that is not full so black.
>
> (IV. iii. 246–9)

The signification of a book in oath is in part both a resurrection and a rejection of the initial ascetic oath, but it is also symptomatic of the structure and affirmation of the sentiment that surrounds the language of the book. It is usually assumed that Berowne's book is a Bible due to the oath-like context; however, given the indefinite article, it could be any book. Equally, within the Neoplatonic context, where Beauty has become the privileged and noble Form, Berowne's book is symbolic of his desire for a sympathetic union of the intellectual trilogy of passion, action, and contemplation.

The play's confrontation with the language of learning, conceptualized in 'the book' and the 'word', undergoes a process of transition and transmutation that is emblematic of a similar journey undertaken by the lovers. The play's relationship with paradox and difference is directly invoked in Berowne's peroration:

> For wisdom's sake—a word that all men love—
> Or for love's sake—a word that loves all men—
> Or for men's sake—the authors of these women—
> Or women's sake—by whom we men are men—

> Let us once lose our oaths to find ourselves,
> Or else we lose ourselves to keep our oaths.
> It is religion to be thus forsworn,
> For charity itself fulfils the law,
> And who can sever love from charity?

(IV. iii. 331-9)

This speech deserves particular and detailed attention, since it juxtaposes, fragments, and reformulates many central and serious elements of discourse. The first four lines, embedded in rhetorical device, employ 'wisdom', 'love', 'word', and 'author', in a dance of meaning that is underscored and harmonized by 'men' and 'women'. Despite the repetition, or ploce, effective in these four statements, none of the sentences are constructed according to the same emphasis or noun definition. The word 'wisdom' enters powerfully as a concept: a word that men love, aspiring to or appreciating that epistemological end; yet, although it is as quickly abandoned in favour of an extended play on 'love', it remains in the shadows of love to support the 'wisdom' of that word and emotion. 'Love's' functions in the second line as a quibble, and according to its specific grammatical disposition, conflates the possessive and the plural in 'love's' and 'loves', exercising word-play at the expense of precision. The second pair of lines is involved in a broader and more essential ambiguity: men, conventionally, are not described as 'authors' of women (or anyone), since they do not bear gestation or labour, yet within this immediate context 'authors' is given the meaning of 'engendered' or 'created'. In the broader context of Berowne's speech and the play, however, the line proposes that men write, engender, or create 'these women' according to their own ideas of self and composition; in other words, they authorize them when they render them communicable in language, or verse. The following line plays upon the ambiguity of the former by allocating women their procreative and supportive role in the development of the male identity. However, rather than function as 'other', in the conventional sense of frictional cipher, women are the formative mirrors of assimilation and reflection; they enable and ignite the subjective self through positioning it in the sensible world.

Within the play, the women represent the ability to recognize, explore, or reject language as an arbitrary and impersonal system of signs. In their recognition of the performance of the 'word', they reject language, like the peripheral space of the park, or the illusory fabric of the masque, as a process of translation in which essence is diluted or even condemned by representation.[62] Just as they stood as theatrical marginalia between the bookmen's voices and pages, the women urge translation not as 'annotational supplement' but as something new. Questioning the status of their poetic invention, the women reject 'copy' and convention. As Brown describes, the residual notion of poetic invention was a static one, and firmly linked to a microcosmic view of language:

> The traditional rhetorical definition of invention refers primarily to the discovery of an idea that already existed, and not to a creation *ex nihilo* . . . . The mind can only comprehend objects with which it is familiar and the process of knowledge is the discovery of resemblances. Invention is not conceived as the discovery of something completely new because there is no room for novelty in a world where everything points to everything else.[63]

What the women seem to want is a world in which everything does not axiomatically point to everything else, a world in which they are not forced to annotate, copy, or marginalize their bodies. Berowne's speech begins to gesture at newness in translation, or the release of meaning from a rigid world order of signs. Women, wisdom, love, and men jostle for a new relationship to each other through the recognition of the fluidity of these words themselves.

The final lines of Berowne's speech temptingly navigate a fundamental point of translation. Arguably one of the most contentious aspects of Tyndale's translation of the New Testament from the Greek in 1526 was his decision to render the Vulgate's translation of 'charity' as 'love'. Berowne's question, 'Who can sever love from charity?', recalls a seminal point in the history of the churches in the relationship between translation and interpretation, symbol and meaning. Berowne's question challenges a composite view of language, and gestures at the language of meaning as in feeling rather than essence. Berowne's gesture retrieves the subjective self from the objective structure: what makes his words meaningful, or anybody's words meaningful, is the journey that they make through both perceptual and cultural signs. Berowne's image

---

[62] Appositely, within the context of this discussion, ' "translation" [is] a synonym for "metaphor" in Elizabethan English'; see Malcolm Evans, 'Deconstructing Shakespeare's Comedies', in John Drakakis (ed.), *Alternative Shakespeares* (London and New York: Routledge, 1996), 75.

[63] Brown, *Redefining Elizabethan Literature*, 45.

juxtaposes a monk who effects a version of charity in his choices and actions with a layman who can accommodate another version of charity through loving a woman. Both men may swear an oath of love, one to God, the other to his wife; both men are forsworn, and both love, but are contracted to different imperatives, and, in the light of this, we might recall Case's analogy with the ineffable nature of God and the romantic affection of marriage.[64] Tyndale's editorial decision, he declared, was based on a desire to 'interpret the sense of the scripture and the meaning of the spirit'; here he deliberately transposes the traditional language of response by 'sensing' the text and 'explaining' the spirit. Such a synthesis of self and meaning underpins the development of the play.

The search to signify the self is localized in the transition from knowledge to self-knowledge, and in the realization that they are not mutually inclusive. Berowne locates the movement of the book from icon to metaphor, from ideology to affection:

> O, we have made a vow to study, lords,
> And in that vow we have forsworn our books.
>
> (IV. iii. 292–3)

However, rather than abandon the premises with which they began, Berowne chooses to translate the idea of the book not only to incorporate women, but also to re-present them:

> Never durst poet touch a pen to write
> Until his ink were tempered with love's sighs.
> O, then his lines would ravish savage ears,
> And plant in tyrants mild humility.
> From women's eyes this doctrine I derive.
> They sparkle still the right Promethean fire.
> They are the books, the arts, the academes
> That show, contain, and nourish all the world,
> Else none at all in aught proves excellent.
>
> (IV. iii. 320–8)

Berowne's 'doctrine' creates a metonymic relationship between women, books, arts, and academes, which he then animates by the correlative verbs of 'show', 'contain', and 'nourish'. This verbal arrangement synthesizes the art of study with the act of procreation to the extent

---

[64] This, of course, is a distinctly Protestant conception, since it is directed through justification by faith, and not by good deeds or coffers, which would register a more Catholic commitment to either love or charity.

that woman and book become mutually absorbed in the act and art of sustaining a world picture. The verbs play upon the visible and physical aspects of pregnancy, whilst at the same time investing the intellectual life with a generative and material power. Here 'show' works to focus the representative potential of women to reproduce their lover and their child as well as imaging the book and the Academe as reflective of knowledge and the bodies who pursue it. Just as desire informed the initial aspiration to study, so here the body contains the presence and potential of all that 'proves excellent'. Even though the speech begins with a certain conventional invocation of love as the essential and poetic Muse, Berowne does acknowledge a dialogic relationship between the lover and his language that requires a process of reflection and engagement. Although Berowne displays a developing awareness of the activity of the word, he continues to deploy his desires through the semiotics of pre-text; and whereas he may push himself beyond a complacent relationship between ink and love, Rosaline will push him back to words that have no textual relief: the 'language' of the speechless sick.

Although for Berowne, the book supports a language of naming, women, desire, doctrine, and love, it remains in limbo. Ultimately the book cannot support what Berowne wants, because the books, the arts, and the academes have been absent or deficient systems of thought throughout the play. In translating the women into the original edict, he moves no further in ascertaining his self or obtaining his desires, for those original ideas were fatally flawed and unstable. Berowne's semantic volte-face does nothing more than alienate the already alienated women. The book as an icon or a metaphor cannot accommodate the lovers, and Berowne terminally misreads his beloved in this transliteration. In sending him into exile with the 'speechless sick', Rosaline condemns any productive or sensible notion of bookishness. The book is redundant. What remains behind—silence, illness, death, and separation—brings the play to a close, and the book becomes part of the fabric of the comedy that never was. The book is the deficient bridge from love to life that will not and cannot travel the distance, from the court to the park, from the mind to the body, from the Academe to the women, and from asceticism to marriage.

Berowne's translation reveals a comprehensive system of expression that is predicated on a value system inherent in the book: 'They are the books, the arts, the academes.' The book began as an instrument of access, via the 'little academe', to the 'wonder of the world', with which Navarre opened the play: the book continues to function as the microcosm, but has since accrued 'love's sighs', 'women's eyes', and, in these, 'the voice of all the gods'. The growth in meaning is born from a parallel expansion in the art of language. Whereas the referent, sign, or emblem could not sustain or animate its essence, the metaphorical or the metaphysical open up a potential discourse between speaker and subject, and in this way the 'copy' is rejected:

> O, never will I trust to speeches penned,
> Nor to the motion of a schoolboy's tongue,
> Nor never come in visor to my friend,
> Nor woo in rhyme, like a blind harper's song.
> Taffeta phrases, silken terms precise,
> Three-piled hyperboles, spruce affectation,
> Figures pedantical—these summer flies
> Have blown me full of maggot ostentation.
>
> (v. ii. 402–9)[65]

Despite the lovers' recognition of the need to re-define themselves and the language of their desires, despite their re-configuration and extension of the structure and demands of the bookish world, they are finally pitched against the judgement of the women, who refer each man to an equitable experience. *Love's Labour's Lost* ends as Armado claims that 'The words of Mercury are harsh after the songs of Apollo', and the juxtaposition of these two gods is usually taken as referring to the sombre entrance of death after the light of love. However, both Apollo and Mercury are astral gods, and the former is associated with music and poetry, the latter with science and travelling. What we might also infer from Armado's closing statement is the power of language and the arts within processes of change. Mercury was, particularly within the field of alchemy, regarded as a potent aspect of change, and in astrology, as a sign of poets or eloquence, as well as mythologically attached to travelling and science. Within the context of these constructions, we might better understand Mercury's role here as symptomatic of the need for fluidity and metamorphosis, for the journey that language must make to confront the world that it encounters.

The women, who refuse resolution, defer expectation, and resist a generic formula, are the keepers of a truth that lies beyond the boundaries of graphic art. Yet, as the play ends with the bookmen packed off into

---

[65] The irony, of course, is that the lines quoted are the octave of a sonnet.

their various spaces of transition or reform, there is a sense in which the play closes as its discourse begins. Each of the men is taken back to the beginning of his journey, only this time in terms outlined by the women. When Berowne explains that from this moment their lives are 'too long for a play', they are returned to words, 'to weed this wormwood from your fruitful brain'; to silence, 'a forlorn and naked hermitage'; to experience, 'a beard, fair health and honesty'; and to thought, after which they will begin their journey into expression once more.

Both *The Taming of the Shrew* and *Love's Labour's Lost* are dramatically supported by a relationship to the book. More particularly, both plays expose how the book can appear to translate systems of value and interpretation from which love can be either defaced or fetishized. In *The Shrew*, the role of the teacher (be he tamer or tutor) is drawn through institutional and anarchic structures of imitation and response. Working with (Lucentio) and without (Petruchio) 'the book', love is identified as a corollary of instruction referred to the body of the woman and the ambivalent socio-eroticism of the institution. Yet, even within a few years, the performance of the book has dramatically changed. In *Love's Labour's*, the idea of the book begins a semantic and metaphysical journey through the terms and forms of represented and representative truth. From the outset, the play scrutinizes and fragments graphic and ideological performances of the book; from the angel knowledge of academia, through rhyme, prose, odes, and inscription to the very ink and page that form the text, each aspect and sign of the written word is subject to accusations of paucity or foppery. Yet neither play concludes comfortably nor celebrates its value system; rather, both plays end with an awkward, unresolved, or ambiguous love. Where we might have begun with a faith in 'translation', from the tutor to the lover, the shrew to the wife, the bookman to the husband, and the Princess to the Queen, not one of these processes of translation is satisfactory. Yet, as the characters unfurl under the semiotic of the book and the auspices of love, it becomes harder to distinguish which—the book or love—has the most power to challenge meaning.

# 4

## 'Marked with a blot, damned in the book of heaven': Word, Image, and the Reformation of the Self in *Richard II*

The book that Richard II places at the heart of his reign and his righteousness is the book of heaven, an inscrutable icon of faith that synthesizes the celestial and temporal worlds: a 'marriage—'twixt my crown and me' (v. ii. 72).[1] The book of heaven is ordained by God in a teleological universe, in which the path of life is justified by the judgement of heaven. This book is strictly bound by the divinity of kings, and it is to these pages that Richard refers his selective conscience for the immutable justification of precedence and power. However, despite the Christian pre-text of this image, Richard appears to create an independent and amorphous space in which he constantly seeks to re-define the limits of his reign. Fashioning himself through theories of un-visibility,[2] Richard harnesses the book to his body, as he later will the mirror to his soul. This book, I shall argue, becomes enmeshed in creating and dissolving representational terms of transparency, which have emerged from the hinterland between Catholicism and Protestantism. On the one hand, the book is iconic, celebrating mystery and divinity through visual suggestion and omnipotent authority; on the other, the book sanctions and justifies private faith and individual free will; it can accommodate the subjective, and write the faithful heart.

---

[1] William Shakespeare, *Richard II*, ed. Stanley Wells (Harmondsworth: Penguin, 1997). All references are to this edition, unless otherwise stated. This edition uses the Folio as the control text.

[2] I use the word 'un-visibility' here, as opposed to invisibility, because Richard negotiates his self-image in terms of what is seen and what might be seen, as though his icons of authority rest from sight rather than deny it.

In this chapter I will examine how *Richard II* uses the spaces between Catholicism and Protestantism to enable signs to move between literal power and figurative freedom; how visual icons emerge to translate each other into effective dramatic weapons; and how the book, drawing on its status as a representational commodity, becomes the token of a faithless self in transition. The figurative scope generated by the arcane book of heaven, in conjunction with the king's self-determined iconography, does not necessarily respond to medieval or even Tudor concepts of kingship, but confronts the relationship between presence and essence. *Richard II* is by far the most complicated play in terms of Shakespeare's idea of the book, for image and word become enmeshed in a shifting religious discourse, as well as theatrical practices of visibility and suggestion. Both the ubiquitous presence of the book and the various devolved icons through which it moves elide our immediate responses to meaning and the sometimes impossible dialectic of truth between word and image.

The book in *Richard II* is never strictly referred to as 'the Bible'; however, Richard's invocation of transcendental support and monarchical authority, his self-righteousness, identification with Christ, and division of the physical and spiritual clearly locate a theatrical synthesis between medieval kingship and post-Reformation supremacy.[3] In religious writings during the latter half of the sixteenth century, the idea of the book often mapped the shift in understanding between the image and the thing itself. The book could accommodate this distance, since it supported both an idea of faith (and therefore became a synonym for the illiterate's visual narrative) and faith itself (the written word of God became the reader's personal devotion). Although we cannot be certain that Richard's book is the Bible as we would recognize it in either the pre- or post-Reformation churches of England, we can begin to explore the way in which both the symbolic and the textual value of the Bible may be absorbed not only into standard humanist culture, but also into representations of power in the relationship between language and image, and, ultimately, how the book becomes essential to an

---

[3] Naseeb Shaheen's study, *Biblical References in Shakespeare's Plays* (Newark, NJ: University of Delaware Press; London: Associated University Press, 1999), claims that, in terms of secondary sources, 'the most significant biblical borrowing is the betrayal of Christ theme taken from Créton and the *Traïson*. But these works contain very few additional references to Scripture, none of which Shakespeare used. . . . As was Shakespeare's usual practice, the many biblical references in the play are largely his own' (p. 362).

exploration of faith, not finally in God, but in oneself. Richard's rather nebulous identification with the book becomes central to how he isolates and represents his own narrative of meaning. That Shakespeare does not nominally, or distinctly, specify the Bible is not unusual, since the word never appears in any of his plays (the exception being a comic reference in *The Merry Wives of Windsor*),[4] but Richard's rhetorical absorption of biblical text into subjective experience, alongside his esoteric relationship with the Word of God, dramatically determines the ways in which the king seeks to augment his self in the book of God and the eyes of men. Although no serious investigation of Shakespeare's books can be considered without an exposition of the role of the Bible, it is important to remember that in *Richard II* the 'book', like the 'glass' or the crown, provides Richard with an empty receptacle for the organization of his reality, and the religious implications do not necessarily mark out the book for spiritual exegesis.[5] As Richard projects himself on to the idea of the book, he seeks to translate the ineffable into private power. Probably the three most important visual signs in this play are the book, the mirror, and the crown; each one is dramatically dependent upon the others, and each article becomes intertwined in the spectacle that seeks to render them meaningless.

The play opens in the middle of the history of the reign of Richard II. Entering the stage in the midst of a murky dispute over loyalty, Richard immediately invokes the 'oath and bond' that binds a subject to protect his king from treason. Despite the history that defines Richard's relationship to the death of his uncle, and Mowbray's and Bolingbroke's parts in it, the play makes no obvious attempt to implicate or narrate the pre-text to this scene. On the one hand, we have an idea of the historical Richard, as we are dramatically thrown into the circumstances of his accession—a story of the death of kings—and on the other, we see

---

[4] Censorship, of course, played a fundamental role in the stage's exclusion of the Bible, and we notice that the escapade with 'the book and the priest' in *The Shrew* takes place off-stage.

[5] 'The Book' is usually understood as a synonym for the Bible, since, according to the *Dictionary of the Christian Church*, 'the word "Bible" derives from a Greek word meaning "books"; as the biblical Books came to be regarded as a unity, the word came to used as a single noun'. The *OED*, however, makes this the fifth definition of the noun. Inherent in the use of 'the Book' as a noun are the concepts of 'unity' and the cohesive authority of the application to and understanding of the text. In *Richard II*, however, the king's understanding of and application to the Book is dependent, not upon its unification of Christian subjects but upon his individual elevation and justification, through the works of God, to the understanding of men.

the Richard on-stage before us, who is apparently entirely contained by the word and voice of divine and monarchical authority.[6] As the scene progresses, we witness Richard presiding over an 'appeal for treason', in which the king has absolute and instant authority to decide justice.[7] As Richard apportions blame and exiles his former allies, he establishes the terms of his power; to Mowbray he declares:

> The hopeless word of 'never to return'
> Breathe I against thee upon pain of life.
>
> (I. iii. 152–3)

In drawing attention to the 'word' of banishment and the imposition of the emotional values of 'hopeless', 'against', and 'pain', Richard breathes his words as statute, writing the air with the irrefutable. Behind his words are the book of heaven and the jurisdiction of God, and Mowbray's anticipation of his exile imagines what Richard has not said—the walking death of silence as an alien in a foreign land:

> Within my mouth you have engaoled my tongue,
> Doubly portcullised with my teeth and lips,
> And dull unfeeling barren ignorance
> Is made my gaoler to attend on me.
>
> .    .    .    .    .    .    .    .    .
>
> What is my sentence then but speechless death,
> Which robs my tongue from breathing native breath?
>
> (I. iii. 166–9, 172–3)

From Richard's 'hopeless word' Mowbray extrapolates the living hell of enforced silence, impotence, and frustration that may remind us of the trials of the Traitors in Dante's book of hell, who were frozen into ice only to watch and murmur away their indefinite time. Mowbray imagines his future in terms that augment Richard's God-like self-image and, in Richard's turning the tongue into a prison, Mowbray

---

[6] Although my study of the book is not based on intertextual sourcing, we might note that 'Shakespeare borrowed more biblical references from it [*Woodstock*] than from any of his other sources': Shaheen, *Biblical References*, 362. In terms of how the play chooses to unfold its history upon the stage, that *Woodstock* contains the prehistory of Shakespeare's Richard and the most secondary biblical references, yet never explicitly defines itself in relation to either, creates a theatrical tension between history and representation on-stage.

[7] As Katherine Eisaman Maus explains, in The Norton Shakespeare, an 'appeal for treason' was when a 'plaintiff and defendant present their cases in their own persons before the King, who instantly dispenses justice' and was 'already archaic in Shakespeare's time' (p. 943).

anticipates the graphic way in which Richard censures life. The word and breath that begin our image of Richard's reign and send his traitors into senseless isolation and speechlessness, 'No never write, regreet, nor reconcile', spreads the written word, and its present history, like a stain or 'blot' across the stage. When Bolingbroke urges Mowbray to 'confess' his treason, he responds: 'No, Bolingbroke, if ever I were traitor / My name be blotted from the book of life' (i. iii. 201–2). This image of the blot, excising or marking a book, introduces an intellectual and visual paradigm that remains powerful throughout the play. The book of life, as compiled by Mowbray, is a long and ubiquitous volume, in which 'life' is a written history of events and effects beyond the instant demands of recorded speech. The weight of Mowbray's book, like his exile, is construed in what is not said: he may be a murderer, but he is not a traitor, and the suggestion of a possible textual truth sets up the book as an image of the competing histories that shadow the stage. Whether 'truth' emerges as determined precedence or suppressed information is evinced by the idea of the book, which supports the various relationships to monarchy and absolutism throughout the play. Working from Richard's own appeal to a divine textual authority, the play exposes how power seeks to augment itself against the graphic stains of history. Whilst Bolingbroke sees himself 'End in a word—such is the breath of kings', John of Gaunt feels his story or 'tale' to have been unheard, and therefore erased by Richard. Following on from his own censure, Gaunt conflates his son's exile with 'this dear, dear, land,' 'leased out' 'Like to a tenement or pelting farm' which has defaced the book of England:

> England, bound in with the triumphant sea,
> Whose rocky shore beats back the envious siege
> Of watery Neptune, is now bound in with shame,
> With inky blots and rotten parchment bonds.
>
> (ii. i. 61–4)

The relationship that Gaunt invokes between the 'leased' land and the rotten fabric of the country may glance at the Domesday Book and Richard's taxation to fund his war with Ireland. Richard's wrongs seep into the pages of his country—imagined as, and recorded in, the book—and the false oaths and bonds through which Richard seeks to consolidate his reign are here evoked as the very land upon which he stands. Shame is the binding of a corrupt text. Calling forth the imperial duty of England's history, Gaunt envisages how Richard begins to rot and stain the pages of his reign, suggesting that both kings and history lie 'writ with blank space for different names'. (*Merry Wives*, II. i. 66). Yet whilst Gaunt images the royal precedent as inexorably linked to its country's textual history, Richard writes his own story, as distinct from that of his subjects, through the symbolic power of what he can either 'show' or 'blot'. As Richard faces Bolingbroke's growing rebellion, he exclaims: 'For God's sake let us sit upon the ground / And tell sad stories of the death of kings' (III. ii. 155–6). For Richard, the earth or 'ground' upon which he sits is ordained by his duty 'for God's sake', and the lives which he will tell bind the narrative of the king to the spine of God's earth. Richard's belief in a pre-ordained existence sets him in a contest between God's spiritual deputy of power and a physical, substantial king of breath. Just before Richard sits upon the ground to find the narrative of kings, increasingly aware of the impact of Bolingbroke's banishment, he declares:

> O that I were as great
> As is my grief, or lesser than my name,
> Or that I could forget what I have been,
> Or now remember what I must be now!
>
> (III. iii. 136–9)

Richard finds himself mortal under the weight of consequence. Setting his 'grief', 'name', and memory upon a scale of impact and authority, Richard turns to the substance of story and matter for the spiritual reassurance in his book of life. Yet the relationship that Gaunt had feared between the earth and the story, rotten and stained by mismanagement, is redeployed by Richard into his language of naming. The distinction that Richard makes here between his grief and his name is symptomatic of the conscious distance he will pursue between the substance and the shadow of representation. Whereas for Gaunt or Mowbray the book of life is a narrative process of representation in the inevitable effects of action, for Richard it is an individual shadow behind the matter of his performance. Yet the figurative potential of the book appears to engage with an overwhelming structure of rightness that will show things not necessarily as they are, but ultimately as what the characters want them to be. Despite the rendition of God's judgement working through the images of earth and story, the relationship to heaven is a consciously theatrical trope. Richard appropriates the image of the heavenly book as one of his tools of representation within the performance of his life. Richard *plays* the book as a mirror in which he will condemn his traitors and confirm his self.

Richard's attention to the 'word', its substance, shadow, and perspective, emanates from his self-reflexive stage. The 'drama' through which Richard emerges is often exposed by the peripheral play-world of the rest of the characters. Yet Richard persists within the language of his own drama—lyrically and intellectually distinct from Bolingbroke, full of scriptural references, and apparent neoclassicism—as he also attempts to direct the image through which he is seen: the mirror, book, 'show'. As the play develops, we begin to notice that Richard becomes involved in a complicated synthesis of Catholic and Reformation ideologies in his relationship to both the *mythos* and the *logos* of expression and communion. Seeking a stage for the oblique representation of the 'inner' man, Richard pursues the word and the image of a relationship to power through God in order to support the terms of his own drama. In the play's presentation of two plays—the self-reflexive world of the player-king and the inexorable vagaries of his observers—*Richard II* stages how the word and image revolve in an apparently unceasing play for authority. Yet, out of Richard's world and into the play as a whole, the media of truth and art become merely delusory tactics sustaining an image that is nothing more than a shadow. Focusing on the moment in *Hamlet* when the Prince notices that his suit of mourning is nothing more than an abstract image of a grief he cannot express—a moment which Robert Weimann observes as 'the rupture in Hamlet himself, between what is shown and what is meant'[8]—O'Connell suggests that in Hamlet's attention to what is 'implicit', he highlights 'the theatrical means by which he, at once character *and* actor, is defining sorrow in visual histrionic terms'.[9] Some six years earlier, in *Richard II*, Shakespeare had composed a similar surface disjunction between 'histrionic' and 'implicit' grief; Richard's poetic complaint that 'these external manner of laments / Are merely shadows to the unseen grief / That swells with silence in the tortured soul' (IV. i. 295–7), also draws attention to the idea that Richard is playing a part, but a part that is in contention with the body and language of expression. However, in Richard, this 'rupture', rather than pointing to the 'theatrical means' by which

---

[8] Robert Weimann, 'Mimesis in *Hamlet*', in Patricia Parker and Geoffrey Hartman (eds.), *Shakespeare and the Question of Theory* (New York: Methuen, 1985), 282.

[9] Michael O'Connell, *The Idolatrous Eye: Iconoclasm and Theatre in Early Modern England* (New York and Oxford: Oxford University Press, 2000), 133.

character and actor negotiate the conditions of the stage, signals the way in which the king understands the 'implicit' as an ontological term of authority. Richard's overwhelming need to seek an expression of authority beyond the grasp of his subjects leads him into a permanent state of projection. Recognizing the mythical power of referred interiority, Richard lurches after spiritual signs of undisputed communion. In insisting on his own inadequate performance or representation, Richard suggests his potential for interpretation beyond the representational requisites of his reign.

In implicating an unrepresentable alternative, Richard refers his presence to what Stephen Greenblatt calls 'symbolic initiative', the 'weapon of the powerless'.[10] The image of the book often appears at critical moments of powerlessness: Gaunt's dying invocation of the rotten parchment of England; Mowbray's application to the book of life; and, in Richard's deposition scene, the terrible turning-point in the relinquishing of his reign. When Richard is asked by his detractors to read a list of his crimes, he responds by turning their deposing into a book:

> There shouldst thou find one heinous article,
> Containing the deposing of a king
> And cracking the strong warrant of an oath,
> Marked with a blot, damned in the book of heaven.
>
> (IV. ii. 232–5)

Richard refuses to read his temporal history, and instead tries to translate his powerlessness into authority through the image of the divine book. In the Bible the 'book of life' appears six times (twice in the Old Testament and four times in the New Testament), and, often in the context of a heavenly ledger, defines the book of life and heaven as interchangeable concepts. The most profound invocation of the 'book of life' occurs in Revelation, when St John sees the book of life as the *other* book distinct from the books of prophecy bound up in the seven seals:

And I saw the dead, both great and small stand before God; and the books were opened, and another book was opened, which is *the book* of life, and the dead were judged of those things, which were written in the books, according to their works. (Rev. 20: 12)

---

[10] Stephen Greenblatt, *Renaissance Self-Fashioning* (Chicago and London: University of Chicago Press, 1984), 78–9.

The book of life is the inexorable record of man's deeds, small and great, observed and invisible. The marginal gloss to the Geneva Bible of 1560 reads: 'Every man's conscience is as a book wherein his deeds are written, which shall appear when God openeth the book.'[11] Yet, Richard's book becomes conflated with the books of prophecy, in which he reads divine exoneration and vengeance written into the reign of kings. Unlike Mowbray's book of life, which marks his conscience and his deeds, Richard's book absorbs the intangible distance between his role on earth and his place in heaven. Despite the Bible's emphasis on both election and good works, Richard traces a direct link to heaven from his temporal royalty that may be described in terms of his mortal effects, but which is not necessarily dependent upon them. However, the profundity of the biblical book of life is dependent upon its nebulous, independent status; calling forth images of the written word, it harnesses our mortal dread of both consequence and annihilation. Glossing the reference in Psalms, 'Let them be blotted out of the book of the life, and not be written with the righteous' (69: 28), the Geneva Bible explains: 'they which seemed by their profession to have been written in thy book, yet by their fruits prove the contrary, let them be known as reprobate.'

Under the language and the presence of the book, this marginal gloss confirms our greatest fears: discovery, censure, and obliteration. However, the book of life is always and only a symbol, partly because, despite scriptural resonance,[12] it depends on ambiguity in order to enable processes of 'reading', and partly because it must remain invisible in order to defy exegesis and support 'faith'. Richard dismisses the stage's visible text, recording the king's 'grievous crimes' as nothing more than an unravelling of his 'weaved-up follies'. In replacing this domestic image with the symbolic book of divine power, Richard tries to reinstate his authority in an inexorable narrative that will unfold upon the heads of his deposers. However, Greenblatt's location of the book as 'the weapon of the powerless' is far more complicated if we consider what 'power'

---

[11] *The Geneva Bible: A Facsimile of the 1560 Edition*, ed. Lloyd E. Berry (Madison, Milwaukee, and London: University of Wisconsin Press, 1969). In all quotations I have modernized the spelling.

[12] 'Rev. 3.5, Bishops': "I will not blot out his name out of the book of life". The Bishops' is the only Bible in Shakespeare's day that has "blot out" in Revelation 3.5. All other versions, including the Rheims New Testament, have "put out" ': Shaheen, *Biblical References*, 367, 382. The 'book of life' is also referred to in Rev. 20: 12, 10: 8, and 21: 27; Phili. 4: 3; Dan. 12: 1; and Ps. 69: 28. According to *The Dictionary of the Christian Church*, the book of life stems from 'the conception of a heavenly register of the elect [which] is based on ideas found in the OT and in 1 Enoch'.

has come to mean. In terms of the images and rhetoric of the Reformers, the book (often Tyndale's *Obedience of a Christian Man* or the English New Testament) suggested a symbolic commitment to God in the face of Marian persecution. Protestants were still persecuted, however, so the book had no temporal power to change their plight, only symbolic power to justify their ways to man and God. Yet, in Protestant polemics, this 'symbolic initiative', pledging 'justification by faith', carried the weight of God's grace, and was surely then more powerful than any temporal outcome. Richard's appeal to the book of heaven initially plays out a sign of being beyond the representable conditions of show. He supports himself through the singular meditative relationship between man and God, which, although augmented by his 'divine right', belongs to Reformation ideologies. Yet the play-world begins to dissolve any associations of power that the divine order of things may carry. The book is always symbolic, drawing on its Christian prehistory of fear and reward, of all-seeing and all-recording; the book moves between the real and the not real as the perfect object of power. As Gaunt referred us to an alternative image of Richard's book in the decaying pages of the country, the Bishop of Carlisle invokes the sanctity of the king's body within the corollary of the body politic. Just before Richard enters, promising his deposers consequences inherent in rupturing the text of determined precedence, the Bishop of Carlisle graphically corroborates this image of the book. Carlisle's speech to Bolingbroke renders Richard's deposition, and damned and blotted book of heaven, as England's atrophy:

> And in this seat of peace tumultuous wars
> Shall kin with kin, and kind with kind, confound.
> Disorder, horror, fear, and mutiny
> Shall here inhabit, and this land be called
> The field of Golgotha and dead men's skulls.
>
> (IV. i. 140–4)

Carlisle, however, is immediately arrested on grounds of 'capital treason', and we realize that in effect Richard has already been deposed. Carlisle's bold rhetoric and images of damnation and decay spill into the scene as a hiatus in Bolingbroke's order of being. Yet Carlisle's language appears inappropriate, and the increasingly violent images of the destruction he 'prophesies' for England merely portray his powerlessness and his expendability. York's arrest of Carlisle confirms that there is no place for him and his ideology within the play. As Bolingbroke and his supporters begin to cleanse the play-world of this kind of rhetorical sway, we realize that when Richard enters to be visibly de-kinged, the *only* initiative left to Richard is symbolic. However, such symbolic initiative is, according to Greenblatt, determined by 'a force outside the self' responsive to God's Word: 'The bible then is the point of absolute, unwavering contact between God and man, the written assurance that God will not be arbitrary, the guarantee that human destiny is not ruled by chance, cunning, or force.'[13] Faith, then, is a symbol of a deferred power that rests with a belief in a teleological universe. The image of a divine book of heaven inherently containing an order of rightness is entirely conventional within a history play of a medieval king. However, in terms of Reformation politics, Richard's relationship to the book charts an uneasy distance between Catholicism and 'Protestantism'.[14] Whilst, on the one hand, the notion of the book of heaven, celebrating and defending the divine right of kings, belongs to an older philosophy of kingship, on the other, Richard places his book as both a literal and an arcane icon, imaging an inward and protective faith that is more responsive to Reformation ideologies.[15] Despite the historical narrative of Richard II, and his infamous self-association with canonized kings, Shakespeare's Richard uses his book in a peculiarly ambiguous religious context. In *2 Henry IV*, the king, weighed down with the uneasiness of 'the head that wears the crown' the night before the battle, exclaims: 'O God that one might read the book of fate, / And see the revolutions of the times' (iii. i. 44–5). Developing his image through how 'chances mock / And changes fill the cup of alteration', he imagines what it might be to read the future, until he

---

[13] Greenblatt, *Renaissance Self-Fashioning*, 111.

[14] According to Brian Moynahan, *If God Spare My Life: William Tyndale, the English Bible and Sir Thomas More—A Story of Martyrdom and Betrayal* (London: Little, Brown, 2002), the word 'Protestant' was coined in 1529: 'It was used to describe the Lutheran princes and cities who had signed a *Protestatio* opposing the Catholic majority at the diet or parliament of Speyer in April of that year. Reformers differed greatly in their own doctrines—already Lutherans, Zwinglians and Anabaptists were at one another's throats, and a score of new sects would soon arise—but the general term "Protestant" was now applied to them all' (p. 176).

[15] Thomas Cromwell imposed the first significant injunctions in 1536, abolishing allegiance to the Pope and instructing the provision of both English and Latin Bibles. There followed a series of more radical measures in 1538, outlawing 'the cult of saints'. However, in 1547, Cranmer published his *Homily of Good Works*, which was 'unmistakably, a manifesto for the forging of the new [religion]'. See Eamon Duffy, *The Stripping of the Altars: Traditional Religion in England 1400–1580* (New Haven and London: Yale University Press, 1992), 398, 407, and 449. Despite Cromwell's foundations, it was Cranmer who effected the most critical changes, in terms of Protestantism, under Edward VI.

declares that 'if this were seen' even 'the happiest youth' 'would shut the book and sit him down and die'.[16] Henry's book, although rhetorically harnessed to his role as King in moving through 'the revolutions of the times', traces the 'mountains', the 'continent', the 'sea', and 'the beachy girdle of the ocean' until it becomes not only Henry's book but one that equally may affect the king and the 'happiest youth' alike. Henry's book carries the fate of his subjects as much as himself, and in this way is distinct from Richard's book of heaven, summoned as the divine protection and justice of his reign. Both Richard's and Henry's books appear to signify an idea of predetermination that denotes an inexorable narrative in which the king is partly author and partly text. But in reading the book that shifts between 'fate', 'heaven', and 'life', these absolutes become synthesized as though they acted as one shaping force. Yet, according to the Reformers, the 'power' of the vernacular New Testament lay in the 'literal text', which offered its readers a direct link to the voice of God within subjective terms and within individual free will. Richard's relationship to his book, however, is not merely individual, it is absolutely exclusive, signifying for him a power and authority beyond the bounds of his subjects and the effects of his reign. When, however, his court, cousins, and advisors ignore and overreach such an image, Richard translates his rendition of iconic power from one symbol into another. Yet the book's relationship to symbolic authority, from Henry VIII's break with Rome (1535) to Elizabeth's Thirty-nine Articles (1563), is profoundly ambivalent. Despite the tremendous political and cultural impact of Tyndale's translation and the visible and social turmoil of the dissolution of the monasteries, the 'book' appeared in many injunctions as simply a pictorial sign.

Reiterating the teaching of the Ten Articles, [Edward] Lee [Archbishop of York] insisted that the people were to be taught "that images be suffered only as books, by which our hearts may be kindled to follow the holy steps and examples of the saints represented by the same; even as saints lives be written . . . for the same purpose". Moreover, a distance must be preserved between the image and the thing imagined, "although they see the image of the Father represented as an old man, yet they may in no wise believe that the heavenly Father is any man, or that he hath any body or age."[17]

---

[16] These lines were not included in the Folio, although they were published in the 1600 Quarto.

[17] Duffy, *Stripping of the Altars*, 413.

Some 'images' were also tolerated as 'unlearned men's books', but in the very process of devaluing the symbol, the book came to offer a transitional language of signification. Since this metaphorical book determines the role of the image as nothing more than a visible suggestion, the semiotic of the book emerges in response to how images should be 'read', and in moving away from the symbol itself, the book seeks to expose a reasonably straightforward relationship between image and meaning that has no inherent value outside the surface on which it is presented. The book here carries no incarnate power, and such a 'distance' between 'the image and the thing imagined' allows the interpretive heart to move within the visual narrative of Christ's life: a narrative, however, which ultimately, and properly, leads to the text. Both the figurative and the symbolic book move forward a process of reading from the visual to the cognitive. Yet, in the devolution of power from the image to the text, the book may culturally begin to absorb the visual role of the icon, which was itself in a state of transition. The limits of idolatry remained ambiguous in this transference of power. Erasmus, in his *A Playne and Godly Exposition or Declaration of the Commune Crede*, responds to the dialectic between the word and the image. Answering a student's anxiety over the worshipping of the name of God as an act of idolatry, as O'Connell explains, Erasmus's response points to a word as 'an arbitrary sign, nothing like the thing represented, and there is no peril that a word should be taken for what it represents'.[18] However, Erasmus's translation of the Vulgate into Greek, and the more general humanist shift to logocentrism, appear in fact to render Christ's body in the Book as an incarnate image: 'For Erasmus—and for humanism more generally—"Christ as text" replaces the painted sculpted Christ. For succeeding reformers Christ's real presence as text would also eclipse his real presence in the visible, tactile Eucharist.'[19] The potential translation of presence from the image to the word in the book of God, and that of the text of Christ to the body of the representational actor, implicated the stage as a possible site of idolatry. Such potential, of course, inflamed anti-theatricalists, and informed many of their invectives against the stage; however, Richard's identification with Christ comes less from his scriptural allusions and pre-texts than from his individual empathy with God's chosen. Richard draws three very powerful parallels between himself and Christ: first, when he accuses Bushy, Bagot, and Green of betraying him: 'Three Judases, each one thrice worse than Judas' (III. ii.

132); secondly, when he uses the same analogy on losing his subjects to Bolingbroke: 'Were they not mine? / Did they not sometime cry "All hail!" to me? / So Judas did to Christ' (IV. i. 168–70); and finally, and contextually most profoundly, in his deposition scene:

> Though some of you—with Pilate—wash your hands,
> Showing an outward pity, yet you Pilates
> Have here delivered me to my sour cross,
> And water cannot wash away your sin.

(IV. i. 238–41)

Richard traces a version of his authority through both the body and the book of God in his identification with Christ. Setting his traitors upon the stage within the names and narrative of Christ's life, Richard seeks to set the Word of God against the word of his detractors, through the body of *his* real presence. The Word of the Bible and the name of God and Christ, despite Erasmus's assertion of the distinction between the word and the thing imagined, represent an ever possible site of presence, and the belief in an effective power of naming, whilst not idolatrous, informs much of the Elizabethan recognition of status. Richard's path to 'the nothing I must be' is consistently informed by his belief in the absolute and incarnate power of names. Confronted by his waning support and authority, Richard exclaims: 'Is not the King's name forty thousand names? / Arm, arm, my name' (III. ii. 86–7). Richard believes in the power of semiotics to direct his subjects and celebrate his being. However, the power of the word is always augmented by its image, and Richard draws his authority through the image of the book, his body, and the mirror, as a theatre in which he fashions himself as an icon. The use of the word or the image to create an inherent force was a deeply contentious issue within the role of theatre; Richard applies his power, and Shakespeare his characterization, to a heady mixture of Catholic idolatry, Christian humanism, and Protestant word and sermon. Yet, within the amplified context of the theatre, Shakespeare does not subject his king to anti-theatricalist charges. Rather, in the single figure of the king, he sustains a distinction between the play-world and the theatre of power. Within these terms, what the book may image and what it may imagine are not inherent in its sign. Whilst the book is on the one hand responsive to the 'old' apotropaic value of icons, on the other it emerges within a shifting system of representation. The distance that Archbishop Lee insists upon, and the intercession of the interpretative heart, are fundamental to the diminishing role of the icon and the rising metaphorical value of the book. There is a distinction here between the 'book' and the Bible. The interpretative contention created by the Reformation, far from establishing and demarcating definitions, provided an amorphous space for interpretation and selective understanding. The metaphorical idea of the book accumulates an ideological power that encompasses both metaphysical and physical responses to a subjective world. However, in accordance with the English New Testament, the Edwardine Books of Common Prayer (1549 and 1552), and the deposing of the icon, the 'book', literal and metaphorical, develops a nebulous power in the re-formation of cultural consciousness.

Given the religious and political history of this image, why does Richard's book emerge at apparently acute moments of powerlessness, particularly if we notice, in contrast, that Henry IV's 'book' emerges at a critical juncture where both power and consequence are still in contention? But when Richard hurls his book of heaven on to the stage, it is too late. In both Catholic and Protestant polemics, the book often appeared as a response to threat. Whilst in the early stages of the Reformation, and particularly under the Henrician regime, images and idols were allowed to remain in churches but only as 'unlearned men's books',[20] in the Marian heresy trials Protestant martyrs went to their death clutching the Book. The book, in both these cases, represents an opposition or alternative to power. Under the counter-reformation of Mary, the pledging of allegiance to the vernacular Bible was a symbolic, but ineffective, act of faith: 'any individual or group confronting a hostile institution that possesses vastly superior force, has recourse to the weapon of the powerless: the seizure of the *symbolic* initiative.'[21] However, the nature of a symbol is that it does not represent itself but something else; the book functions to represent a relationship between man and his faith: the body and the soul that may be imagined in the idea of the book, which in turn represents the teaching and love of Christ. Thus, as the book emerges in Reformation politics as a material object through which man may read and interpret grace, it also functions as a sign of independent and ineffable communion. John Foxe notoriously ritualizes the exhibition of the devout and 'inward' soul in *Acts and Monuments* (1563). His spectacular and detailed accounts of devout Protestants being burned, hanged, strangled, and quartered for their

---

[20] See Duffy, *Stripping of The Altars*, 428–9; cf. O'Connell, *Idolatrous Eye*, 38.
[21] Greenblatt, *Renaissance Self-Fashioning*, 78–9.

beliefs often centralize the place of the 'book' during their execution. John Bainham, like many others, went to his death holding Tyndale's *New Testament* and the *Obedience of a Christian Man*, and as Greenblatt rightly claims, 'what rivets our interest in the case, almost lost in the great mass of Foxe's famous work, is the critical role taken, at the height of the drama of abjuration and relapse, by the printed book'.[22] However, Greenblatt firmly posits a developing sense and expression of interiority in the appropriation of the vernacular Bible and other English works of scriptural and spiritual guidance, particularly in their value as symbolic resistance. Whilst this may be true in its development over a period of time, the role of the book in heresy trials and Foxe's *Acts and Monuments* performs a distinctly theatrical and visible role, which externalizes the concept of inward commitment and moral righteousness. The 'spectacle' of the book served both the martyrs on trial and those who put them there. For the proponents of the Marian regime, the vernacular Bible being extinguished with the dying 'traitor' acted as a deterrent to would-be reformers; similarly, for the martyr and his proponents, it symbolized a visible commitment to belief. The role of the book in heresy trials dramatically materialized the 'inward' man. Foxe was perfectly aware of this, and in his infamous championing of the printing-press, he rendered the 'book' a powerful tool of action rather than meditation:

The Lord began to work for his Church . . . not with sword and target to subdue His exalted adversary, but with printing, writing and reading. . . . How many printing presses there be in the world, so many blockhouses there be against the high castle of St Angelo, so that either the pope must abolish knowledge and printing or printing at length will root him out.[23]

The book will 'root out' the authority of the Church, since it returns us to the 'work' of the Lord himself, and thereby encompasses and represents a power far greater than the intercession of aggressive or aggrandizing temporal authority.[24] Whilst in Reformation politics the book could emerge, at least according to Foxe, as a weapon to rival that of the 'sword and target', it also promised the private salvation of man or woman living by the justification of faith. Equally, the absorption of Scripture into humanist education and commonplace book culture facilitated the words of God through the everyday experience of comfort

---

[22] Ibid. 76.     [23] As cited by Greenblatt, ibid. 98–9.

[24] Foxe's 'root out' is a significant choice of rhetoric, since Shakespeare often uses the phrase in relation to sedition or regicide in the history plays, including the three parts of *Henry VI*, *Henry VIII*, *Richard III*, and *Henry V*.

or fear. The physical nature of the book, as opposed to the priest as mediator, promised its faithful a private recognition of the words of God, and as an icon it could overwrite the images of the Church as a narrative and pre-text. In his use of the book of heaven, Richard, like Mowbray and Gaunt, imagines the trajectory of man's life, and, like Carlisle, he augments this image with a faith in the absolute sway of the king as the Lord's anointed. However, in his scene of deposition, Richard further complicates the prehistory of his book in translating his iconic self into a material mirror. Richard begins by making himself visible through the blazoning of his body on to his self-imposed de-crowning, and in setting his body against the requisites of the king, Richard will go on to invoke his soul. In Richard's self-image and emphasis on show, the play confronts the extent to which reinterpretation exposes failure. The deposition scene highlights a fissure in the order of the king's image of authority.[25] From the initial power of the word, 'the breath of kings', and the book of life, Richard had projected an idea of his authority in response to his unknowable and invisible communion with God. Here, however, in recognition of his powerlessness in the face of Bolingbroke's preference for action over words ('What my tongue speaks my right-drawn sword may prove' (i. i. 46)), he tries to become a self-generated idol. Much of the dramatic power of Richard's deposition emerges when he chooses to portray the moment as visible, and in so doing moves from the idea to the image. Since there is no precedent or efficacy in Richard's de-crowning of himself, the moment is usually considered as Richard's tragic attempt to wrest some form of 'symbolic initiative' from Bolingbroke. In grasping the language of ceremony from the 'silent king', Richard shows himself to 'play many persons in one part'. However, in Richard's particular attention to his body, his image, and the inherent power he believes to be supported by that image, he uses his theatre of power to portray himself as an idol, as a visible and effective image that Bolingbroke can re-define but not destroy:

> Now mark me how I will undo myself.
> I give this heavy weight from off my head,
> And this unwieldy sceptre from my hand,
> The pride of kingly sway from out my heart.
> With mine own tears I wash away my balm,
> With mine own hands I give away my crown,

---

[25] This scene was not published until the fourth Quarto of 1608, and provides the basis for the Folio.

> With mine own tongue deny my sacred state,
> With mine own breath release all duteous oaths.
> All pomp and majesty I do forswear.
> My manors, rents, revenues I forgo.
> My acts, decrees, and statues I deny.
>
> (IV. i. 202–12)

Richard's use of the singular 'I' rather than the royal 'we' recognizes that he has already lost the crown, but, in recalling the language of a coronation ceremony, Richard stages a theory of power, in which he reasserts not only his divine, 'chosen' right, but also the very body that stands before them. The acute attention to his body in collaboration with the physical sacraments of ceremony define Richard's space as controlled by his presence—his body and hands, heart, head, tongue, breath, and tears—at once 'both character and actor'. As Michael O'Connell explains, 'art' and the visual aesthetics were 'bound up in the hermeneutics of religious culture', as was *particularity*: 'At the centre of the iconoclast case that the image itself is worshipped has always been the charge that a particular image commands more devotion than another.'[26] Richard's ecphrastic rendition of his self animates only the particular parts of his body associated with sacred power; where the hands, tongue, and breath denote his monarchical and religious authority (to pronounce sentence or pray), the tears are often associated with the worship and justification of images (we need only think of the many instances in which graven images were reported to have wept in proof of their apotropaic value). Equally, Richard's sense of *particularity* has informed his self-image throughout the play, not only in his elegiac characterization, but here in his self-reflexive ability to appropriate initiative, symbolic or otherwise, from out of Bolingbroke's hands. In elaborately and specifically performing the 'undoing' of himself, Richard foregrounds his visible body to create, in 'complex layers of cultural meaning', himself as idol and image. As O'Connell explains, both the majesty and the mystery associated with the veneration of idols and ceremony may invoke a sense of magic, but 'rather than magic, what is at work is a response to multivocality, response to the complex layers of cultural meaning bound up in the object of devotion and its site'.[27]

Richard suggests that he may be divorced from his signifying crown, but he remains within a multivocal process of image and response.

---

[26] O'Connell, *Idolatrous Eye*, 58, 59.     [27] Ibid. 59–60.

Reinstating the complexity of the divine king, Richard believes he can transcend systematic processes of reading through laying claim to an interpretative value beyond the bounds of signification.

Richard's shift from the figurative to the visual is developed through an application to his face. Reminding his subjects of his imprint on coinage, he moves that face into a double perspective:

> And if my word be sterling yet in England
> Let it command a mirror hither straight
> That it may show me what a face I have
> Since it is bankrupt of his majesty.
>
> (IV. i. 263–6)

Richard's play on currency not only marks the authority of the king's stamp as it runs through the daily transactions of his subjects, but reaffirms his reflection as effective authority. Richard's attempt to reappropriate power is practised through his application to 'things'. But even as he turns his word into a currency, Richard cannot relinquish his idea of symbolic majesty and moves his body into a position wherein he will show, by virtue of a mirror, the dual aspect of a king. Consciously working within terms that Bolingbroke neither understands nor recognizes, Richard tries to reinstate an image of his self within the anamorphic perspective of visible and un-visible. Appealing at first to the invisible and ubiquitous book of heaven, Richard traces the signifier, by virtue of his body, to the sign of the mirror:

> They shall be satisfied. I'll read enough
> When I do see the very book indeed
> Where all my sins are writ; and that's myself.
> *Enter one with a glass*
> Give me that glass, and therein will I read.
> No deeper wrinkles yet? Hath sorrow struck
> So many blows upon this face of mine
> And made no deeper wounds?
>
> (IV. i. 272–8)

Although the 'very book', or the book of books, by definition, should be the Bible, Richard invokes this image within the immediate context of himself and the visible body through which he stands on the stage and in front of his deposers. The book of self is often used by Shakespeare to support imaginatively the idea of a (in)discernible being, wherein, for a moment, the soul or body may be read by the observer, whether it is for love, conscience, secrets, or lies. Almost always this book emerges to engage with a process of reading, to offer the observer, if only briefly, a possible revelation of feeling or vestige of truth. For Richard, however, the image is powerful because it cannot present him to his observers. Despite calling upon processes of reading and reflecting, Richard denies the appropriate potential of such processes to accommodate either history or truth. It would seem, therefore, that in consciously offering the potential of seeing, Richard seeks only to highlight the inadequacy of the visual. Paradoxically, in order to amplify the absolute intelligibility of his bodily relationship to heaven and himself, Richard translates the book into the mirror: two signs that are here dependent upon their transparency.

The mirror appears on-stage to translate reading into looking. But just as we could not see Richard's book of heaven, neither can we see his reflection. The divine right that Richard had tried to invoke in the book is reorganized into show through a twofold relationship to the mirror. On the one hand, the mirror is reflective of man's microcosmic image of God and world, and on the other, the mirror plays out on-stage Richard's dialectic between the icon and the interior. Richard's insistence in the play that he must be both seen and not seen mystifies his interiority as the site of authority. The book of heaven, blotted by Richard's deposition, is reorientated by the mirror and its shards.[28] Richard's shattering of the mirror is theatrically complicated, since, although a king would certainly have owned a crystal mirror, it is unlikely that the Chamberlain's Men could have afforded to own, let alone break, one. It is much more likely that the actors used a tin mirror, more common and more affordable; but a tin mirror would not shatter. Dramatically, then, Richard's act is literally symbolic, but his iconoclasm, and his verbal representation of it, is extremely complex. On one level we must look at how the mirror (as opposed to the stage or painting) reflects, and, on another, how, in terms of that reflection, the body is defined. Alongside questions of reflection or depiction is the

---

[28] The mirror in itself has a complex and arcane history. The relationship between the mirror and God may be understood, for example, in the depiction of the mirror and our visual absorption of the requisites of *seeing* as reflective of God's eye (Jan van Eyck's 'Arnolfini Marriage', e.g.), and in the fifteenth century 'word spread that a convex mirror, by capturing a wide-angle view, would absorb the healing radiance of holy relics. . . . Once you had your mirror, you found some suitable vantage point—even the city walls were crowded—where you could hold the mirror aloft, the longer the better, as if it were a third eye, allowing it to be imbued with the rays of holiness': John Man, *The Gutenberg Revolution: The Story of a Genius and an Invention that Changed the World* (London: Review, 2002), 63.

status of the icon, and what substance, symbolic or literal, is attached to the image, and where, if at all, its power lies. Jonathan Miller, in his discussion of the mirror in painting, makes an important distinction between depiction and representation. The painting, he explains, depicts something or someone because it acknowledges its own surface area; the mirror, however, denies that surface area and transparently images an image; it both depends on that transparency and denies it:

> But when the reflective surface is smooth, flat and colourless, the images which appear in it are qualitatively indistinguishable from the real thing, so that the only way of telling that they are or might be reflections is purely circumstantial. That is to say it depends on something other than the quality of the imagery itself.[29]

What Richard is or might be depends upon the circumstances he creates around self-reflexive articles of representation or reflection. The stability of the referent is important only inasmuch as Richard locates the mirror's presence on-stage; what becomes much more significant is the way in which the mirror will circumstantially perform. We know that the mirror provides his reflection, yet not his representation, because of the imagery through which he builds and rejects the vision.

The 'something other' that locates the mirror is the imaginative preparation through which Richard advances his self-image. The problem of perspective, acutely drawn by Bushy in his interview with the Queen ('Like perspectives, which, rightly gazed upon, / Show nothing but confusion; eyed awry, / Distinguish form' (II. ii. 18–20)), is here translated into a language of representation. Icons were flat images, although often wrought in ivory or mosaic, which were painted onto wood surfaces. As I have suggested, in Richard's undoing of himself he uses language to paint his body on the surface of a scene that has been established to deny him: 'that in the common view / He may surrender'. Having created an image of himself, he commands a mirror in which to observe the 'truth' of that image and the 'reality' of the occasion. On looking at his reflection, Richard claims that he does not see what he expects to see: 'Hath sorrow struck / So many blows upon this face of mine / And made no deeper wounds?' (IV. i. 276–8). Yet Richard is in control of this image, for it is his reading that turns our eyes to his reflection. Richard portrays his reflection as flat, as showing only the

[29] Jonathan Miller, *On Reflection* (London: National Gallery Publications Ltd., distributed by Yale University Press, 1998), 86.

surface, rather than the 'deeper' story of the soul, and it is through his disengagement with his reflection as well as its apparent one-dimensional nature that, paradoxically, we recognize the ambivalence of the object. When he shatters the mirror, he does so for its material inadequacy, because it is merely a symbol of his body, not a representation of it. Richard thus divorces his symbolic self from his bodily self, and in so doing plays out the final stages of his own deposition. In an attempt to redeploy his royal mystery, he turns all symbols out with the king and all representations in with the subject; representation itself becomes the desired state. Up until now Richard had amplified the symbolic value of the king through the book of heaven and the divine right of God's ordination; in translating this symbolism into the shattered mirror, he dreadfully destroys everything that had once held him together. When Bolingbroke replies to the broken mirror, he declares: 'The shadow of your sorrow hath destroyed / The shadow of your face' (iv. i. 291–2). The 'shadow', like the imprint on the coin, or the crown, or 'kingly sway', was only ever an image that applied itself to Richard in his state as king. Bolingbroke, too, recognizes that Richard's symbolic role is over, and only the substance of a subject remains.

Yet, prior to his deposition, Richard had begun to imagine himself as both the king and the subject. Despite the disparity between them, 'all this while' Richard has lived as a king yet needed as a subject:

> Throw away respect,
> Tradition, form, and ceremonious duty;
> For you have but mistook me all this while.
> I live with bread, like you; feel want,
> Taste grief, need friends. Subjected thus,
> How can you say to me I am a king?
>
> (iii. ii. 172–7)

Yet the disparity arises because tradition, form, respect, and ceremonious duty are presented as incompatible with 'want', 'grief', and 'friends'; thus, the idea of king and its incumbent ceremony, like theatre, appears to deny inwardness whilst at the same time acknowledging the very fragility of those structures to be representative. Richard's destruction of the mirror violently acknowledges his status as existing always and only within the bounds of the symbolic. Richard is spectacularly denied a claim to authenticity outside his own structures of value; the book of life, the crown, the mirror, and the stage will not retain an inherent power beyond the strains of the visible. Richard's contest between symbol and representation is complicated by the nature of the theatre or show through which he exists. In order to apprehend not only an appearance of 'reality', but also a faith in the relationship between sign and signifier, certain conditions need to remain stable. But as Richard sanctions his identity between the icon and the image, we, like his subjects, lose faith, in what he represents and what he believes represents him. Despite his powerful collaboration with his authorized book, body, and mirror, the ultimately transparent nature of these images denies any signification beyond the instant in which they are formed. Tragically, even pathetically, it is an image that York knows only too well:

> As in a theatre the eyes of men,
> After a well graced actor leaves the stage,
> Are idly bent on him that enters next,
> Thinking his prattle to be tedious.
>
> (v. ii. 23–6)

York's theatre both celebrates and denies Richard's performance, crediting him with a role but denying him a reality, York wryly appreciates mock majesty. Yet, part of the theatre of Richard's reign is to invoke his symbols of being even in his absence. Alongside his bodily presence, Richard projects his transparent icons to suggest his un-visible—yet powerfully authoritative—interior self. Richard tries to effect an alternative potential in constantly suggesting the possible self that cannot be defined in 'these external manner of laments', or represented in the 'tradition', 'form', and 'ceremony' of king. This sense of potential is linked predominantly to God and to the mysterious ways in which faith can sanction an authentic self. However, Richard's relationship to his idols of being and meaning are, despite the play's many scriptural allusions, not responsive to a consistent Church.

The Elizabethan emphasis on *The Homily of Disobedience* holds it a sin to overthrow a monarch or commit any act of treason, upon which the perpetrator 'will never enter the kingdom of heaven'. However, Calvinist doctrine states that the 'sword is given into the people's hand when tyranny takes over'. Although the Elizabethan state in no way absorbed a Calvinist codicil on tyranny, within the shifting religious context of the play, the relationship between the book of heaven and the monarch can only be harnessed absolutely if there is faith in the righteousness of his reign. The prehistory of the book of heaven in the history plays is often translated into a more humane discourse on the composite nature of history and effect. Yet Henry IV's book of fate, in which may be recorded the 'revolutions of the times', is a conventional poetic image, and in this way serves to highlight the dramatic significance of an apparently similar image in *Richard II*. Whilst in *2 Henry IV* the book of fate is present to attune our sympathies to the nature of responsibility and fortune in the unfolding of events, in *Richard II* the image of the book serves, on the one hand, to highlight an 'old world' picture in contest with the emerging 'new', and on the other, to offer a symbol of individual and subjective power. Yet the sign and the idea chart a process of cognitive and dramatic development in the king in which we witness the semantic and ideological field through which Richard determines action. The significance of the book of heaven in his deposition scene is the way in which it traces metonymic values of representation in search of an idol. Apart from its historical pre-text, the book here has no form; if it has pages or parchment, binding or text, they are born from the figurative potential of the imagination to harness symbolic authority. But the idea of God as the ultimate repository of devolved power shadows the play in the single conscience as much as the divine king. When Bolingbroke ends the play determined to absolve himself of the stain of Richard's murder, he decides on a spiritual journey to make his peace with himself through God. But this is not Richard's God, or even a God who determines the place and power of kings (since, if it were, how could Bolingbroke have deposed 'God's chosen'?),[30] but rather a private resurrection of his faith and purpose with distinctly individual aims. The figurative potential of the book emerges from itself to generate its own semantic and representative scope.

However, part of the complexity of this scope is consciously imposed through Richard's attention to his own unrepresentable self. Our understanding of the translation of the spiritual into the dramatic often emerges through the idea of the invisible and indefinable soul in search of expression. Katherine Eisaman Maus points out that the very stage and space of theatre makes this an ineluctable task. Maus argues that the theatre both plays with and problematizes the interior self through its attempts at representing both silence and subjectivity in an arena dependent upon visual and audible presence.[31] However, this

[30] It is interesting to remember that in *Henry VI*, all three parts of which were written before *Richard II*, Richard's deposition by Henry's grandfather, Henry IV, dreadfully dogs the validity of his reign.

[31] Katherine Eisaman Maus, *Inwardness and Theater in the English Renaissance* (Chicago and London: University of Chicago Press, 1995). Maus refers to Hamlet's grief-stricken response to his mother's marriage, in which Hamlet specifically sets up the

sense of the interior in communion with God was a particular product and impetus of the Reformers, as well as central to the opportunities made available by the Bible in English. In Tyndale's preparation and privileging of the vernacular New Testament, he urges the 'plain text' and 'literal sense' as 'the unselfconscious language of the inner man'. Although Tyndale's task here is to effect an uncomplicated narrative and lift the veil from dogmatic Catholic mystification, the sense of 'plain' and 'literal' is that it is not mediated by complex taxonomic or cultural imperatives. Thus, the plainer and more literal the language, the more likely it is not only to reach the truth of the 'inner man', but also to express that 'truth'. Within these terms the dramatic book can often emerge as a text dependent on its reading, in which the 'inner man' can be revealed only in his twofold relationship to the book; he must acknowledge the potential reading in order to suggest its absence. Reading the soul through the body can be compared to the Reformers' project of retrieving the plain text from ceremonial illusion, since the body often represents the 'actions a man might play', through which one must pass to find the 'true' and 'inner man'. Shakespeare often describes the soul or conscience in bookish terms, wherein processes of reading and misreading expose the possibilities of the private self in conversation with others. Equally, however, the plight of Everyman on-stage, within his Christian narrative and moral responsibility to a faithful life, began the public history of theatre within a Christian domain. Where the spiritual and the secular, the effable and the esoteric, merge or even begin in theatre is always a site of contention—particularly in a period in which negotiations of power, consensual or personal, became central to the relationship between Church and monarch. Despite the synthesis of the body and the soul in the rhetoric of evangelism—Bunyan's description of how 'Texts "tear and rend" his soul, "touch him", "seize" him, [and] "fall like a hot thunder-bolt" upon his conscience', or Tyndale's instruction to 'suck out the pith' and feel the impact of Scripture upon the heart—Richard's bodily awareness accompanies, even directs, his kingly performance rather than his 'private self'. Yet, according to David Daniell, 'Shakespeare's theory of drama is

opposition between the outward, articulate self and the inward, ineffable self, within the conditions and requisites of theatre. This dialectic between the performed, ritualized, social self and the inward, absent self positions 'truth' at an oblique angle to reality, since reality is contained within the collective, communicable matrix of a society in which 'art' verifies life.

of bodily presence.... That body is in interior, human, conflict.'[32]
For Daniell, Shakespeare's animated dramatization of human conflict
is tantamount to rendering the Gospels both visible *and* subjective.
However, Richard's animated human conflict is always dramatically
referred to a performative image: heaven's book, 'a glass', and, finally,
the sermon of the prison.

The prison scene is the first and only time we see Richard alone
on-stage; unlike in many of Shakespeare's dramatic soliloquies or single
performances, the place serves only to highlight his ignominy, rather
than his potential. The notion of 'privacy', interior or physical, appears
complex, since despite the possibility of individual potential, the very
notion images the alien: 'If privacy as we think of it existed at all, it
was regarded as a negative—as the absence of station, of authority,
of the divinely bestowed right or ability to lead a nation. Being a
public person, on the other hand, seemed automatically to confer these
qualities on individual persons, whether priests, kings or prelates.'[33] In
*Richard II*, the private space is manifest as a prison constructed explicitly
for the removal from society of the outsider who has deviated from
the consensual vision. However, rather than harness his interiority in
estrangement, Richard fabricates an audience:

> I have been studying how I may compare
> This prison where I live unto the world;
> And, for because the world is populous,
> And here is not a creature but myself,
> I cannot do it.

> (v. v. 1–5)

In 'studying' Richard has tried to apply his normal conditions of reality
and being to the situation—both alien and alienating—in which he
finds himself. And because he cannot reconcile the world in which he
exists with the world in which he finds himself, he turns to the 'word':

> As thoughts of things divine, are intermixed
> With scruples, and do set the word itself
> Against the word; as thus: 'Come, little ones';

---

[32] David Daniell, 'Shakespeare and the Protestant Mind', *Shakespeare Survey*, 54 (2001), 10–11.
[33] Cecile M. Jagodzinski, *Privacy and Print: Reading and Writing in Seventeenth-Century England* (Charlottesville, Va., and London: University Press of Virginia, 1999), 23–4.

> And then again,
> 'It is as hard to come as for a camel
> To thread the postern of a small needle's eye.'

>                     (v. v. 12–17)

As Richard 'studies' and turns to 'thoughts of things divine', imagining a peopled world and the text of St Mark (10: 14), he becomes almost entirely caught up within a cerebral process of orientation. The only manifest or material authority to which Richard now applies himself is a quotation from the Gospels, which sets the word of God against the scruples of man. Richard's dramatic centrality, rendition of the frailty of man in relation to the imperatives of faith, allusions to the Gospels, and projected audience combine to suggest a Protestant sermon. O'Connell explains that despite Reformation emphasis on the disjunction between Protestantism and theatre, 'The preacher . . . assumed a prophetic role and aimed at an actorly delivery, [but] did not portray another with his physical body.' However, 'The sermon can be understood perhaps as the quintessential form of Protestant drama, one in which a solitary figure assumes the role of conveying and interpreting God's word.'[34] This may be the only time in the play that Richard 'does not portray another with his physical body'; bereft of his icons of authority, of his populous, and even his awareness of the physical self, Richard stands alone on the stage to face both himself and the audience within man's abjection and God's word. Richard ends his life in the prison with the comfort of a love that notices his idea of redemption; as the bells combine with the music, sounding both his madness and his healing, he translates the dwindling noise of his life into a reciprocal voice of love:

> Yet blessing on his heart that gives it me;
> For 'tis a sign of love, and love to Richard
> Is a strange brooch in this all-hating world.

>                     (v. v. 64–6)

In imagining himself beloved like rare beauty in a hostile world, Richard once again makes visual contact with his sense of self. When he finally dies, Richard sees his body fall to the earth upon which he once sat to tell sad stories of the death of kings, and, as he does so, he once more observes the ineluctability of his divine condition:

---

[34] O'Connell, *Idolatrous Eye*, 90.

> Exton, thy fierce hand
> Hath with the King's blood stained the King's own land.
> Mount, mount, my soul. Thy seat is up on high,
> Whilst my gross flesh sinks downward here to die.
>
> (v. v. 109–12)

I do not pretend to answer any questions as to the particular religious direction of either the play or Shakespeare; rather, through the image of the book, I suggest that *Richard II* tackles a perspective on the way in which faith and authority create, in search of infallibility and recognition, icons in language and language in icons, and in so doing, attempts to uphold the role of interpretation in representations of power, private or public, through which we constantly search for a reflection of the ways in which we live. For those who seek to be loved and feared in the absence of righteousness, the book is a symbol of, and a companion for, the journey from life to death, and from living to being. The idea of an authorized self makes sense of the fragility of human history and a fugitive God; for Richard, the book of heaven was both his justification and his joke in a world where no one saw his 'gross flesh' sink 'downward here to die'.

# 5

## 'Minding true things by what their mockeries be': Forgetting and Remembering in *Hamlet*

When Horatio apprehends Hamlet, shortly after the spectacle of his mother's marriage, Hamlet suddenly declares: 'My father—methinks I see my father.' 'Where, my lord?', asks the trepid Horatio; 'In my mind's eye,' replies Hamlet (I. ii. 184–5).[1] We too have seen his father, stalking the battlements, silently, and fully clad for war. The internal vision that Hamlet lays claim to will shortly be followed by a discernible image of his father as a ghost. Hamlet, in his 'mind's eye', recalls an image of his father; the stage projects another. Together, the image and the thought culminate in the Ghost's central injunction to Hamlet: 'Remember me'. Hamlet's response to this request begins the play's search for truth, a search and a truth that are predicated upon processes of remembering and forgetting:

> Remember thee?
> Ay, thou poor ghost, while memory holds a seat
> In this distracted globe. Remember thee?
> Yea, from the table of memory
> I'll wipe away all trivial fond records,
> All saws of books, all forms, all pressures past,
> That youth and observation copied there,
> And thy commandment all alone shall live
> Within the book and volume of my brain,
> Unmixed with baser matter.
>
> (I. v. 95–104)

---

[1] William Shakespeare, *Hamlet*, ed. G. R. Hibbard (Oxford and New York: Oxford University Press, 1998). All references are to this edition, which uses the Folio as 'the control text'. Relevant departures from the Folio are noted.

Hamlet expresses this confrontation with the ghost of his murdered father in terms that negotiate the classical and humanist art of memory. The art of memory, as it was understood through the anonymous ancient text *Ad herennium*, and set down by Cicero and Quintilian, suggests that the brain organizes *loci,* places, in which the mind may write and overwrite images for the purpose of recall. Hamlet, however, prepares himself to remember only one thing: 'thy commandment all alone shall live / Within the book and volume of my brain'. In order to commit himself to the Ghost's command, and the revenge inherent in it, Hamlet decides to terminate and erase all relationships with his past and recently present self. Hamlet's commitment to memory begins in forgetting; books, humanism, history, and study are worthless companions to the new book and volume of his brain: a book, singularly inscribed, pure and 'Unmixed with baser matter'. Hamlet's commitment to memory hauls back the dead from the mind's eye to set the image and the word to war. Our journey with Hamlet's books begins both in the past and in the present. Emerging from his studies as an emblem of the past he must reject, and becoming his mind as the present he must enforce, the book is both a social structure and a private distress. This chapter will explore how Hamlet uses the material and metaphorical book to manipulate the social and mystify the subjective self, and, ultimately, how memory—remembering and forgetting—provides the language through which the book moves to retrieve the immediate and improvised body from the spectacle of performance.

Of all the characters that Shakespeare presents us with, Hamlet stands alone as the icon of the scholar self; fresh from the Protestant academy of Wittenberg, to which his mother begs him not to return, fiercely intellectual and self-scrutinizing, he epitomizes the humanist dialectic between knowledge and self-knowledge, individual aspiration and social harmony. In modern terms, 'to be or not to be' has entered the language as the aphorism of the existential intellectual, and Hamlet persists as the bookish icon of the restless mind. Yet, in terms of Shakespeare's play, this iconic Hamlet is a retroactive construction, for, early on in the play, he denounces all that humanism prized—the book, the academy, and the past. The 'table of memory' from which Hamlet wipes away 'all trivial fond records, / All saws of books, all forms, pressures past, / That youth and observation copied there' is both his material commonplace book and his mental storehouse of thought and learning. Hamlet's violent rejection in response to the Ghost's command indicates a relation-ship between his books and his task, also understood as a relationship between the past and the future that is no longer tenable. The commonplace book into which Hamlet may have copied such youthful observations would have been predicated upon a scholarly attitude to humanist endeavour, synthesized with social and political aspirations. The substance of a commonplace book expresses the relationship between education and intellectual integrity, tracing the projections of the mind through the vagaries of experience and aspiration. Importantly, as Mary Carruthers explains, the notion of a commonplace book supported an 'ethical rhetoric', or, as P. K. Ayers elaborates, 'the shared texts, shared experience, shared culture, and shared ideological assumptions of Medieval and early Tudor humanism'.[2] In erasing his education within the context of his commonplace book Hamlet simultaneously censures the pressures, forms, and inscriptions that have organized and represented him until now, and rejects the 'ethical rhetoric' of a shared culture, which may evolve from shared texts, but does not reproduce shared values. Yet the concept of the book is not thrown out with its contents or form, for Hamlet makes the space available for a new book, written, as it were, with the eternal memory of his father's living death, a memory and an imperative for which he has no pre-text. That Hamlet will reject all he knows for that which he does not know in a quest for truth is one of the many paradoxes that drive his world.

The relationship between the printed book and memory was an unstable one. Although the art of memory, as advocated by Quintilian and, to a lesser extent, Cicero, became absorbed into the visual fabric of manuscript and medieval practices of memory and Prudence, the printed book made the traditional arts of memory seem 'old fashioned'. Erasmus, for example, merely advocated 'study, order, and care' for the retention and decorous retrieval of information, rather than the more complex art of *loci* and *summa*. The classical art of memory was gradually replaced by an independent and more empirical relationship between the book and the body. The human body, no longer reliant upon the 'art' but simply on an awareness of how the mind could engage with the material, became 'itself a sort of book, or rather . . . a support for cognitive memory work'.[3] Hamlet's mind turns away from material aid to the recesses of his private body. In storing the image

---

[2] P. K. Ayers, 'Reading, Writing, and Hamlet', *Shakespeare Quarterly*, 44 (1993), 430. I quote Mary Carruthers from this article.

[3] Mary Carruthers, 'Reading with Attitude, Remembering the Book', in Dolores Warwick Frese and Katherine O'Brien O'Keefe (eds.), *The Book and the Body* (Notre Dame, Ind., and London: University of Notre Dame Press, 1997), 1.

of his father in his 'mind's eye', Hamlet makes way for a vital and explosive relationship between image and action that is symptomatic of his conscious destabilization of perceived truths.

Yet, having rejected the material volume, including its content, only a few lines later Hamlet declares:

> My tables,
> My tables—meet it is I set it down.
> That one may smile, and smile, and be a villain!
>
> (I. v. 107–9)

Although most modern editors[4] include a stage direction here, '*He writes*', this does not appear in the Folio, and since Hamlet intends only to include acute and apposite information in the book and volume of his brain, such an injunction to himself—'meet it is I set it down'—appears to be both a trenchant response to his previous rejection of 'All saws of books' and a mental note to the new cognitive work predicated on the murder of his father. But Hamlet does not write, since, as we will soon discover, he makes a very particular distinction between the internal and the external book; where as one harbours truth, the other carries him into his first encounter with the court, having learned of his father's murder. The two 'books' that Hamlet isolates, the material and the metaphorical, become his companions in the ways in which he will begin to negotiate his two versions of being and seeming, creating—for the audience, at least—two possible sites of interpretation. If we understand Hamlet, according to his own imperatives, to have noted the awesome dissimulation of a smiling villain in his developing mental repertoire, we might also notice that the next time we see Hamlet, he is reading a book. Yet, as Hamlet throws out his learning and attends to his tables, we begin to wonder whether this alternative commonplace book, based on the evolving book and volume of his brain, records advice or admonishment: 'That one may smile, and smile, and be a villain!'. Is this Hamlet's final and ironic repulsion of the book, sending it out of his mind with a text of duplicity and turpitude, thereby rejecting the mark of the book in its appallingly inadequate, even banal, relationship to the reality of experience? Or does Hamlet earnestly copy this maxim into his new 'book', the one in which only a few moments ago he had determined to keep 'alone' the

---

4 Including those of the most popular editions: the Oxford, Arden, Norton, and Cambridge.

Ghost and his commandment? In a recent exposition of 'table-books', a number of distinguished scholars gathered evidence to suggest the 'ubiquity', 'erasability' (containing erasable leaves for the rewriting and overwriting of information), and 'portability' of the Renaissance tables.[5] Exposing the significance and proliferation of table-books, this article suggests that tables could simultaneously function as companion models to the art of memory and as an 'antithetical model of the mind: a model of the most unreliable of traces and of human forgetfulness'.[6] Thus the relationship between the table-book and memory and forgetting is always in a state of crisis; the book aids memory, yet reminds us that we forget. Montaigne goes so far as to declare that he can only remember a 'charge' if he writes it down:

> Memory is an instrument of great service, without which, judgement will hardly discharge his duty whereof I have great want. What man will propose unto me, he must doe it by peecemeales: For, to answer to a discourse that hath many heads lieth not in my power. I cannot receive a charge, except I have my writing tables about me [*Je ne saurais reçevoir une charge sans tabelettes*].[7]

If Hamlet did not write down his observation on the smiling villain, would he forget it? The bitter humour with which these lines are construed suggests that Hamlet intends neither to remember nor to forget the merry perfidy of his uncle, but to satirize the role of the written. The relationship between writing and remembering becomes absurd in the light of individual tragedy, when the self becomes fragmented in the very act of its own observations. Once Hamlet renders his thoughts as text, the problem arises as to whether those thoughts remain effective or oblique; does writing remember or forget the self? Montaigne, in his search for and presentation of the self within his writing, is acutely aware of this dialectic, and it is one that he tries to confront through synthesizing the physical, cerebral, and continuous 'I'. Terence Cave explores the impasse between the writing and experiencing self in Montaigne:

> The writer reflects on writing, it seems, in order better to reflect the total self; the book of *essais* separates itself like a mirror so that it may represent a living being. Yet, on the other hand, this duality is unstable because it can never be

---

[5] Peter Stallybrass, Roger Chartier, J. Franklin Mowery, and Heather Wolfe, 'Hamlet's Tables and the Technologies of Writing in Renaissance England', *Shakespeare Quarterly*, 55 (2004), 410.
[6] Ibid. 411.    [7] As quoted by Stallybrass *et al.*, ibid.

fully resolved either in unity or in antithesis; also because it is generated wholly by the writing process itself.[8]

Hamlet, however, seems to separate himself like a mirror from the 'book and volume' of his brain, so that he may see his imperative but not his being. This duality in the idea of the book provides the metaphorical space for dissimulation, projecting both a shared rhetoric and an isolated authority.[9] Later, Hamlet, Polonius, and Ophelia will all play the book for its dualism.

In the light of Hamlet's fierce rejection of his learning against the discovery of his father's murder, the book—in all its forms and representations of pressures past—appears as blindingly incompatible with experience. Hamlet's reaction seems to present his predicament as a contest between experience and the book; and the book makes him radically ill equipped for such a task. Yet Protestant humanism, of which his education at Wittenberg makes him an example, determined its course of learning on a decorous synthesis of intellectual integrity and practical experience. The book, at times, became either superior to, or a synecdoche for, experience; whilst Roger Ascham, in *The Schoolmaster*, claimed that 'learning teacheth you more in one year than experience in twenty', Juvenal's Satire no. 1 states: 'Everything mankind does, their hope, fear, rage, pleasure, joys, business, are the hotchpotch of my little book.' In *Othello*, written only a year or two after *Hamlet*, Iago says of Othello that

> . . . his unbookish jealousy must construe
> Poor Cassio's smiles, gestures and light behaviour,
> Quite in the wrong.
>
> (IV. i. 99–101)

According to Iago, to be 'unbookish' is to be inexperienced, to misconstrue, which here, quite literally, means to misread or mistranslate. Whilst for Iago to be bookish is to understand things as they really are—to 'construe' rightly—for Hamlet it is contrary to the right relationship between observation and action, appearance and understanding. Montaigne, however, appears to note a tension in the

---

[8] Terence Cave, *The Cornucopian Text: Problems of Writing in the French Renaissance* (Oxford: Clarendon Press, 1979), 273.

[9] In a different context, we might remember that in *Cymbeline* Posthumus distrusts the book he finds when he wakes from his dream, suspecting it to be deceptive: 'A book? O rare one, / Be not, as is our fangled world, a garment / Nobler than that it covers' (v. iv. 133–5).

relationship between learning and experience when he writes: 'There is no desire more natural than the desire for knowledge. We try every means that may lead us to it. When reason fails us we make use of experience.'[10] Experience seems to rescue knowledge in the absence of reason; yet, at the same time, Montaigne's expression presents experience as a continuum that is not excluded by knowledge. Leonard Barkan, however, distinctly locates 'reading' in Shakespeare as 'part of a textual alternative to actual experience'; he explains that 'the texts of grammar, rhetoric, and literature, when rendered *as* texts, are in a profound sense bracketed—as are, of course, the characters who import them. Brilliant or foolish, these individuals speak of that which is external, unlived, or, at best, exemplary rather than real.'[11] Barkan is referring to intertextual references or allusions, and not necessarily to the presence or invocation of the book on-stage. What he notices is that 'imported' texts appear to create bridges out of the immediately dramatic into the abstract or commonplace world of generality. Knowledge, when rendered textual, effects a shared space which seems 'external, unlived' or 'exemplary', by virtue of its graphic invitation to a common site. Although Hamlet, alone, reacting to the Ghost, rejects the book for precisely the reasons Barkan gives, when he re-enters the world of the court, he manipulates these same observations for the ways in which they enable integration. Here, however, Hamlet excludes the book from his reality by shifting its status and significance from shared text to private imperative. But as Hamlet turns away from his books to experience, he cannot help but render that experience textual, setting it down in his mental commonplace book. Unlike Titus, who finds Lavinia's experience 'patterned by the poet' in Young Lucius's book, Hamlet finds no such precedent. Yet, as the play develops, Hamlet will extract patterns from poets to explore a voice he cannot make particular. The confusion that Hamlet suffers, the shock of discovery and the fear of ignorance, is manifest in the way he moves from the literal to the figurative, from education to experience, the past to the present, and the ways in which he tries to redeploy his now suspended emblems of authority into a meaningful relationship with the moment.

[10] Michel de Montaigne, *Essays*, trans. J. M. Cohen (Harmondsworth: Penguin, 1983), 343.

[11] Leonard Barkan, 'What did Shakespeare Read?', in Margreta de Grazia and Stanley Wells (eds.), *The Cambridge Companion to Shakespeare* (Cambridge: Cambridge University Press, 2001), 39.

To some extent Hamlet's creation of a reciprocal relationship between the figurative and material book complicates the role of either in the formation of his consciousness, since, on the one hand, the table of memory and the 'book and volume' of his brain form an imaginative wax tablet on which he may seek to inscribe only the information he requires, irrespective of present forms or pressures past; on the other hand, the material book, particularly in response to his scholarship at Wittenberg, denotes a particular textual fabric of transmission that is external to Hamlet. Hamlet rejects the material book according to the shared context in which it has hitherto existed. Instead, developing his own metaphorical control, he ushers in a cognitive and mnemonic image in which he may define and accommodate a singular existence. The table of memory and the 'book and volume' of the brain all begin to share a shaping semantic force, which is ultimately realized in 'The Mousetrap'. The purpose of this play is to provoke memory, harnessed and articulated by 'the conscience of the king', which involves the same process of remembering forced by Hamlet from Gertrude in the picture of the brothers and the mirror of words of truth. The powerful link that Hamlet makes between the literal and the imaginative book, and the way in which it will begin to forge his direction, and dissimulation, begins the play's confrontation with mnemonic triggers and visual truths, 'minding' and 'mockeries' (IV. o. 53).[12]

However, the performative potential of the book to control appearance and obscure 'reality' shifts its status out of the particular humanist fabric of Hamlet's education and into the role of a theatrical object. Hamlet both rejects and appropriates the book according to its ability to 'perform' within a dramatic context. Whilst, on the one hand, such performative potential re-emphasizes the passive ideological role which the book takes in shared spaces, on the other, such passivity and ideology provide potential for subversion. A little later, anxious to discover the cause of Hamlet's madness, Polonius manipulates a relationship between his daughter and the book in order to observe Ophelia and Hamlet 'alone'. Having already established that he and Claudius, 'seeing unseen', will spy on the couple, Polonius sends

---

[12] *Henry V*, Chorus. Although the Norton edition glosses 'minding' as 'imagining', the *OED* cites 'the action of remembering, regarding, paying attention to, caring for' as the earliest extension of the verb 'to mind', substantiating this definition with quotations from the fifteenth and sixteenth century.

Ophelia into an apparently isolated space under the guise of private devotion:

> Read on this book,
> That show of such an exercise may colour
> Your loneliness.

(III. i. 45–7)

Polonius uses the book to create an idea of privacy, one that will 'colour' his and Claudius's presence as much as Ophelia's solitude. Polonius refers the responsibility for his plan to the religious nature of Ophelia's book. Protestantism has long been held by historians to be responsible for the cultural shift from the collective to the individual.[13] The autonomous relationship to Scripture made available by the devolution of worship from the priest to the patriarch, the shift from the icon to the word, and the encouragement of private reading outside church all have emphasized the Protestant impetus to interiority.[14] Under the auspices of Protestantism, 'privacy' moves away from its medieval associations of suspiciousness and duplicity, and achieves a respectable status as a condition of deeply personal introspection, self-awareness, and integrity.[15] Yet, in 'show', 'colour', and 'loneliness' [aloneness], Polonius unwittingly returns Ophelia's seclusion to a state of anxiety, amplified by the duplicitous conditions of seeming and being that support Elsinore. Claudius, noticing this irony, augments the moment with an aside: 'The harlot's cheek, beautied with plast'ring art, / Is not more ugly to the thing that helps it / Than is my deed to my most painted word' (III. i. 52–4). The 'painted word' begins to emerge here

[13] Although I refer specifically to Protestantism, if Ophelia is carrying a Book of Hours, it is, of course, a medieval production, and therefore Catholic. However, whilst the book itself may be a Roman Catholic article, the nature of both privacy and independence in her association with the book are more responsive to Reformed ideas of individual worship.

[14] This is a crude summary of the seminal impact of sectarianism on the reading and book-buying public, and although, under the authority of Protestantism, the book is a habitable space for the private self and for individual communion with God, this should not be taken in antithesis to Catholicism, since reading remained an equally important part of it. Cecile M. Jagodzinsk, in *Privacy and Print: Reading and Writing in Seventeenth-Century England* (Charlottesville, Va., and London: University Press of Virginia, 1999), explains that private reading became increasingly important within the Catholic faith as the Reformation made it impossible for Catholics to worship publicly: 'English Catholics borrowed devotional techniques from the continent; with the suppression of Catholic writing and the liturgy in England, translations of prayer manuals and other devotional works abounded' (p. 28).

[15] Ibid. 3–12.

in both its material and metaphorical capacity. Ophelia's status and 'solitary' female space suggest her to be carrying a book of devotion, possibly a Book of Hours, which may contribute to Hamlet's 'nunnery' comment, since such a book directed the time and prayers of a nun's daily worship, as well as the laywoman's.[16] A Book of Hours is also a literal testimony to the painted or illuminated word; moreover, the kind of 'plast'ring art' to which Claudius refers locates the ability of the word, like appearance, to deceive and colour. The severance of the word from meaning, and the dramatic resonance of Claudius's response, is more profoundly exposed when Claudius admits that 'words without thoughts never to heaven go'; but here we observe the book in its ability to inform superficially and contain a social space. The book, as held by Ophelia, and positioned by Polonius, is used for its capacity to enable processes of dissimulation. Although a Book of Hours may also perform some sort of apotropaic role, standing between Ophelia and Hamlet's potentially threatening madness, the object itself is a mere accessory to the ideological context it supports. The practice of reading signified by a woman and a book denote a private space of devotion, which socially accepts the observed or encountered single female. Through Ophelia, we are shown visually and textually how the book supports dual versions of reality, and how, by its very appearance, it becomes complicit in the world of 'seems'. The moment of 'reading', which allowed the presence of Ophelia to accept the entrance of Hamlet, is referred back to the hidden observers in an apparently endless process of misreading. The dramatic space abounds with misinterpretations that are symbolically reflected by the role of the original object; Polonius and Claudius watch and misread the lovers' conversation, and the lovers condemn their intimacy to confusion as Hamlet makes increasingly obtuse and cryptic responses, which develop a momentum toward annihilating Ophelia: 'you jig, you amble, and you lisp, and nickname God's creatures, and make your wantonness your ignorance. Go to, I'll no more on't, it hath made me mad' (III. i. 145–7). It is also possible that Hamlet's famous vitriol, 'Get thee to a nunnery', is, in part, a response to the gross deception he knows Ophelia to be playing with a book of

---

[16] Like Hamlet, Ophelia could in fact be carrying any book, since its performance in this scene is strictly 'theatrical'; in other words, it is a prop or disguise to facilitate a dialogue or an effect. However, Polonius's direction suggests a devotional book, which, within this period, could be anything from Psalms, *The Book of Common Prayer*, homilies, or a book about devotion. Dramatically, it is also possible that Ophelia and Hamlet in fact use the same book to 'colour' the real purpose of their presence.

devotion.[17] When Polonius sends his daughter out to trap Hamlet, book in hand, he comments that 'with devotion's visage / And pious action we do sugar o'er / The devil himself' (III. i. 48–50). The book in this scene synthesizes the duplicity of Claudius, the devil himself, and the sexual and spiritual betrayal of Gertrude, her visage of devotion toward her dead husband's brother. The violence with which Hamlet casts Ophelia into his repulsion of women, sinners, and 'breeders of sinners', may be augmented by her entrapment 'with devotion's visage'. Finally, Ophelia's comment that Hamlet was 'Th' observed of all observers', and cry: 'O woe is me / T'have seen what I have seen, see what I see' (III. i. 155, 161–2) condemns the scene's dependence on seeing to dreadful irony. Yet, even before finding Ophelia 'read[ing] on this book', Hamlet has manipulated his own relationship to reading and seeing.

When Hamlet enters, half-way through Act II, scene ii, reading a book, the King and Queen have been discussing, with Polonius, the state and cause of Hamlet's madness. Polonius, believing Hamlet to be mad for the love of Ophelia, chastizes himself for having instructed her to repel him. In hindsight, he wishes he had 'played the desk or table-book' or 'looked upon this love with idle sight' (II. ii. 135, 137). Here, within the context of his relationship with Ophelia, and indeed the book itself, Polonius's comment returns us to Hamlet's initial erasing of such forms. In the 'desk or table-book' Polonius would have positioned himself as the text between the lovers, conveying or being the keeper of words of love or 'remembrances'; the phrase is an image of all that Hamlet appears now to detest about the book, its ability to suggest a public bridge into a private world, and practice inclusion in a personal context. Hamlet's second 'public' appearance on-stage is announced by Gertrude's exclamation, 'But look where sadly the poor wretch comes reading' (II. ii. 168). Among the eleven definitions the *OED* gives for

---

[17] Although the text is somewhat ambiguous as to whether Hamlet knows he is being observed, most directors seem to read his question to Ophelia, 'Where's your father?' as an indication that he knows that Polonius is there. Carol Chillington Rutter, in *Enter the Body: Women and Representation on Shakespeare's Stage* (London and New York: Routledge, 2001), draws attention to Olivier's film version when, in this scene, 'As Hamlet quizzes Ophelia, they move around a stone prie-dieu, which stands between them like a desecrated sacrament. She hears her mistake as soon as she answers "At home my lord", for both of them know Polonius is behind the arras. As her betrayal catches in her throat, she reaches out her arms to Hamlet, but the shot cuts them off, making the appeal grotesque. Hamlet, savage, throws her on her knees to resume her fake attitude of prayer' (p. 34).

'sadly', eight are now obsolete; however, both 'in earnest, gravely' (†7) and 'steadfastly, fixedly' (†5) were last used to a similar effect as Gertrude in the early seventeenth century, and may cast Hamlet within a more precise visual context than the modern understanding of 'sorrowfully'. Both 'gravely' and 'steadfastly' direct Hamlet to an intense relationship with the book as he enters the scene; and yet we know that he has also assumed an 'antic' disposition, committed himself to the revenge of his father's murder, and has abdicated from his role as the scholar, son, lover, and prince. Like Polonius's decision for Ophelia to 'colour' her presence by virtue of the book, Hamlet refers to the book for a similar confusion of appearance and motive. If Ophelia's text allows for the single woman of status to be found alone in a social space, how does Hamlet's book perform?[18] Hamlet's concerted attention to the book, as noticed by Gertrude, is clearly an assumed posture, and presumably works to one of two ends: either Hamlet aims to be ignored because he is thought to be so involved in his book, or he knows that an appearance of studiousness will elicit the kind of response he gets from Polonius. Since the latter seems more likely (given that if Hamlet wanted to be ignored, he surely would not have entered a space so committed to observing), the book emerges as Hamlet's platform for performance; it enables his 'madness' to emerge, and stands between him and his observers. The physical role that the book takes on-stage frequently carves up the dramatic space for the inclusion, seclusion, or redirection of the interrelationships of the characters in place. Hamlet finds his own theatre as he holds the book between him and the bodies of his observers to direct the misreading of his presence. The book seems to create a space of anamorphis; it directs the mind outward to constructions of reading (books or bodies), whilst simultaneously occupying an independent space of peculiar visual clarity and form. Initially, however, like Ophelia's volume, Hamlet's book provides a mutual point of contact for the characters on-stage. Yet, whereas Hamlet violates the form of Ophelia's text, here both Gertrude and Polonius find Hamlet through the presence of his book. Hamlet's entrance 'reading' immediately locates him within a self-referential or solitary space of thought. Ophelia has already reported the state of

---

[18] Technically, there are various different books referred to in *Hamlet*; these include the 'tablet' or commonplace book, the devotional work, the metaphorical book of the mind, memory, and soul, and the generic book of education. However, each of these books function in opposition to, or in confrontation with, experience. Whatever the original and literal status of the books, they tend to shift into a figurative and metaphysical context that encompasses multiple meanings.

Hamlet's madness: 'with his doublet all unbraced, / No hat upon his head, his stockings fouled, / Ungartered, and down-gyvèd to his ankle' (II. i. 79–81), and, to some extent, we might hear Gertrude's comment as one of relief; that the 'sad wretch' is 'reading' signifies a hopeful return to the scholarly status with which she is familiar. Equally, Polonius's attempt to engage with Hamlet through his reading material signifies the book as providing an access to the Hamlet he recognizes.

The Folio's stage direction '*Enter Hamlet reading on a book*' positions the scholar holding a book, probably open, with his head bowed. Yet the text is neither specifically identified nor intertextually supported. Scholarship has variously tried to identify this book. T. W. Baldwin suggests Cicero; Leonard Barkan, noticing 'the satirical slave', postulates Juvenal; others have implicated Montaigne.[19] However, although we might more easily identify Hamlet's object as his own commonplace book—following on from his tables, his recent observation of the smiling villain set down and new commitment to a blank tablet from which his erased memory may proceed—his garbled refusal to accommodate any textual stability shows Hamlet to obfuscate keenly any specific identification. It is simply Hamlet's book, and one that he deconstructs to support his madness and make a strategy for sanity.

Initially it appears that Hamlet chooses to enter reading in order to defer his 'real' presence; his book as a companion allows him to enter the space of his mother and uncle without the absolute responsibility of interaction, for it allows him a certain privacy associated with reading, as well as providing a brief stability in the recognition of his scholar self. However, although the book may begin as a refuge from public interaction, it is quickly appropriated as a vantage-point by the other characters. Polonius's question, 'What do you read, my lord?', far from initiating the discourse he expects, in which he too believes the book to stand as a refuge between himself and Hamlet's 'madness', releases a display of the very condition he feared. Hamlet's response, 'Words, words, words', instantly devalues any role that the book has as a meaningful or social sign. Hamlet's description of the matter he reads falls as a stricture on not only the humanist enterprise of

<hr />

[19] T. W. Baldwin, *William Shakespeare's 'Small Latine & Lesses Greeke'*, i (Urbana, Ill.: University of Illinois Press, 1944); Barkan, 'What did Shakespeare Read?', 39. I have extrapolated the suggestion that Hamlet may be reading Montaigne's *Essais* from the work of Cave, *Cornucopian Text*, and Eric Auerbach, *Mimesis: The Representation of Reality in Western Literature*, trans. Willard R. Trask (Princeton: Princeton University Press, 1974).

imitation, or copia, but also on the signification of meaning. When Hamlet declares the 'words, words, words' of his book, he instantly severs any relationship that Polonius may try to make through the referent, as well as emphasizing the vast gulf between his matter and his meaning. In Hamlet's 'obliteration' of 'referentiality', Ayers marks this moment as 'anticipating Derrida by some three and a half centuries, and announcing nothing less than a radical reformation of conventional ways of looking at words, texts, and the process of reading itself'.[20] However, Hamlet's reaction, rather than anticipate a profound post-structuralist fissure in the order of signification, seeks to establish an isolated space independent of the order of communication. Hamlet's response to Polonius uses the book and its 'words' as both defence and attack, in order to sever himself from shared lines of meaning, not to re-negotiate them. Hamlet's response makes no attempt to include his companions in a discourse on signification; rather, he simply replies to Polonius's question literally and turns Polonius back to the bare sign, the 'word', and not away from it. For the audience, however, Hamlet's response returns us to the erasing of his books, which he acts out for his spectators, on the one hand divorcing the 'matter' from any signification and, on the other, gambolling through a seething mishmash of proverbial wisdom: the 'dead dog' 'kissing carrion', 'backward crab'; classical satire, 'satirical rogue' who 'says here that old men have grey beards'; and contention with the graphic sign, since 'all which, sir, though I most powerfully and potently believe, yet I hold it not honesty to have it thus set down' (II. ii. 200–2). Although Hamlet may 'powerfully and potently believe' something, it is not honest to have it written down, for truth cannot be honoured by the written word. In 'words, words, words' Hamlet condemns the idea of meaning as it is reflected by the book. Hamlet's violent reappraisal of the book excludes him from precisely the kind of assumptions that Polonius makes between meaning and matter.

The relationship between meaning and matter was often explicitly emblematized in the book. Much of sixteenth-century discourse saw the book as not only representative of meaning but also its precedent; the book visually and textually promised knowledge. In Gregor Reisch's *Margarita Philosophica* (1503) and Francis Bacon's *The Great Instauration* (1620), for example, a virtue is made of blazoning knowledge. The former depicts Grammar opening the gate to the 'castle of knowledge'

---

[20] Ayers, 'Reading, Writing, and Hamlet', 424.

with a key in one hand and an alphabet in the other,[21] and the latter shows an image of a ship sailing towards the two pillars of learning beyond which stretches an endless horizon of knowledge. Humanist endeavour is entirely supported by the trading of knowledge as both a cognitive and a literal commodity, and the printed book became emblematic of the material and metaphorical journey that knowledge and the reader could make. In contrast, in Montaigne's *Essais*, a retreat from the public life becomes synonymous with a sceptical and thorough examination of how the 'self' achieves and recognizes meaning within an order of its own making. In declaring words as empty transactions that only replicate the gulf between expression and experience, Montaigne observed something similar to Hamlet when he said: 'Our disputes are about words. I ask what is Nature, Pleasure, a Circle, and a Substitution. The question is couched in words, and is answered in the same coin.'[22] Although the subjective 'author' and singular 'I' increasingly began to find a voice towards the end of the sixteenth century,[23] Montaigne appears to be doing something different. In contrast to Robert Burton, for example, who, like Montaigne, appears to explore 'la condition humaine', when he declares 'Thou thyself art the subject of my discourse',[24] Burton contains his 'I' within a consensual academic fabric of recognized values that seek only to reaffirm those values in reflecting, and creating, an image of himself: 'Concerning myself, I can peradventure affirm with Marius in Sallust, "That which others hear or

[21] As described by Anthony Grafton, *New Worlds, Ancient Texts: The Power of Tradition and the Shock of Discovery* (Cambridge, Mass., and London: The Belknap Press of Harvard University Press, 1995), 16.

[22] Montaigne, *Essays*, 349.

[23] Alongside the more generally recognized inflection of the 'individual' in the sixteenth century famously discussed by Jacob Burckhardt in *The Civilisation of the Renaissance in Italy*, 2 vols. (New York: Harper & Row, 1958), and explored more anecdotally in the work of New Historicism, Douglas Bruster draws attention to an equally important emergence of the 'personal', i.e. 'embodied writing': 'a kind of text and textual practice that, increasingly during the 1590s, put resonant identities and physical forms on the printed page'. Bruster specifically locates the rise of satire, particularly the Marprelate tracts, *à clef* and erotic writing, the increasingly powerful relationship between the author's death and the popularity of his works (suggesting a celebration of the 'author'), and, of course, the embodied presence of writing on-stage: 'Granting bodily presence to fictional characters, and a fictional identity to real bodies, this writing mediated the imaginary and the actual in its bodily address': *Shakespeare and the Question of Culture: Early Modern Literature and the Cultural Turn* (Basingstoke and New York: Palgrave Macmillan, 2003), 65–93.

[24] Robert Burton, *The Anatomy of Melancholy*, ed. Holbrook Jackson (New York: New York Review of Books, 2001), p. 20.

read of, I felt and practised myself; they get their knowledge by books, I mine by learning." '[25] Burton scrutinizes and recognizes himself within terms and conditions that are already set down; Hamlet, however, wrenches himself from those terms, words, or matter which contain an order of communication not predicated upon independent experience. Hamlet's determined misconstruing of Polonius amplifies both the arbitrary nature of language to represent meaning—brilliantly exposed in Hamlet's perfect misinterpretation of 'matter'—and the necessity of meaning to reflect relationships. Polonius's observation that 'Though this be madness, yet there is method in't' sanctions Hamlet's oblique drive for truth beyond the 'painted word', 'suits of woe', or smiling perfidy that supports the dualism of Elsinore. However, both Polonius and Claudius suggest in their reading of Hamlet's madness that there is meaning behind his 'antic' and 'divided' self, particularly in contrast to the outright alienation of mad Ophelia. When things 'seem' to be something, they threaten the very order upon which 'seeming' survives.

The auspicious entrance of the players into Hamlet's world enables him to advance his developing practices of meaning. Hamlet casts himself into the world of theatre and theories of playing through the murky space between naturalism and realism. Caught between the potential reality of the play and the effects of a player's reality, Hamlet is confronted by his own theories of representation and truth:

> What would he do,
> Had he the motive and the cue for passion
> That I have? He would drown the stage with tears
> And cleave the general ear with horrid speech,
> Make mad the guilty and appal the free,
> Confound the ignorant and amaze indeed
> The very faculties of eyes and ears. Yet I,
> A dull and muddy-mettled rascal, peak
> Like John-a-dreams, unpregnant of my cause,
> And can say nothing.
>
> (ii. ii. 548–57)

Hamlet adumbrates the representational difference between the appearance and the reality of truth; whilst truth should behave with horrid speech to amaze both the eyes and ears, in reality it says nothing. Yet where, for Hamlet, the book afforded no outlet for the expression of

[25] Ibid. 22.

life, the theatre, in enclosing life, will give reality the opportunity to disclose itself on the margins of the contained. From the outset, Hamlet enters into questions of truth bound up in the vagaries of 'seeming'. Yet, condemning his books, erasing his memory, and living only with the commandment of the Ghost, Hamlet finds truth in the battlements, cellar, and shadows of Elsinore. Truth emerges as the obverse to art and, in confronting what art has come to mean, subjects reality to the pressure of perception. According to Francis Bacon, 'the nature of things betrays itself more readily under the vexations of art than in its natural freedom.'[26] Bacon's contention is that man's mind is as 'an uneven mirror', which, in receiving impressions, 'distorts the rays of objects according to its own figure and section', and therefore 'cannot be trusted to report them truly, but in forming its notions mixes up its own with the nature of things'.[27] Although the mirror was a commonplace conceit for the mind of man, as much as it was for the theatre, Bacon's observation recalls Hamlet's play as it subjects the nature of things to the dual process of vexation and observation. Hamlet, like Bacon, seeks to enforce a linear perception, understood in terms of the objectivity of truth, by pressurizing nature into an even space of reflection. The art itself is nature according to where the mirror, as it were, is placed:

Suit the action to the word, the word to the action, with this special observance, that you o'erstep not the modesty of nature. For anything so overdone is from the purpose of playing, whose end, both at the first and now, was and is to hold, as 'twere, the mirror up to nature: to show virtue her own feature, scorn her own image, and the very age and body of the time his form and pressure. (III. ii. 16–23)

The mirror stage must reflect nature in its art; yet the auditorium must betray its art in the modesty of nature on-stage. Ultimately it is the mirror of nature on-stage that will vex the art of the auditorium into reporting itself truly. For Hamlet, the vexations of art, construed as theatre, perform the function of what Foucault calls a 'man-made sign', which not only derives its power from its 'fidelity to natural signs', but also 'draws the dividing-line between man and animal; that transforms imagination into voluntary memory'.[28] The language with

---

[26] Francis Bacon, *New Atlantis, and The Great Instauration* (1620; rev. edn., ed. Jerry Weinburger Wheeling, Ill.: Harlan Davidson, Inc., 1989), 28.

[27] Ibid. 25.

[28] Michel Foucault, *The Order of Things: An Archaeology of the Human Sciences* (London and New York: Routledge, 2000), 62.

which Hamlet negotiates his theatre recalls his rejection of the book; the 'form and pressure' so essential to the effect and purpose of playing were also aspects of his learning erased for the memory of his father. However, where 'all saws of books' simply re-presented the pressures past as natural signs of the known and knowing world, uncontested by the man-made relationship between experience and meaning, the theatre confronts memory in the embodied imagination of reflection and remembering. Hamlet ushers in the theatre to affect the manner of a man-made sign, transforming what appears to be imagination into the voluntary memory of Claudius. Where as Hamlet's books took him only into the terrain of a shared ethical rhetoric, condemned by their form to transform matter into meaning, his theatre projects the spectator into a site of inner struggle.

Antonin Artaud in his extraordinary work *The Theatre and its Double* develops an analogy between the plague and the theatre that begins in the imaginative relationship between conflict and memory: 'like the plague, theatre is a powerful appeal through illustration to those powers which return the mind to the origins of its inner struggles.'[29] The relationship that Artaud makes between the plague and the actor is symptomatic of the relationship between Claudius and the stage:

The condition of a plague victim, who dies without any material destruction, yet with all the stigmata of an absolute, almost abstract disease upon him, is in the same condition as an actor totally penetrated by feelings without any benefit or relation to reality. Everything in the actor's physical aspect, just as in the plague victim, shows life has reacted to a paroxysm, yet nothing has happened.[30]

Hamlet's theatre turns Claudius into the actor, 'totally penetrated by feelings without any benefit or relation to reality', suffering the paroxysms of memory, 'yet, nothing has happened'. Or, rather, nothing has *apparently* happened, since the theatre pretends to contain its action within the character and the stage. Yet Hamlet's ostensible attention to both decorum and text, warning the actors against improvisation and excess, allows the extended space for imitation to occur outside the playing space. The play is presented as a contained text, devoid of 'the motive and the cue for action' of real experience or feeling, and what occurs outside the play, in the audience, is the potential mimetic space. Hamlet 'set[s] down' a 'speech of some dozen or sixteen lines' (II.

[29] Antonin Artaud, *The Theatre and its Double*, trans. Victor Corti (Montreuil, London, and New York: Calder, 1999), 20.
[30] Ibid. 15–16.

ii. 529), and performs it for the players as he will have it performed: 'Speak the speech, I pray you, as I pronounced it to you' (III. ii. 1). Despite his original injunction, Hamlet returns to his humanist roots, providing both text and imitation in order to effect action and response. Yet the play itself is a copy or imitation of an event, so that reality, text, performance, and mimesis converge as a recursive process, ultimately finding their point of completion in the bodies of the audience.

Theatre, however, captures a sense of immediacy associated with the direct relationship between thought and action, feeling and response; such an immediacy lies at the heart of retrieving the self from its textual precedent: 'Both improvisation and inspiration are concepts which seek to erase the wealth of pre-existing written materials and represent discourse as arising immediately from the mind, breath, or voice of the speaker.'[31] Hamlet began the play erasing a wealth of pre-existing discourse in order to determine a way of retrieving the unmeditated. The dialectic between shared experience and private imperative makes the book a volatile companion. Returning to his classical learning, Hamlet extracts moments which justify or accept his emotions. When Hamlet recalls Pyrrhus's revenge of his father's death—'One speech' which he 'chiefly loved, 'twas Aeneas' tale to Dido, and thereabout of it especially where he speaks of Priam's slaughter' (II. ii. 437–9)—he asks the theatre to regain the moment of contact between text and experience, which has been condemned by the book.

Through theatre, Hamlet translates his relationship to the book from reader to writer:

Succeeding the Author, the scriptor no longer bears within him passions, humours, feelings, halts, impressions, but rather this immense dictionary from which he draws a writing that can know no halt: life never does more than imitate the book, and the book itself is only a tissue of signs, an imitation that is lost, infinitely deferred.[32]

Although Barthes is talking about the 'death about the author' at a particular moment in history, he speaks for the crisis of the book. Hamlet is forced by his own predicament, like a 'dull and muddy-mettled rascal' to deny his 'passions' and 'humours', in saying 'nothing'. Instead, drafting his own play through the pre-text of 'The Murder

---

[31] Cave, *Cornucopian Text*, p. xii.

[32] Roland Barthes, 'The Death of the Author', in David Finkelstein and Alistair McCleery (eds.), *The Book History Reader* (London and New York: Routledge, 2002), 223.

of Gonzago', Pyrrhus, Priam, or Hecuba, he draws from 'an immense dictionary', the 'book and volume' of his brain, a 'tissue of signs' to set memory in motion through the mimetic life of the spectator/reader. The bridge from art to life is forged by the transformation of the imagination into memory. The processes of remembering and forgetting that drive so much of the play move through the book to retrieve the improvised self in the theatre. Later, when Hamlet recounts his discovery of Claudius's plot to kill him as he sails for England, he tells Horatio:

> Being thus benetted round with villains—
> Ere I could make a prologue to my brains,
> They had begun the play—I sat me down,
> Devised a new commission, wrote it fair.
> I once did hold it, as our statists do,
> A baseness to write fair, and laboured much
> How to forget that learning.
>
> (v. ii. 30–6)

Improvising his theatre, 'Ere I could make a prologue to my brains', Hamlet remembers his part through the clerical terms he had hoped to forget. Writing himself back from forgetting, Hamlet enters into the immediate world of action through the language of theatre. When Hamlet rejected the book initially, he did so for its flat representation of consensual experience; when he appropriates the theatre, however, he re-ignites the writing hand as a powerful tool of anamorphis. Issuing the stage with a mirror that can provoke both remembering and forgetting, Hamlet organizes his words to provide the graphic images of the heart. Where as 'The Mousetrap' offers Claudius an image of himself—or, as Cassius says to Brutus, 'you cannot see yourself / So well as by reflection'[33]—Hamlet's words, as he advances on his mother, become a mirror to her memory:

> You go not till I set you up a glass
> Where you may see the inmost part of you.
>
> (III. iv. 20–1)

Where as the actual mirror in *Richard II* failed to represent his 'inmost part', reflecting merely the 'external manner of laments' signifying nothing, Hamlet's mirror, glistening with the truth hitherto denied by Gertrude, reflects her very soul. Gertrude, terrified of Hamlet's vitriol and responding to his being 'thought-sick at the act' asks:

[33] *Julius Caesar*, I. ii. 69–70.

> Ay me, what act,
> That roars so loud and thunders in the index?

(III. iv. 53–4)

Gertrude's reference to 'the index' forces the image of the book back into contest with its representative potential. Gertrude is probably specifically referring to 'a table of contents prefixed to a book' or 'a sign, token, indication *of* something' (*OED*, 4.b., 5.†a), suggesting that Hamlet's accusations have yet to reveal the argument or 'act'. However, Gertrude's exclamation may also glance at the *Index librorum prohibitorum*, a book issued by the Catholic Church listing forbidden books, or the *Expurgatory Index*, a sub-volume of the *Index* listing passages to be excised or altered, amplifying the image of the book within the context of sin.[34] In *The Cardinal* (1641), James Shirley has Antonio advise his companion on how to approach his love for a woman with 'a little stain' upon her honour:

> First I would marry her, that's a verb material;
> Then I would print her with an *index*
> *Expurgatoris*; a table drawn
> Of her court heresies; and when she's read,
> *Cum privilegia*, who dares call her whore?[35]

Despite Antonio's context of exoneration, the idea of the '*index*' is clearly associated with sexual transgression and sin. On the one hand, Gertrude's response declares that she understands Hamlet's accusations to condemn her not only graphically, but before the act has either occurred or been understood; on the other, however, if we accept a possible reference to the *Index*, Hamlet's condemnation is not simply private or domestic, but, within a public moral fabric of absolute judgement, indelibly set down. Having set himself up as the mirror to Gertrude's soul, Hamlet forces her eye to the image of her husbands:

> Look here upon this picture, and on this,
> The counterfeit presentment of two brothers.

(III. iv.55–6)

---

[34] Although the *Index librorum prohibitorum* was formulated under the Council of Trent and published by Pius IV in 1564, the *OED* does not cite the first reference in English until 1613. Equally, the *Expurgatory Index*, although published under Phillip II in 1571 in Antwerp, is not cited in English until 1611.

[35] James Shirley, *Dramatic Works and Poems* (London: John Murray, 1833), V. II, p. 337.

The relationship between the word and the image is brought together by Hamlet's initial declaration that he will set his accusations against her as a mirror to her 'inmost part'; the metaphorical mirror appears in Gertrude's forced confrontation with an image of herself, as set down by Hamlet, and an image of her betrayal as pictured by her husbands. The literally visual (the picture) and the materially inscribed (the index) are conflated with the metaphorically visual (mirror) and imaginatively inscribed (soul). Again, it is the improvised, immediate self that forces the eyes inward to the memory of the soul. Confronted with the shards of Hamlet's truth, Gertrude sees her son's words written in her heart with the black ink of sin:

> O Hamlet, speak no more.
> Thou turn'st mine eyes into my very soul,
> And there I see such black and grainèd spots
> As will not leave their tinct.
>
> (iii. iv. 80–3)

From Hamlet's mirror of words, Gertrude configures her individual book of sin, although condemned in the eyes of God and the Church, stained to her private soul. Yet, contrary to the prohibited passages or books in the *Index*, the black ink of Gertrude's soul cannot be excised. The soul as a tablet upon which words or images may be impressed was central to the art of memory, and in devising their systems of memory, both Plato and Cicero attach a value system to the soul. Where as Cicero identified Prudence as a central aspect of the right understanding and application of memory, which was later powerfully appropriated and amplified in the works of Albertus Magnus and Thomas Aquinas, Plato, through the idea of the, literally, impressionable soul, develops a relationship between memory and the soul as a temporal reminder of Ideal Form.

In *Phaedrus*, in which Plato expounds his view of the true function of rhetoric—which is to persuade men to the knowledge of truth—he again develops the theme that knowledge of the truth and of the soul consists in remembering, in the recollection of the Ideas once seen by all souls of which all earthly things are confused copies.[36]

Likewise, Plato's use of 'the seal imprint metaphor in the famous passage in the *Theaetetus,* in which Socrates assumes that there is a block of wax

---

[36] Frances A. Yates, *The Art of Memory* (London: Pimlico, 2001), 51.

in our souls—varying quality in different individuals—and that is "the gift of memory, the Mother of the Muses," '[37] presents the wax tablet of the soul in terms that recognize its value according to its mnemonic imprint. The soul is a repository for truth in relation to its seal of impression. Hamlet, before he enters his mother's closet, ascertains that his soul will not 'seal', receive the impressions of, the words he will use against her:

> I will speak daggers to her, but use none.
> My tongue and soul in this be hypocrites—
> How in my words somever she be shent,
> To give them seals never my soul consent.
>
> (III. ii. 379–82)

Although Hamlet will disgrace his mother and rebuke her actions, he cannot 'seal' them with a belief that she is truly profane.[38] The entrance of the Ghost corroborates Hamlet's decision not to 'seal' his words in his soul. Old Hamlet appears to warn Hamlet of his anger toward his mother, to 'step between her and her fighting soul!', and to re-engage Hamlet, since 'the soul never thinks without a mental picture'.[39] The Ghost returns us to Hamlet's conviction for truth in the command 'Remember me'. *Ad herennium* propounded the use of 'active' or 'dramatic' human figures for recall, which is not only exemplified in 'The Mousetrap', but also here when the sudden entrance of the Ghost, at this apparently unnecessary moment, amplifies the role of visual memory in action. Although Quintilian preferred the art of memorizing whole passages of books, often in visualizing the said passages or pages, he notices a particular relationship whereby the image becomes the word: 'Images are as words by which we note things we have to learn, so that as Cicero says, "we use places as wax and images as letters".'[40] Aristotle, in *De anima*, claims that memory 'belongs to the same part of the soul as the imagination' and that 'Imagination is the intermediary between perception and thought'. Through Aristotle's 'imagination' we can observe how Foucault's man-made sign is indicative

[37] Frances A. Yates, *The Art of Memory* (London: Pimlico, 2001), 50

[38] Although I accept that 'seal' can equally refer to the mark of a legal document, implying that Hamlet will not set down his words in jurisdiction, given the scene's emphasis on the soul, and the play's emphasis on memory, I think it more likely that Hamlet uses 'seal' in the context of the wax tablet of the soul.

[39] Yates, referring to Aristotle's 'De anima', *Art of Memory*, 47.

[40] Yates, *Art of Memory*, 40, 38.

of the cognitive process that occurs when the mind negotiates sign and meaning through both the familiar and the strange.[41] When Hamlet rejected 'all saws of books' in favour of the 'book and volume' of his 'brain', he began a process of forgetting and remembering based on subjecting forms of representation to pressures normally on the margins of their meaning—hence the book to experience, words to matter, the stage to the spectator. Yet, when Hamlet reintroduces the words of his play, or classical allusions on to the stage, he re-engages the sign with its lost journey: to transform imagination into memory by way of 'truth'.

Hamlet begins his journey to truth through a double process of reflection; the metaphorical mirror in his play and confrontation with Gertrude apparently start with linear representation, but then, as 'A natural perspective, that is and is not' moves the soul toward her bias, it turns the 'inmost' out.[42] The mirror works when it both reflects and turns the seeing eye: 'the eye sees not itself but by reflection.' Yet, according to William Baldwin in *The Mirror for Magistrates*, and Lady Percy in *2 Henry IV*, the metaphorical mirror is the imitative and reflective article to educate and gentle the human soul.[43] For Lady Percy, her husband 'was the mark and glass, copy and book, / That fashioned others' (II. iii. 31–3). The book and the mirror in this context are interchangeable artefacts of material and metaphorical signification in and through which men may aspire and imitate. The humanist paradigm is thus amplified within a metaphysical, even Platonic, aspect of becoming what you see or read. But Hamlet reverses the aspirational and the benign; the theatre, which is the devolved site of the mirror, must reveal the evil rather than inspire the good. It is no longer a site to teach, but to punish. The theatre was both born from, and often justified by, a didactic imperative; but Hamlet's play cannot redress evil by means of the virtuous mirror, it can only re-present things as they already are:

---

[41] Although I choose to develop Foucault's comment in the context of Aristotle's *De anima*, I do not mean to suggest an ideological relationship between the philosophers. I am aware that Aristotle refers to 'things past' within the context of what Plato would develop into Ideal Forms, but here I simply observe the cognitive process which affects its own system of meaning.

[42] I have taken the quotation and idea from *Twelfth Night*, v. i. 214, 257, wherein Orsino sees Cesario's transformation into Viola as an optical trick 'making one image into two', and Sebastian comments on his marriage to Olivia (as she thought, Cesario) as nature ultimately, even inexorably, bending toward the 'right', straight course.

[43] Kinney observes the great number of titles that were published during this period which included the word 'mirror' as a metaphor for the exemplary or didactic nature of its content. See *Shakespeare's Web*, 6.

'to show virtue her own feature, scorn her own image, and the very age and body of the time his form and pressure'. Theatre interacts with life as a parallel image, but, crucially, according to Hamlet's remark that men may 'declare' themselves at plays in response to the imaged self, it has the capacity to uncover life and provoke truth.

The idea of the mirror brings the word and the image together to challenge representation and reveal the soul. In isolation, the image is always in a state of flux, the 'seeming', 'observed', 'seen unseen' world of Elsinore undermines any sense of even perspective; something Hamlet suddenly remembers in his treatment of Laertes: 'That to Laertes I forgot myself; / For by the image of my cause I see / The portraiture of his' (v. ii. 77–9). By contrast, the 'mind's eye' takes the shape of truth: 'O my prophetic soul'. The 'book and volume' of Hamlet's brain ushers in memory as it erases all pressures past for the immediate theatre of the mind's eye.

## 'WHILE MEMORY HOLDS A SEAT IN THIS DISTRACTED GLOBE'

In 1550, Guilio Camillo's treatise for the construction of a memory theatre was published. *L'idea del Theatro* quite literally reflects the synthetic relationship between word and image, and the potential memory holds for a temporal and celestial order. Out of the Platonic idea of 'copies' Guilio Camillo designed a 'Theatre of Memory'. Camillo's fame was due partly to his ingenuity and partly to his eccentricity. His elaborate appropriation of the ancient art of memory, its ascent (or descent) into the occult, and its theatrical presentation won no favours with humanists, who preferred the more rational, methodological treatment of Quintilian. However, Viglius Zuichemus visited Camillo's Theatre and wrote to Erasmus concerning what he saw:

He calls this theatre of his by many names, saying now that it is built or constructed mind and soul, and now that it is a windowed one. He pretends that all things that the human mind can conceive and which we cannot see with the corporeal eye, after being collected together by diligent meditation may be expressed by certain corporeal signs in such a way that the beholder may at once perceive with his eyes everything that is otherwise hidden in the depths of the human mind. And it is because of this corporeal looking that he calls it a theatre.[44]

---

[44] Quoted in Yates, *Art of Memory*, 136–7.

Camillo's Theatre is important, not for its Platonic or arcane implications but simply because it overtly synthesizes the theatre and the
unconscious. The Theatre aims to retrieve the spectator's hidden mind
and make it visible, corporeal. This process involves reversing the traditional layout of a theatre by making the observer also the observed.
'There is no audience sitting in the seats watching a play on stage:
the "solitary" spectator of the Theatre stands where the stage would
be and looks toward the auditorium.'[45] By reversing the relationship
between spectator and spectacle, the Theatre overturns the linear relationship between observation and outward form. The Theatre projects
the unconscious in 'certain corporeal signs', and retrieves the hidden
depths of the human mind. When Hamlet devises the play for the King
and Queen, he devises a theatre of memory, a projection of corporeal signs that reflects the dark recesses of his spectators' minds. Yet,
although we may notice structural similarities between these theatres of
memory, both Hamlet and Camillo project their spectator imaginatively
or literally on to the stage; both devise 'corporeal signs' supported by
text, for Hamlet inserts 'some dozen or sixteen lines', and Camillo puts
scraps of Cicero into drawers beneath the stage; and although they
may both work toward hidden truths, what they reveal, and what they
want to reveal, is very different. Camillo's memory theatre is strictly
committed to retrieving the Ideal Forms of the fallen mind, and aims,
in triggering and recovering memory, to return the mind to its perfect
origins. Hamlet's theatre, by contrast, although striving for truth, will
remove a veneer of what 'seems' to reveal the evil that lies beneath.
As Hamlet fulfils the command of the Ghost to 'Remember me', he
projects his spectator on to this mirror stage and holds up a glass to the
mnemonic soul.

When Thomas Heywood, in *An Apology for Actors*, claims that 'All
men have parts, and each must act his own', he suggests that finding
your world is finding your part in it: 'The World's a Theatre, the
earth a Stage, / Which God, and nature doth with Actors fill'.[46] When
Hamlet hauls Claudius's life on to the stage, he re-engages with the
relationship between the theatre and the world, showing Claudius the
part he played, in nature and before God; or, as Jonson claimed, 'all
Representations . . . eyther have bene, or ought to be the mirror of mans

---

[45] Ibid. 141.

[46] Thomas Heywood, *An Apology for Actors Containing Three Brief Treatises* (London:
Nicholas Okes, 1612), A4ᵛ.

life.'[47] The 'true transparent crystal mirror' of the stage does not simply reflect the world but reorientates 'each man [to] act his own' part. Where as the book could only ever represent a partial self, a self of words, and a form of experience, the theatre effects a reconciliation of the art itself as nature. Heywood recalls an incident with 'a company of our *English* Comedians', in which a woman, watching the performance of a particular method of murder, became 'with great gravity strangely amazed' and 'with a distracted and troubled brain oft sighed these words: Oh my husband, my husband!' A few days later, the sexton, having discovered the skull of a man murdered similarly to the man in the play, makes it known to the churchwarden, and 'the woman, out of the trouble of her afflicted conscience discovered a former murder'.[48] The play, it seems, catches the memory of the spectator.

Since Hamlet forgot his books and remembered his father, etched a commonplace in the teeming volume of his brain, turned out the court with his companion to madness, and wrote the theatre of his revenge, the book has moved to and from the social and the subjective, providing the refuge of a shared rhetoric and the violence of a private passion. As the book enables Hamlet to move between the worlds of public drama and private tragedy, it becomes his most powerful weapon against the conscience and consciousness of his being. There is a dreadful complexity in the book, which the play chooses never to ignore: whether it is Hamlet's mind, his past, his reading, or his 'matter', Ophelia's devotion, talisman, or entrapment, Polonius's regret that he had not played the table-book or his misreading of madness for method; the book is an idea and an image that the play depends on for the volatile dynamic between a cultural language and a dangerous mind.

---

[47] Jonson's prefatory note to *Love's Triumph*, as quoted by Andrew Gurr, *The Shakespearean Stage 1574–1642*, 3rd edn. (Cambridge: Cambridge University Press, 2003), 25.

[48] Heywood, *Apology for Actors*, G2$^v$, G2$^r$.

# 6

# 'Rather like a dream than an assurance': *The Tempest* and the Book of Illusions

When Peter Greenaway entitled his adaptation of *The Tempest* 'Prospero's Books' (1991), he foregrounded the magus and his material as the iconic authority through which the film moved. During the course of the film, Greenaway puts twenty-four books into the hands of Prospero, each one a testimony to the independent power of the book to both create and reflect its subject: in *The Book of Water*, for example, 'As the pages are turned, the watery elements are often animated. There are rippling waves and slanting storms'; or in *The Book of Languages*, where 'Words, sentences, paragraphs and chapters gather like tadpoles in a pond in April or starlings in a November evening sky.'[1] For Greenaway, these books belong to an arcane corpus synthesizing humanist aspiration and the self-fulfilling agencies of the natural and the cosmic world. They appear to belong to Prospero, as their pages unfold in sympathy with the magus, offering the depths of their illusions to the strength of his desires. The visual impact of Greenaway's imagination, and the lengths to which his cinematic licence go, are evidence of the power of the book in this play. In Shakespeare's *The Tempest*, however, no single book is named; nor do any appear on-stage.[2]

---

[1] Peter Greenaway, *Prospero's Books: A Film of Shakespeare's* The Tempest (London: Chatto & Windus, 1991), 17, 21. Although the film claims twenty-four books, only twenty-two actually appear, and, as Daniela Carpi suggests, 'the missing books are the most fundamental ones, or rather, the volume containing all Shakespeare's works including *The Tempest*': 'Prospero's Books *and* The Tempest: *Science, Magic and Painting*', in Patricia Kennan and Mariangela Tempera (eds.), *Metamorphosing Shakespeare: Mutual Illuminations of the Arts* (Bologna: CLUEB, 2004), 110.

[2] It is possible that when Prospero talks of drowning his books, he performs the act on-stage. However, not only does his speech of abjuration anticipate, rather than direct, the act, but it is unlikely that the characters are standing on the shoreline at this point; also, since the book is to be buried 'deeper than did ever plummet sound', Prospero would need to be quite far out to sea.

The Tempest, unlike any other play discussed here, does not support an inclusive attitude to the book; it does not engage the audience or the play-world in a reciprocal relationship with the book. In Shakespeare's plays, the book, material or metaphorical, is almost always manifest in relationship to the stage, enlarging or reducing our understanding of its presence beyond the requisites of the drama. Prospero's books, however, do not appear to exist beyond the limits and imagination of the scaffold; yet that is where they reside for the duration of the play. The paradox of these books is that they cannot visually support the illusions they claim to sustain. Although such books enter the play almost immediately, they come not on their own, but out of a tale some thirteen years old alongside the 'stuffs and necessaries' of Prospero's past. Prospero's books begin their voyage into our imaginations through allegory, emerging apparently unchanged from a dubious 'tale' of immorality and selfishness. Whilst Antonio 'Made such a sinner of his memory / To credit his own lie', Prospero, as his 'state grew stranger', allowed his library, 'poor man', to become 'dukedom large enough' (I. ii. 110–12, 76, 110).[3] 'Rapt in secret studies', 'transported', and 'neglecting worldly ends' (I. ii. 76, 77, 89), Prospero does not situate his books amidst good government or Christian humanism, and as they arrive on the island and in to the play, they come bearing the tales of trauma and tempests, alienation, secrecy, and greed. The journey which the books make from Milan to the island, from usurpation to the command of spirits, and the retaining of their significance and shape in both places, suggests their allegorical function in the play. The role of the books in both narratives appears to promise disclosure or revelation, definition or design. Within the play, however, Prospero's books fulfil none of these roles. Whilst on the one hand they offer an image of the world through which The Tempest will move; on the other, they deny us a vision of that world. What we see instead is the illusion of order and the chaos of art.

The relationship between illusion and oppression has often fore-grounded the book in post-colonialist readings of the play, so that the object, like Prospero's art, becomes enmeshed in taxonomic or cultural materialist theories of authority and surveillance.[4] Equally, the book

---

[3] William Shakespeare, The Tempest, ed. Virginia Mason Vaughn and Alden T. Vaughan, The Arden Shakespeare, 3 ser. (Walton-on-Thames: Thomas Nelson, 1999). All subsequent references, unless otherwise stated, are to this edition.

[4] See, e.g. Paul Brown, ' "This thing of darkness I acknowledge mine" ', in Jonathan Dollimore and Alan Sinfield (eds.), Political Shakespeare: Essays in Cultural Materialism, 2nd edn. (Manchester: Manchester University Press, 1994), who suggests that The

may surface through intertextual interpretations or source hunting, as
we trawl for traces of Virgil, Ovid, Montaigne, Strachey, or Hakluyt
in the sea or along the shore of the island.[5] Francis Barker and Peter
Hulme, however, broadened these interpretative scopes by focusing on
what they term 'con-texts', which, as in post-structuralism, seek to
break away from the 'autotelic' text and 'from the inequality of the
usual text / context relationship'. The relationship between text and
context is read as a text, and not as something that 'simply make[s]
up the background'.[6] But even though Barbara Mowat, for example,
may claim that 'No play by Shakespeare gestures toward the book
as pervasively and as importantly as does *The Tempest*', she not only
relegates this leading comment to a footnote, but goes on to discuss
what she calls 'infratexts', or a system of intertextual interpretation.[7]
But, despite this almost ubiquitous awareness of the book, *The Tempest*
denies it a local habitation and a name, preferring instead the airy
nothing of magic and the insubstantial pageant of art. There is no
language of the book, no rich landscape where the idea or object can
be harvested or ploughed. The book is what Milan and the island
share and what apparently begins and ends the drama of Prospero: it is

*Tempest* 'serves as a limit text in which the characteristic operations of colonialist discourse
may be discerned—as an instrument of exploitation, a register of beleaguerment and a site
of radical ambivalence' (p. 68). Aimé Césaire's *Une tempête* is a significant contribution
to the relationship between *The Tempest* and colonialism, since, in this play we see
Caliban 'fight back', exposing 'how colonisation decivilizes the coloniser'; as Césaire's
Caliban reclaims his island, he translates the underside of *The Tempest* into a fight against
the ignorance of Protestant White oppression.

[5] Donna B. Hamilton, in 'Re-Engineering Virgil: *The Tempest* and the Printed English
*Aeneid*', in Peter Hulme and William H. Sherman (eds.), *The Tempest and its Travels*
(London: Reaktion Books Ltd., 2000), shows how the *Aeneid* was a commonplace text
for appropriation: it was published and republished, translated and retranslated, as a
polemical model for both propaganda and public expression. Hamilton gives examples of
the varying translations, dedications, and interpolations that accompanied the publication
of the text during the Reformation, Counter-Reformation, and intermediate union with
the Habsburgs (pp. 114–20). Montaigne's 'On Caniballes' (1603) is thought to have
influenced Gonzalo's commonwealth speech; William Strachey's 'True Reportory' (1625)
gestures at the opening scenes, and a few later references to 'dissensions, conspiracies, and
retributions'; and travellers' tales, including Richard Hakluyt's 'Principal Navigations'
(1589, 1598–1600) and Samuel Purchas' 'Pilgrimage' (1613), are testimony to an
emerging climate of discovery and story.

[6] Francis Barker and Peter Hulme, 'Nymphs and Reapers Heavily Vanish: The
Discursive Contexts of *The Tempest*', in John Drakakis (ed.), *Alternative Shakespeares*
(London and New York: Routledge, 1996), 192–5 n. 7.

[7] Barbara Mowat, ' "Knowing I loved my books": Reading *The Tempest* Intertextually',
in Hulme and Sheman (eds.), *The Tempest and its Travels*, n. 275.

an object of possession and destruction, of aspiration and valediction. What seems to bring the two worlds together is the transformative power of illusion; magic shapes the order of *The Tempest*, and converts chaos into mimesis. Order, however, the privilege of representation and the Aristotelian tenet of mimesis, no longer rewards impasse with the extravagance of the extraordinary, but becomes it: the *deus ex machina* is the great creating nature of action and the thesis of art. The relationship between allegory and the supernatural is predicated upon the emblematic and unrealistic gestures and happenings of chance and magic, happenings normally excluded by the probability and predictability of aetiological order. Yet *The Tempest* perverts the allegorical structure, allowing the irrational to take responsibility for explanation and effect, and the rational to lurk illogically behind the order of chaos. When Gonzalo admits that the island is a place where no man is himself, or Alonso dreams of his son deep mudded in the ooze, or the lovers are resurrected to a game of chess, or the tramping hounds of conscience emerge amidst the sweet airs of celestial music, art jostles art for the argument of design. The island cannot, then, support the linear form of narrative, probability, cognition, or genre; the book, however, can and does, which is why, in the library, the boat, the ooze, and the cave, it lies out of sight, concealed from the 'fabric of this vision' that makes a mystery of the ordinary. Why, then, is the book so central to our awareness of the play, to Greenaway's film, critical theory, academic thought, and performance? And, perhaps more importantly, why does it trace the shadows of the island, chart the trajectory of the play, harness Prospero's magic, his reward and nemesis, Miranda's tuition, and Caliban's sedition?

As the play opens and the tempest subsides, Prospero takes Miranda through 'the dark backward and abysm of time' of her own history, and recalls the great service that Gonzalo did them on their expulsion from Milan:

> Out of his charity—who, being then appointed
> Master of this design—did give us, with
> Rich garments, linens, stuffs and necessaries,
> Which since have steaded much; so of his gentleness,
> Knowing I loved my books, he furnished me
> From mine own library with volumes that
> I prize above my dukedom.
>
> (I. ii. 162–8)

As Prospero recalls his and Miranda's dramatic escape, the corruption of his brother, and the life-threatening conditions through which they travelled, he remembers his books and his library; amidst 'stuffs and necessaries', Gonzalo also remembers Prospero's library, and knowing both Prospero and his books, he manages to find and transport those volumes that he prized above his dukedom. Yet these books are not 'necessaries', but come from the 'gentleness' of Gonzalo, a mark of his kindness and nobility in recognizing Prospero's desires as well as his needs. The journey that Prospero makes with Miranda is redeemed by his books, bringing with them some of that 'gentleness' or nobility through which they were exchanged, and translating the island, from a barren exile of subsistence into a potential place of development and order. However, despite the consequences of his bookish seclusion in Milan, Prospero replicates the secrecy and isolation on the island. Although Prospero may have schooled Miranda, and Caliban will sell his self for the destruction of the magus and his books, initially Prospero admits that he appears to his daughter as 'thy no greater father', 'master of a full poor cell', and that she is 'naught knowing / Of whence I am, nor that I am more better / Than Prospero' (I. ii. 21, 20, 18–20).

The relationship that Prospero makes between his dukedom and his library, his self and his study, is the most composite image the play provides of the nature of Prospero's books. The passage that the books make from Milan to the island is accommodated by the idea of the library and the status of a duke. Anthony Grafton describes how the library functioned in fifteenth-century Italy: 'The serious humanist's library not only mapped the intellectual territory he knew best but provided in its notes of acquisition and marginal annotations a record of the social and intellectual networks that sustained him.'[8] Although Prospero may be sequestered by his 'secret studies' and the 'closeness and bettering' of his mind, the sustenance of the margins, of the relationship between himself and his books, and the transactions made over the pages and amidst the walls, provide a *habitas* for the book to emerge. Prospero refers back to his library and his dukedom in remembering the journey of the books. They belong, for him, to the network that sustained him in Milan, and they are not socialized or translated by their new habitat. Yet Prospero does not tell Miranda of

---

[8] Anthony Grafton, *Commerce with the Classics: Ancient Books and Renaissance Readers*, Jerome Lectures, 20 (Ann Arbor: University of Michigan Press, 1997), 104.

his renown as either man or magus; despite his learning and his art, to Miranda he is 'thy no greater father'. The order from which the books emerge remains with them in the shadows of the play: their status as commodities is not defined by a use- or trading value, but through possession or destruction. Prospero's possession of his books appears distinct from his magic, as Miranda notices them only in connection with her father's routine, when she tells Ferdinand that he will be 'hard at study', and therefore 'safe for these three hours' (III. i. 20, 21). These books are apparently linked to Prospero's art, yet also distinct from his behaviour on the island, since Miranda is, until now, ignorant of their history, or the intellectual and social world that lies beyond the shores of her home. Amid the story of her past, Prospero reminds Miranda that

> Here in this island we arrived, and here
> Have I, thy schoolmaster, made thee more profit
> Than other princes can that have more time
> For vainer hours, and tutors not so careful.
>
> (I. ii. 171–4)

Although Miranda has been taught by her father, perhaps schooled in at least the *trivium* as would befit 'princes', she clearly has no idea of the significance or prestige of learning. It is difficult to imagine what Prospero has taught Miranda, since the humanism that he makes so much of requires not only knowledge of the classics, but an intellectual and spatial awareness of the relationship between the past and the present. As Prospero recounts his past for Miranda, tracing a particular image of his endeavours and aspirations, moving from the 'liberal arts' to being 'rapt in secret studies', dedicated to the 'closeness and bettering of my mind', and being 'reputed', 'without a parallel', for his study, we become aware of the kind of vacuum into which Prospero's books have entered on the island: there is no 'house' to 'deck withal', no networks of communication, or marginal referencing, and Miranda is unaware of the price that they have both had to pay:

> And Prospero the prime Duke, being so reputed
> In dignity, and for the liberal arts
> Without a parallel; those being all my study,
> The government I cast upon my brother.
>
> (I. ii. 72–5)

In tracing that 'dark backward and abysm of time', Prospero tells his daughter the story of his usurpation as it becomes the story of his books; Antonio, who 'made such a sinner of his memory / To credit his own lie',

> To have no screen between this part he played
> And him he played it for, he needs will be
> Absolute Milan. Me, poor man, my library
> Was dukedom large enough. Of temporal royalties
> He thinks me now incapable.
>
> (I. ii. 107–11)

In contrast to the limitless trust that Prospero placed in Antonio, as well as his boundless appropriation of power, the library, like the 'closeness', appears as a private and contained space, apparently divorced not only from 'temporal royalties', but also from the time and place of the polity and *populus* that surrounded him.

> I thus neglecting worldly ends, all dedicated
> To closeness and the bettering of my mind
> With that which, but by being so retired,
> O'er prized all popular rate.
>
> (I. ii. 89–92)

Prospero is blinded by his books, removed from 'worldly ends', and ignorant of the 'popular rate'; his study turns in on him, and knowledge appears to close down the active world of living. In his move to the island, however, Prospero appears to try and recoup a vestige of the under-prized 'popular rate' he once ignored. Prospero replicates his bookish secrecy on the island; but rather than exclude him from the rites of power, his books form the infrastructure of his mini-state, tutoring his daughter, his erstwhile companion, now slave, Caliban, and his command over Ariel. Wherever these books may lie, and whatever they are, they appear to operate an invisible government, directing, supporting, and enabling manifestations of Prospero's authority. The notion of a library as housing the voices and ghosts of its authors, guiding from the spines, and speaking from the pages, is not unusual. Montaigne discussed in some detail the location and precepts of the library space, and a century earlier, Leonello d'Este describes an imaginary place in which books are ordered, among other things, in categories 'to be read rather than reread', and 'the paving, the wall, the beams' are to be 'polished' and 'elegant'. For Leonello, the library is the supportive space that promotes the mental leap into perfection, a structure that is well governed and ordered, decorous and aesthetic, advancing an image of a similar mind. For Giovanni Gualengo, who was one of Leonello's 'circle', the intellectual colony is the intertextual companionship of the authors: 'When I look at and study the ranks of my books—for I have put the name of each author on the binding—I feel as if I am looking at the holy graves of those who wrote them.'[9] Where as here the book may provide a sympathetic model for the mind's assimilation and application of knowledge, which is responsive to the active world, for Prospero it remains in antipathy to the visible order of being. The voices or 'holy graves' that Prospero imports onto the island are not those of authors or texts, but the illusions of an art independent of any visual or intellectual relationship to books. Despite Prospero's inability to reconcile learning and good government, Jonathan Bate, in his essay 'The Humanist *Tempest*', sees the play as an exercise in humanism, wherein good and bad humanism emerge in their relationship to good polity and, ultimately, Christianity. As Bate claims, despite the wealth of critical discourse dedicated to the play's relationship to colonialism:

Throughout the first act . . . there is persistent recourse to the lexicon of learning and education: this, surely, is a more dominant con-textual discourse than that of colonialism, which is barely mentioned in the seed-bed act, save in the passing references to the 'still-vexed Bermudas' and the Patagonian deity Setebos.[10]

Our first encounter with Prospero and Miranda unfolds as if it is in a schoolroom, as Prospero the tutor checks Miranda's attention, rebukes her apparent lack of concentration, and compliments her line of questioning: 'Well demanded, wench: / My tale provokes that question' (I. ii. 139–40). Prospero appears to continue in this attitude for most of the play, until the moment when he tells Ariel, 'The rarer action is / In virtue than in vengeance' (v. i. 27–8), replacing trial with patience, punishment with grace. Prospero's anagnorisis illuminates not simply his driving quest for retribution, but his punitive methods of teaching that begin not in example, but in fear. As Prospero tests Miranda's concentration, he also tests Ariel, threatening him with his own memory into obedience: 'I must / Once in a month recount what thou hast

---

[9] Quoted ibid. 33.
[10] Jonathan Bate, 'The Humanist *Tempest*', in Claude Peltrault (ed.), *Shakespeare, La Tempête: etudes critiques* (Besançon Cedex: Université de Franche-Comté, 1993), 13.

been, / Which thou forget'st' (I. ii. 261–3). As in *Hamlet*, memory and theatre become central to the play's processes of rectitude and realism; yet, for Prospero, and despite the humanist emphasis on memory in the five parts of rhetoric, they are linked to neither his learning nor his books. Prospero holds memory, as he holds illusion, in the wings of his theatre, to manipulate anxiety and to teach.[11] From the outset, the play appears to support a moral maze, but, as Prospero warns, censures, condemns, rewards, and punishes, the root of this moral structure is unclear. Although much of Prospero's ethical authority is assumed in his guise of pedagogue and magus, the relationship between the book and teaching is ambiguous. Despite the tremendous presence of this authority, ideas and practices of teaching appear as perversions of traditional modes of thought. Miranda reminds Caliban that she

> Took pains to make thee speak, taught thee each hour
> One thing or other. When thou didst not, savage,
> Know thine own meaning, but wouldst gabble like
> A thing most brutish, I endowed thy purposes
> With words that made them known.
>
> (I. ii. 355–9)

But Caliban admits, 'You taught me language, and my profit on't / Is I know how to curse' (I. ii. 364–5). In explaining that his only 'profit' is to curse, Caliban takes a fundamental precept of humanist teaching, associated with Horace's famous dictum of 'profit and delight', and travesties it. Perverting order, meaning, and language is Caliban's good learning. As he takes possession of cursing, Caliban condemns the decorous self-images of Miranda and Prospero, abusing meaning for his order of reality. Caliban's delightful profit is in the destruction of the 'art . . . of such power' (I. ii. 373), not its imitation.

When Stephano and Trinculo find Caliban amidst the stench of another storm, the identity of all three characters is thrown into doubt: 'In a poor isle', 'When no man was his own' (v. i. 212, 213). Caliban's status as a monster is confirmed, rather than questioned, by his ability to speak 'our language', and Stephano, the 'drunken butler', becomes a god. When Caliban recalls the beginnings of his relationship with

---

[11] Bate picks up an interesting link within the play's treatment of theatre and humanism: 'The education of Ferdinand and Miranda into virtue, which in their case Prospero makes synonymous with chastity, continues, through the masque. This introduces the possibility that theatre can do what humanism traditionally relied on books to do', ibid. 17.

Prospero, he remembers being given 'Water with berries in't', and how Prospero 'strok'st' him and 'made much of' him, teaching him

> To name the bigger light and how the less
> That burn by day and night. And then I loved thee
> And showed thee all the qualities o'th' isle.

(I. ii. 336–8)

In remembering both the loving and the reciprocal relationship he once shared with Prospero, Caliban recollects a drink that is probably alcoholic, either some sort of wine or possibly a version of the spirit Gin, made from juniper berries, which although it was not first produced as such until the seventeenth century in the Netherlands, possibly existed in some form before then. There is perhaps also some quibbling on the word 'spirit' in the play, which not only refers to Ariel, the ethereal and incorporeal spirits, those things that are held in higher esteem than the body, but also alcohol.[12] When Stephano first uncovers Caliban, he exclaims: 'The spirits torment me! O!' (II. ii. 63); although on an immediate level he speaks of the tormenting sprites of Prospero's magic, Stephano responds to give Caliban a 'taste of my bottle', and there may be a play on the nature of spirits both to falsely empower a man and to transform him into a mockery.[13] Although this is no more than a possible interpretation, it becomes clear that Caliban associates both affection and servitude with 'Water with berries in't', as well as 'celestial liquor'. Caliban's relationship with Stephano begins in associating his 'celestial liquor' with the power of a god: 'That's a brave god and bears celestial liquor. / I will kneel to him' (II. ii. 115–16). The drink becomes an object of idolatry and exchange, and as both a product and an article, it acquires a power and a use-value. Stephano has a 'whole butt' of sack, giving him both a possession and a home: 'My cellar is in a rock by th'seaside, where my wine is hid' (II. ii. 131–2). When Stephano describes his escape, he synthesizes his rescue with a place on the island and the butt of sack itself. Using the bottle to harness Trinculo's right to his survival, he asks:

Swear by this bottle how thou cam'st hither. I escaped upon a butt of sack, which the sailors heaved o'erboard—by this bottle, which I made of the bark of a tree with mine own hands since I was cast ashore. (II. ii. 118–21)

---

[12] Ben Jonson in *The Alchemist* used the word 'spirit' in the context of some sort of process of distillation: 'He's busy with his spirits, but we'll upon him' (II. vi. 1).

[13] Rabelais's *Gargantua and Pantagruel* brilliantly synthesizes the book and alcohol in its search for the 'Holy Bottle'.

Stephano, in using the bottle as an oath and the means of his escape, brings some kind of apotropaic value into play, which is amplified by Caliban's reaction. Caliban immediately responds to the bottle, and Stephano's bearing of it, in servitude: 'I'll swear upon that bottle to be thy true subject, for the liquor is not earthly' (II. ii. 122–3). When Stephano calls to Trinculo to 'kiss the book', he brings in tavern humour for a pledge of loyalty and a celebration of their survival. The anarchy of delusion, the muddled motion of misplaced authority and acute power, is paraded in drunkenness. As these bodies reel across the stage through various notions of supremacy and self-belief, the idea of the book waits in the wings as the still silent voice of order. 'Kissing the book' is a direct travesty of the pledge of the faithful, who, in kissing the Bible, commit not only to God, but also to truth. Elizabeth I in her pre-coronation procession through London famously exemplifies the iconography of such an act. As the progress reached its climax in a conduit in Cheapside, the Queen was presented with a book: 'But as soon as she had received the book, kissed it, and with both her hands held the same, and so laid it upon her breast, with great thanks to the city therefore.'[14] Elizabeth's gesture marks a moment of stillness in the motion of her authority. Kissing the book represents and reaffirms an order of absolutes, wherein the book stills the spectacle of pageant to celebrate Elizabeth as both defender of the faith and governor of the Church.[15] Yet, unlike with Elizabeth, the book here is not the book, but the bottle, and the symbolic order of being and authority is overturned as Stephano, capitalizing on the value of the sack, his own survival, possession, and 'cellar', brings his new comrades to heel with the command of a tapster. The reeling idiocy of the two men coupled with Caliban's foolish naïvety parodies the presence of the book in the effects of alcohol. All that we see of the book—magic, illusion, trauma, tempests, inanity, and drunkenness—is the chaos of its absence.

[14] James M. Osborn (ed.), *The Quenes Maisties Passage through the Citie of London to Westminster the Day before her Coronacion* (facsimile of the publication on 23 Jan. 1559), (New Haven: Yale University Press, 1960), 48. I have modernized orthography and typography.

[15] Although the title 'Defender of the Faith' was awarded to Henry VIII by the Pope in 1521, and revoked in 1534 when Henry broke with Rome, Henry claimed it back in 1544 in accordance with being 'Defender of the True Faith of the Reformed Church'. Elizabeth I was not crowned Supreme Head of the Church, like her father, because Mary revoked the Act of Supremacy during her reign; however, about six months after her coronation in 1559, Elizabeth became the Supreme Governor of the Church.

The act of kissing the book not only travesties the Bible; it also replicates the relationship between sin and servitude signified by the Faithful's response to, and atonement in, religious dogma. Prospero's godlike status is notoriously ambiguous; whilst, on the one hand, the island offers a space of independent authority, a no-place upon which music, howling, 'sounds and sweet airs', 'a thousand twangling instruments', 'open', 'rich' 'clouds', and dreams suggest a pantheistic harmony of self-generating agencies; on the other hand, the profusion of languages, cursing, wonder, vengeance, and ubiquitous authority signifies an ambiguous place of pre- and post-lapsarian texture, where Ariel can tell his terrified diners that the storm was created by 'powers' who 'not forgetting, have / Incensed the seas and shores—yes, all the creatures— / Against your peace' (III. iii. 73–5). Against Caliban's avenging angel, Prospero stands as a 'god of power': 'so rare a wondered father and a wise / Makes this place paradise' (IV. i. 123–4).[16] Gonzalo's attempt to make his own vision of heaven, his utopian commonwealth, and perception of Prospero's banquet, over which Ariel presides as a harpy, 'Who, though they are of monstrous shape, yet note / Their manners are more gentle, kind, than of / Our human generation you shall find / Many, nay, almost any' (III. iii. 31–4), claims a particular vision of the island as beautiful and humane against Prospero's rendition of hell: 'Thou hast said well, for some of you there present / Are worse than devils' (III. iii. 35–6).

Amidst the heaven and hell of the island, the potential of the 'books' shifts between the arcane, the humanist, and the biblical. In Marlowe's *Doctor Faustus*, written twenty years earlier, heaven and hell are juxtaposed in an analogous exploration of books and magic.[17]

---

[16] There is some editorial contention over the word 'wise', which in Rowe's 1709 Folio was printed as 'wife' and continued to be so until the nineteenth century. However, I disagree with the current editors of the Arden edition, and suggest that 'wife' is the more likely reading within the context of Ferdinand's sentiments. Ferdinand imagines a 'paradise' in which they are the pre-lapsarian trinity: Father, Adam and Eve. Tiffany Stern also points out that 'the word is not in fact "wise" but "wife" with the integument on the "f" broken off leaving the letter resembling a long "s" ': *Making Shakespeare: From Stage to Page* (London: Routledge, 2004), 155.

[17] Cosmo Corfield sees Ariel and Caliban as fulfilling analogous roles to those of Faustus's good and bad angels: 'Caliban externalises Prospero's propensity to evil just as Ariel represents his aspiration toward good. Marlowe, of course, does something similar when he situates Faustus' conscience between a good and bad angel—in other words, a Holy Guardian Angel and a Malevolent Demon': 'Why Does Prospero Abjure his "Rough Magic"?', *Shakespeare Quarterly*, 36 (1985), 34. Although Prospero's comment, 'this thing of darkness I acknowledge mine', often situates Caliban as the demon in

For Faustus, however, the material drive beyond the limits of allowed knowledge is internalized, as the soul and its consciousness become the site of turmoil. Here, Marlowe makes an ambiguous journey from the book to damnation, setting Faustus first within the study of humanist inquiry and then in the devil's library, by way of necromancy. The book is central to Faustus's path to hell, which is amplified by the choices he makes and the attitude with which he makes them. Marlowe continues to pave the way to the devil with books, and it becomes clear how dangerously ambivalent books are as both the victims and enablers of profane transgression. Marlowe's attention to the books leaves no doubt as to their role in the evolution of the play, and, like Prospero's books, they begin and end a personal journey. The problem of Prospero's books—what are they?—might to some extent be explored through Marlowe's play, since he makes explicit the role they play in the transition from humanism to the occult. Yet we must be careful, since in *Faustus* the heavy-handed exploration of moral integrity makes a sharp distinction between the good and bad pursuit of individual aspiration and desire, whereas in *The Tempest* the book becomes enmeshed in a broader discourse of personal power complicated by illusion and imagination.[18] Although Prospero was 'all dedicated' to study, without parallel in the 'liberal arts', and his 'library / Was dukedom large enough', and full of books he in fact 'prize[d] above' his dukedom, the play makes no attempt to present or expose what these books might be. Rather, the books trace the play's journey from Prospero's expulsion with his books to his return to Milan without them. Like Marlowe's Doctor Faustus, Prospero is a man caught between the humanist and the magus, between the 'liberal arts' and the occult. Both Faustus and Prospero are dedicated to their books; yet, whilst Marlowe particularly explores Faustus's education, celebrating him as 'the flowering pride of Wittenberg', whose journey into the damnable arises from his frustration with the limits and rewards of knowledge, neither the trajectory nor the motivation of Prospero's

---

Prospero, it is difficult to claim this as a consistent reading within the play. Caliban's shifting status from loved companion to abhorrent slave to freed individual in search of grace is not consistent with a demonic reading. Caliban's responses of affection, vengeance, violence, and penitence are too closely linked to Prospero to recognize an inner or ulterior 'darkness' under suppression.

[18] Although Marlowe makes the moral dialectic explicit in his use of Christian emblems, our response to Faustus is not as clear-cut. Despite the didactic nature of the play, Faustus is and remains an alluring character, and his pursuit of the profane is often exciting and seductive, complicating a righteous reading of his performance.

education is so clear. That both men begin as humanists and move into magic, and that both plays celebrate the power and destruction of the book, creates a critical relationship between the two.[19] Whereas Peter Greenaway may put books into his film, books which are themselves a conceptual testimony to the imagination, mystery, and magic of the play, visually synthesizing art and allegory, Faustus's books are a more literal abstraction of the epistemological discourse of the late sixteenth century. There is no clear point at which we become aware of Prospero's move from the liberal arts to the occult (although we might imagine that such a practical transition occurred when he arrived on the island and released Ariel from the cloven pine), and the very ambiguity of the book keeps it from passivity; one way or another, its pages have a story in the development of the brilliant or flawed sinner. If the idea of the book supports some sort of generic transition from the magus to the monster by way of the devil, how does it also support great learning and imperial pride? Is the relationship between these conditions so fragile?

In *Faustus*, as the doctor turns his back on the depths of his learning toward a profane desire for the knowledge of power, we learn what books have contributed to the 'flowering pride of Wittenberg'. Whilst Faustus refers to Aristotle, Galen, Justinian, and Jerome's Bible, Valdes talks of '[Roger] Bacon's and Abanus' works, / The Hebrew Psalter, and New Testament' (i. 153–4).[20] Despite Faustus's pact of power and omnipotence with the devil, he still pursues knowledge through the book, asking for 'a book wherein I might behold all spells and incantations, that I might raise up spirits when I please' (v. 166–8), or 'a book where I might see all characters of planets of the heavens, that I might know their motions and dispositions' (v. 170–2). The scholar

[19] It is worth remembering, however, that the title-page woodcut of *Doctor Faustus* in 1631 'is matched by one to the prose history *The famous historie of fryer Bacon* published in 1627 by Francis Grove, and later, in 1630, used for the play *Friar Bacon and Friar Bungay*. That woodcut also includes the sphere and the shelf of books; indeed, the two illustrations may consciously recall one another—each story concerns an academic who is also a conjurer or magician—but the fact that a study in Wittenberg (*Dr Faustus*), and Brasenose College, Oxford (*Friar Bacon and Friar Bungay*), are depicted so similarly also points towards a consensus as to what a stylised "study" should contain': Stern, *Making Shakespeare*, 99–100. The reproduction of these images suggests that along with the stylized study is the stylized idea of the book that lies behind the story of the scholar-magus.

[20] Christopher Marlowe, *Doctor Faustus*, ed. John D. Jump (London and New York: Routledge, 1988). This edition is based on the B text. All subsequent references are to this edition.

has learned through the book, and it seems that for heaven or hell, knowledge or trickery, it remains the object through which his desires move. For Faustus, all that is knowable is contained in the book. Perhaps more than this, the book is the only reasonable or performable idea of power available to the mind's eye. The idea of the book familiarizes and orders his recognition of learning. Despite having the devil at his beck and call, Faustus continues to want books, pleading 'for one book more, and then I have done' (v. 174). Yet Faustus feels cheated, thinking that the devil's books do not contain all he wants, to which Mephostophilis replies, 'Tut, I warrant thee', assuring Faustus of the material. The devil knows that the book is the limit of knowledge, the capacity of cerebral need, and where he, Mephostophilis, cannot answer Faustus's questions, the book can, warranting the scope of Faustus's enquiries. To Faustus there is, or must be, some book containing the subjects of his desires, and if it does not appear, it is because the devil withholds it rather than denies its existence. This conversation is a moment of profound irony, since there is a sense in which Faustus could almost have acquired the books themselves, without committing his soul to damnation. The fact that we can envisage them, imagine their touch, recognize their size and shape, unlike Helen of Troy or the Pope's chambers, sets them about the play as objects that stand between the natural and the supernatural, the material and the illusory worlds. Unlike Prospero, we not only know what Faustus reads; but we also know what he wants to read and how he reads; we know that books give order and shape to his devilish pact; they make it real for him in a way that Mephostophilis's equivocation and show cannot. Whereas in *The Tempest* the book is denied its dramatic space, to enable chaos to control the mimetic order, in *Doctor Faustus* the reverse takes place. The supernatural denies mimesis: Mephostophilis cannot describe heaven or render the terrors of hell; magic stretches to nothing more than out-of-season strawberries or popish impostors, and what reality there is lies with the book, with the scholars, the study, and the plausible limits and images of knowledge. Despite the often-claimed allegorical nature of Marlowe's play, it speaks far less to allegory than *The Tempest* does. The nature of the book, from the study to the consuming fire, supports a reasonable and contained order of reality above and beyond devilish apparitions, angels, and time-travel.

Faustus's need for knowledge within the bound volume of a book continues to inscribe the process by which the hero arrived at both his aspirations and his limits, and consistently returns us to his position as a scholar, and the terrible power of the book to celebrate or condemn its reader. Yet this is no war of absolutes, no clear-cut contest between good books and bad books; reading and, perhaps more dangerously, intellect are always in the process of re-forming the material. Envy, frequently associated with ignorance, during the parade of the Seven Deadly Sins, declares: 'I cannot read and therefore wish all books burned' (vi. 131–2). Envy's destruction further betrays her ignorance in condemning the very chance of change. Although Envy's sentiment ironically looks forward to Faustus's terrible plea before the devil takes him, the book here is very particularly the victim and not the culprit. Throughout Marlowe's play the book undergoes a trial: on the one hand, the reader must take responsibility for the content; and, on the other, the book itself is an independent and powerful entity that has the power to change and organize its universe. This may seem an entirely predictable sentiment to emerge from a period that witnessed such material changes, even revolutions, as the vernacular Bible, pocket-book, and literature in translation. The book was everywhere and nowhere, lining the stalls of St Paul's whilst being evicted from the utopias of Jack Cade and Gonzalo.[21] Francis Bacon's famous synthesis of gunpowder, the printing-press, and compass shows the powerfully equivocal nature of these objects to simultaneously advance and condemn their legatees. Whereas *The Tempest* may question the ethical limits of Prospero's art, *Doctor Faustus* is more inclined to its dramatic readers. When Robin finds one of Faustus's books, we know the potential danger that lies in misuse: 'I have gotten one of Doctor Faustus' conjuring books, and now we'll have such knavery as 't passes' (vii. 1–3); whereas we may fear Faustus's reading, here we fear Robin's misreading. It is Faustus's ability to 'read' that unleashes his profane desires from 'that damned book' and turns his soul away from Jerome's Bible. Towards the end of the play, when Faustus, terrified of his fate, declares, 'O, would I had never seen Wittenberg, never read a book' (xix. 45–6),

---

[21] As part of Cade's revolution, he calls for the expulsion of all books save the 'score and tally', and makes a particular relationship between the book and magic, which amplifies his view of their potential for oppression or mystification; referring to the Clerk's 'book in his pocket with red letters in't', Cade replies, 'Nay, then he is a conjuror' (*2 Henry VI*, IV. ii. 80–1). Gonzalo too—although with very different motives—views his commonwealth without books: 'For no kind of traffic / Would I admit, no name of magistrate; / Letters should not be known' (*Tempest*, II. i. 148–50).

Mephostophilis returns him to the critical moment when he mentioned 'Jerome's Bible':

> When thou took'st the book
> To view the Scripture, then I turn'd the leaves
> And led thine eye.

(xix. 94–6)

In turning the leaves, Mephostophilis appears to close the Bible and turn Faustus's reading eye away from the pages of Scripture to damnation; the devil holds Faustus between two books, one of sin, the other of salvation. Yet we also know that the devil has no real power over the faithful, and Faustus's eyes must have already stopped reading and have been turned away for his soul to come into jeopardy. Despite Faustus's self-aggrandizing pride, and lust for 'wealth, power, and omnipotence', it was his rejection of God's text that made him prey to the devil, and, emblematically, both books visually dramatize this choice. Although the book in all its vagaries appears consistently throughout Marlowe's play, tracing Faustus's wants and the intellectual scope through which his hunger moves, it ultimately remains an emblem of Christian humanism which furnishes and expands the mind alongside the right application of prudence and virtue. As Faustus becomes increasingly seduced by the delights of the devil, begging for 'one book more, and then I have done, wherein I might see all plants, herbs, and trees that grow upon the earth' (v. 174–6), and the good and bad angels increasingly image the turmoil of a sinning soul, we become aware of how the play's Christian dialectic is dramatized by the book. Faustus's frenzied cry, 'Come not, Lucifer; / I'll burn my books!' (xix. 189–90), theatrically realizes the role of the book, as Faustus is also consumed, suggesting the trial and execution of a condemned heretic. The book performs alongside Faustus, playing out of the shadows of his part. However, whereas, in *Doctor Faustus* the play navigates a direct juxtaposition between 'Jerome's Bible' and 'that damned book' of necromancy, the role of the book in *The Tempest* is profoundly ambiguous. Whilst Prospero may chart his own moral crusade, exacting vengeance, manifesting Ariel as a harpy, fabricating and interfering in the fates of others, and shaping the island as a place of rectitude and grace, both his books and his reading remain in the metaphysical hinterland of the play. When Faustus declares, 'Is to dispute well logic's chiefest end? / Affords this art no greater miracle?' (i. 8–9), or laments 'Yet, art thou still Faustus, and a man' (i. 23), we know that Faustus wants to make an explicit leap beyond his own experience and capabilities. Yet, when Prospero describes his renown in the liberal arts, the closeness and bettering of his mind, and his oblivion to worldly matters, being 'rapt in secret studies', we do not know the extent to which he has, or will, betray the ethical limits of power.

Part of the problem of Prospero's power and its ethical limits is the extent to which it relies on illusion. Illusion is difficult to police; trading on its non-reality, illusion blurs our ethical boundaries when trauma or desire survive under the guise of fantasy.[22] Hamlet notoriously faces such a question in the midst of the appearance of his father, as do the lovers in *A Midsummer Night's Dream*, and Posthumus in *Cymbeline*, yet what becomes important is the extent to which illusion is absorbed or accommodated by realism. Prospero's assurance that the wedding party were neither hurt nor drowned may affect Miranda's reality, but it does not affect ours; we do not know the limits of Prospero's power, and it is the effects of his art that organizes *The Tempest*'s realism. When the play opens, it is with a vivid and emotional rendition of fear and frenzy, a frantic scrabbling for life through an idea of hell: Miranda tells us that

> The sky, it seems, would pour down stinking pitch
> But that the sea, mounting to th' welkin's cheek,
> Dashes the fire out.

> (I. ii. 3–5)

Unlike Hamlet's 'seems' ('Seems, Madam? Nay, it is, I know not "seems" '), Miranda's 'seems' is our reality, and how we might imagine the storm to have been. Where Gertrude must move beyond what seems to that 'which passeth show', we must take the trappings, and that which a man might play, as the thing itself. Miranda's 'seems' is all we have. We believe in the power of suggestion to sustain our visual imagination and animate the presence of the play's fabric. Equally, when

---

[22] Frank Kermode, in his Arden edition of *The Tempest* (London: Methuen and Co. Ltd., 1954), notes the ambivalence between demon and daemon: 'The relationship between Prospero and Ariel is perhaps not theurgically pure, since it appears to contain elements of black magic—Ariel is bound by pact, like his namesake in the Faust-books, and it is sometimes possible to see him as a "familiar". "Come with a thought," orders Prospero; and though this was well within Ariel's powers . . . the ability to arrive "as quick as thought" was sometimes required by goetists of their demons. These traces are no doubt due to the element of popular demonology in the play, and it would be foolish to expect absolute lucidity and constancy in the treatment of theses ideas': Appendix B, 'Ariel as Daemon and Fairy', 143.

Ariel describes the desperate bid the men made for their lives in leaving the tormented ship, we must follow what seems into the reality of an experienced illusion:

> All but mariners
> Plunged in the foaming brine and quit the vessel;
> Then all afire with me, the King's son Ferdinand,
> With hair up-staring (then like reeds, not hair),
> Was the first man that leapt, cried 'Hell is empty,
> And all the devils are here'.

> (I. ii. 210–15)[23]

Our first encounter with Prospero's art is in its ability to imagine disorder; our first encounter with the book, however, is its potential order: the walls of the library, the seven parts of the liberal arts, the confined body, and the rapt mind. And although Prospero's neglect of the state enables the chaos of Antonio's usurpation, it is Prospero, and not his books, that precipitate the breakdown of good government. Prospero's storm begins the play's journey through the imagination to urge into play the hypnotic power of illusion. The dream-like substance of Prospero's magic opens the play into a meta-theatrical world in which the supernatural assumes the mimetic order. The extraordinary design of art or magic appears to present an order of probability and happenings that, unlike allegory, do not defy mimesis but become it. Every chance happening has its teleology and aesthetics, Caliban's four legs, spun by the storm and Trinculo, Ferdinand's labour, the game of chess, or the invisible hounds of conscience. The *deus ex machina* becomes mimetic in the theatre that makes sense of the absurd. The rational logic of the book, powerfully supported by the direct relationship between knowledge and effect in both *Faustus* and *The Tempest*, cannot be dramatically accommodated into a structure that has begun to find meaning in perversion. In the context of allegory, Angus Fletcher refers to the *kosmois*, an image which 'contain[s] the cosmos of those works where they appear. They contain the universe and at the same time they have magical power, for good or evil, or as more usually is the case, for both good and evil commixed.' However, 'The curious fact', he explains, 'is that the best instances of kosmoi are all objects toward which a degree of ambivalence is felt; they are both good and bad at

---

[23] The air drawn vision of horror glances at *Macbeth* and the similarly strange relationship between witchcraft and desires in the projection of both fear and ambition.

once.'[24] In *The Tempest* the book becomes such an image, containing and supporting the universe of the play-world. However, whilst its ambivalence may appear to reside in the commixture of good and bad, freedom and oppression, its real ambivalence, its theatrically effective ambivalence, lies in its ubiquitous absence. The mystery of Prospero's books—what they are and, more importantly, where they are—sustains the play-world's commitment to magic as the dominant aesthetic form. The ritualistic, almost hypnotic, nature of illusion supports the notion of a multi-layered but authentic representative order, at the root of which true meaning lies. Yet, unlike most allegories, in which the dual plot lines or images support a compatible narrative, the relationship of the books to magic is ambiguous, appearing on the one hand to engender, sustain, and contain Prospero's art, but on the other hand theatrically refusing to absorb it. The illusive nature of Prospero's books, in accordance with the play's passionate acknowledgement of them, proposes that they must lie outside this artistic world in order to remain whole, even real.

The visual memory is central to the way in which the play organizes its infrastructure of power. Challenging the three men of sin through the ambiguity of his presence, Ariel works to disorientate their sense of judgement and perspective, which in turn will challenge their personal sense of right and action. Ariel's performance as a harpy reinvokes the storm, guiding the diners through their sins: 'Which here, in this most desolate isle, else falls / Upon your heads—is nothing but heart's sorrow / And a clear life ensuing' (III. iii. 80–2). Ariel's role turns the men inside out, and forces them to visually confront a semblance of conscience, long buried by their ambitions and achievements. This tempest could be the work of God or the devil, or, as Miranda says, 'any god of power'.[25] Martin Luther, in his 'Preface to the Psalms' (German Bible, 1528), used a storm as a metaphor in which the heart is vexed into truth:

The human heart is like a ship on a stormy sea driven about by winds blowing from all four corners of heaven. In one man, there is fear and anxiety about impending disaster; another groans and moans at all the surrounding evil. One

---

[24] Angus Fletcher, *Allegory: The Theory of a Symbolic Mode* (Ithaca, NY: Cornell University Press, 1964), 219.

[25] A tempest may, of course, function at many levels, and is clearly recognized as a structural emblem of prose romance; it may also recall certain historical encounters in contemporary travels, including, among others, Hakluyt's voyage to the Bermudas, and possibly the fortuitous storm of 1588.

man mingles hope and presumption out of the good fortune to which he is looking forward; and another is puffed up with a confidence and pleasure in his present possessions. Such storms, however, teach us to speak sincerely and frankly, and make a clean breast.[26]

For Luther, a tempest is both an analogue to, and a reflection of, the journey a man's heart makes from self-knowledge to God. The tempest here is life, and the capricious sea reflects the ways in which we realize and respond to anxieties and desires. As the heart travels on the stormy sea, it is, faced with its own illusions, forced into a confrontation with the kind of troubles that can find solace only in truth. Under conditions of extremity, each man brings his particular self-image to bear on a situation in which both his instincts and his delusions are challenged. Yet, when the heart is tested by the 'winds from the four corners of heaven', new beginnings and self-knowledge become possible. Prospero's tempests usher in a similar path to resolution through anxiety to 'a clear life ensuing' or a 'clean breast'. By virtue of this analogy the sea becomes a cognitive link to the unconscious, in which exposure looks forward to truth. However, after Faustus has been contracted to Lucifer, one of the things that Mephostophilis does is give him a book on which 'iterating of these lines brings gold / The framing of this circle on the ground / Brings thunder, whirlwinds, storm, and lightening' (v. 160–2). Later in the play Prospero will frame a circle, but here in his 'art', his magic, he shipwrecks the party for justice and for 'truth', precipitating the tale for Miranda in which he will 'make a clean breast'. Like Luther's storm, Prospero's is a performance in which the returning wedding party must learn the lines of their own human hearts, and, like Lucifer's storm, it is conjured from the idea of the book.

More than any other play by Shakespeare, *The Tempest* challenges the meaning of the book. Faustus's devilish books are representative of the soul tumbling into chaos, of earthly confusion, and of profane desires. Although ultimately we see Caliban seeking 'grace' and Prospero union and humility—most acutely suggested by the drowning of his books—the iconic role of the book is never explicitly good or bad,

---

[26] Quoted by John Martin, 'Inventing Sincerity, Refashioning Prudence: The Discovery of the Individual in Renaissance Europe', in Keith Whitlock (ed.), *The Renaissance in Europe: A Reader* (New Haven and London: Yale University Press in association with the Open University, 2000), 23. Martin examines the shift in the idea and application of 'sincerity' in the context of a changing climate of self-expression, from the collective ideology of predetermination to the conflicting sense of belonging and displacement that found expression in both emotional honesty and expedient dissimulation.

devilish or heavenly. The book most clearly signals authority, but that authority is both enabling and reductive. Prospero recognizes the power of his 'art' to invoke fear, observing his enemies' 'distractions': 'My high charms work, / And these, mine enemies, are all knit up / In their distractions. They are now in my power' (III. iii. 88–90). Yet when he employs his 'high charms' later for the marriage masque of Miranda and Ferdinand, it is different; the sinister, punitive aspect has gone, and Prospero enjoys the illusory and ephemeral effects of his power: 'These our actors, / As I foretold you, were all spirits and / Are melted into air, thin air' (IV. i. 148–50). Since this 'insubstantial pageant' fades, leaving not a 'rack behind', we see no trace of the magic or actors who filled the time—the moment is absolutely and entirely gone. The book, however, will remain, and, unlike his art, staff, robe, or person, Prospero's books have a realm of their own that cannot be visualized by the play. Although the idea of the book seeps into the air of the island, tracing the shapes of power and supremacy, it never appears in a form we would recognize. It never appears as itself.

When Stephano asks Caliban to 'kiss the book', he does so in honour of Caliban's adoration and servitude. To mark his supplication, Caliban declares, 'I'll show thee every fertile inch o'th' island, / And I will kiss thy foot. I prithee, be my god' (II. ii. 145–6). That he 'will kiss thy foot', is not only in itself a mark of subservience but, in Prospero's terms, a sign of the pupil's relationship to the master. When Miranda tries to tell her father how to treat Ferdinand, Prospero indignantly replies: 'What, I say, / My foot my tutor?' (I. ii. 469–70). Caliban falls unquestioningly into his role as servant and pupil to Stephano the demagogue. Yet, despite Caliban's developing sedition, he almost directly reflects his early supplication to Prospero, calling Stephano a 'wondrous man' and declaring:

> I'll show thee the best springs; I'll pluck thee berries;
> I'll fish for thee, and get thee wood enough.
>
> (II. ii. 157–8)

Although Caliban pledges his servitude before Stephano asks him to 'kiss the book', there is deep irony in Stephano's choice of phrasing, which seals Caliban's commitment and draws from him a strangely recursive response. Together the book, the god, wonder, and delirium confirm Caliban's commitment to service. Yet, almost immediately, Caliban's servitude becomes 'ridiculous' to Stephano and ridiculed by Trinculo, who 'will laugh' himself 'to death' at the sight. They make a mockery of his iconophilic response to the bottle, not knowing that for Caliban the bottle may resemble the book. Caliban's reflex response to his own servitude, his feelings of love and awe, and his keenness to show the fruits of the island are reminiscent of his initial relationship with Prospero, and the ease with which Caliban transfers these feelings to Stephano suggests the lucidity of taxonomy. The men's offering of metamorphosis triggers the memory of Prospero, who, within the frame of master / servant, is now a 'tyrant', just as the notion of 'wonder', so particularly associated with Miranda, is foregrounded in Caliban's naming Stephano a 'wondrous man' and Trinculo's ironic repetition: 'A most ridiculous monster—to make a wonder of a poor drunkard!' (II. ii. 162–3). Yet, despite Caliban's transferral from one authority to another, he strangely translates his new servitude into freedom: 'Ca-caliban, / Has a new master, get a new man. / Freedom, high-day; high-day freedom; freedom high-day, freedom' (II. ii. 180–2). Caliban is still a servant, and Prospero a master, for he must 'get a new man', and 'Freedom high-day,' celebrates the drunken servitude into which Caliban has fallen, hailing every day as a 'high-day', or holiday. Caliban anticipates misrule replacing rule, yet both conditions require his servitude:

Caliban expresses his freedom by deconstructing the name that Prospero has given him; the vigorous rhythm of his song is an affront to Prospero's rod-like pentameter world. . . . For Shakespeare's Caliban "Freedom, high-day!" is an illusion: he has merely exchanged one master, one god, for another.[27]

Although Bate sees Caliban's self-referential song as a direct affront to Prospero's rule, Caliban is still operating within the terms of Prospero's rule. Caliban does not want to pervert the lines of power, only transliterate them. 'Freedom, high-day' is an illusion, because Stephano's authority is a drunken dream, just as his bottle is no 'art of such power'. Caliban appears used to recognizing metamorphosis as power, Sycorax's spells, Prospero's books, and Stephano's liquor. An uncanny relationship between art and alcohol is later suggested when Trinculo exclaims: 'The folly of this island! They say there's but five upon this isle; we are three of them. If th' other two be brained like us, the state totters' (III. ii. 4–6). The irony, of course, is, that the state indeed 'totters': not only Antonio's 'state' as Prospero plots his revenge, or Alonso's 'state' as Sebastian contemplates his murder, but if 'th' other two' are Miranda and Prospero, one is 'brained' by love and the other, having lost his

---

[27] Jonathan Bate, 'Caliban and Ariel Write Back', *Shakespeare Survey*, 48 (1995), 158.

state, compelled by magic to revenge. Recalling how Prospero lost his dukedom through the book, we return to Stephano's image of the book and the bottle to see the state 'totter' on the island, and Milan towards Prospero's reclamation. Caliban, however, despite his pledged servitude, begins to assume authority in alliance with Stephano over Trinculo, encouraging that Trinculo be beaten for insulting them:

> Beat him enough; after a little time,
> I'll beat him too.

> (III. ii. 83–4)

Caliban again asserts an authority in the knowledge of the island, and the idea of Prospero's books:

> Why, as I told thee, 'tis a custom with him
> I' th' afternoon to sleep. There thou mayst brain him,
> Having first seized his books.

> (III. ii. 87–9)

He goes on to delegate the *coup d'état*:

> Remember
> First to possess his books, for without them
> He's but a sot, as I am, nor hath not
> One spirit to command. They all do hate him
> As rootedly as I. Burn but his books.

> (III. ii. 91–5)

Here both cause and effect are absorbed by the book, which becomes the central object of their obligation to change. If, as Caliban claims, Prospero is a mere 'sot' without his books, then are we to believe that all of the magic and the magus lies with the book? By taking his books before he kills Prospero, Caliban seeks both to disarm and to punish his erstwhile master; yet if such power—the power that separates the sot from the magician—lies with the book, why does Caliban seek to annihilate rather than appropriate it?[28] Everything that Caliban despises about Prospero's art, he associates with his books, for he appears to want to destroy '*but* his books' and retain his 'brave utensils', '(for so he calls them) / Which, when he has a house, he'll deck withal' (III. ii. 96–7). Although Caliban's idea of 'freedom' may still be supported by servitude, he does not anticipate the power he might have or the

---

[28] It is intriguing to note that a sot is also 'one who drinks too much' (*OED*).

island he might recoup. Prospero's books are emblems of something repellent to Caliban. In anticipating the murder of Prospero, Caliban takes possession of Miranda only to offer her, and some idea of imperial power, to Stephano, telling him how Miranda will 'become thy bed' 'And bring thee forth brave brood' (III. ii. 104, 105). Under Caliban's instruction, the island becomes available for Stephano to be 'king' of, taking Miranda as his 'queen' and 'Trinculo and thyself will be viceroys' (III. ii. 108). Yet, despite his eagerness, Caliban does not take the task upon himself, telling Stephano: 'Within this half hour will he be asleep. / Wilt thou destroy him then?' (III. ii. 113–14).

Whilst Caliban finds 'freedom' with Stephano, Ferdinand is in bondage, performing the task Caliban rejected, collecting wood. As Miranda watches her lover, she reassures him that Prospero is 'hard at study', 'safe for these three hours', suggesting that this is Prospero's routine, even though he is watching them 'unseen'. Despite the apparently impassioned and candid responses of the lovers to each other, there is a strong sense that Prospero has created this love through his art. Observing the initial meeting between his daughter and Ferdinand, Prospero exclaims: 'It goes on, I see, / As my soul prompts it' (I. ii. 420–1). 'Soul' here, according to the Arden note's citation of the *OED* means 'an intellectual or spiritual power, distinguished from physical'; spiritual power, with the nuance of wish or desire, suggests the inclination of Prospero's magic. After observing Miranda's proposal, and Ferdinand's acceptance, Prospero declares:

> So glad of this as they I cannot be,
> Who are surprised withal, but my rejoicing
> At nothing can be more. I'll to my book,
> For yet ere suppertime must I perform
> Much business appertaining.
>
> (III. i. 92–6)

Prospero returns to his books, presumably to make arrangements, not only to avenge Sebastian, but also for the marriage of his daughter and Ferdinand. Although on one level we are made to believe that in the strength of the lovers' feelings their attraction is independent of Prospero's art, Prospero's direction of, and desires for, the union, as well as his presence and organization, strongly link the couple's love to his magic. Miranda and Ferdinand play out their love for one another according to the allegory of Prospero's art. The order of the wood-bearing scene, the mesmerizing masque of the 'airy spirits', and the perfect symmetry of the game of chess, expose the brilliant puppeteer, Prospero, organizing art to imitate art.

The play is deeply suggestive of the possible relationship between Prospero's books and art. The union between Miranda and Ferdinand appears on the one hand to celebrate the power of those 'rapt' and 'secret studies', and on the other to reclaim and surpass the ducal power that Prospero compromised and lost in his library. Through Miranda, Prospero looks forward to a version of kingship, and a memory, even rack, of that authority will always remain. In Alonso's imagination we see the bedded ooze where he fears his son to lie:

> The winds did sing it to me, and the thunder—
> That deep and dreadful organpipe—pronounced
> The name of Prosper. It did bass my trespass.
> Therefore my son i'th' ooze is bedded, and
> I'll seek him deeper than e'er plummet sounded,
> And with him there lie mudded.
>
> (III. iii. 97–102)

Alonso extrapolates the death of his son from the low 'bass' of his 'trespass', burying him deep in this place of prolepsis. Yet Alonso misreads the singing winds, for this is not where his son lies, but where we will leave Prospero's books at the close of the play. Perhaps the sea's rejection of Alonso's nightmare and reception of Prospero's books signals the end of one state and the inception of another, the government and rule of Miranda and Ferdinand:

> O heavens, that they were living both in Naples,
> The king and queen there! That they were, I wish
> Myself were mudded in that oozy bed
> Where my son lies.
>
> (v. i. 149–52)

Or perhaps the oozy bed is the site of the confrontation between dream and substance, between the duration of the play-world and what remains behind, the landscape of the book that lies beyond the winds of the stage.

Prospero seems to look forward to relinquishing his art as, advancing toward the sanctification of Miranda and Ferdinand, he begins to disseminate his authority, telling Ariel:

> Go bring the rabble
> (O'er whom I give thee power) here to this place

Incite them to quick motion, for I must
Bestow upon the eyes of this young couple
Some vanity of my art.

(IV. i. 37–41)

As Prospero charges Ariel with the control of 'thy meaner fellows', or subordinate spirits, he, for the first time, refers to his art as a trick, an illusion, even a passing entertainment. The 'vanity' of his art, which may glance at Agrippa's *De vanitate*, is suggestive of something 'worthless' or 'unprofitable' (*OED*, 1.a, b), a trick, by which he presents his art as nothing more than the 'thin air' of an 'insubstantial pageant', to be enjoyed within the frame of its finality: 'We are such stuff / As dreams are made on, and our little life / Is rounded with a sleep' (IV. i. 156–8). Whereas, for Hamlet, the 'undiscovered country' of death is an extension of the sleep or dream, for Prospero, life is the dream that prologues the sleep of absence. The self-reflexive images of the Globe and the theatre, dependent alike on the figurative world and stage, promote the ambivalent relationship between theatre and dream, sleep and performance end. As Prospero associates himself and the lovers with the heavily vanishing nymphs and reapers, art and life become bound to the theatre of illusion. Actor and character become enmeshed in this insubstantial pageant, and, as 'our little life is rounded with a sleep', death, absence, and the play's close compete for the final meaning. Just after Prospero admits that: 'They being penitent, / The sole drift of my purpose doth extend / Not a frown further' (v. i. 28–30), he traces a circle,[29] during which he claims:

But this rough magic
I here abjure; and when I have required
Some heavenly music (which even now I do)
To work mine end upon their senses that
This airy charm is for, I'll break my staff,
Bury it certain fathoms in the earth,
And deeper than did ever plummet sound
I'll drown my book.

(v. i. 50–7)

---

[29] Whilst all modern editions state that Prospero '*Traces a circle*' at the beginning of this speech (v. i. 33–57), the Folio's direction follows the speech, stating '*They all enter the circle which Prospero had made, and there stand charm'd.*' I have modernized typography.

According to the Folio, 'solemne musicke' begins at the end of this speech, which is when Prospero will fulfil the actions of his promises. Like almost all Shakespeare's music, the function is symbolic and, as in *Lear*, it may signify a kind of healing and resolution, or possibly in its solemnity a funereal procession, signifying a ritualistic ending to what we have come to know. It is not clear, however, when the opportunity arises for him to 'bury' his 'staff' or 'drown' his 'book', and these actions are therefore probably meant to happen off-stage. However, despite Prospero's abjuration of his magic, the tracing of a 'circle' is particularly associated with both witchcraft and protection against evil.[30] Thomas More in his *Dialogue Concerning Heresies* (1529), explains: 'Negromancers put their trust in their circles, within which thei thinke them self sure against all ye devils in hel.' Ironically, in *Faustus*, Mephostophilis gives Faustus a book on which 'iterating of these lines brings gold / The framing of this circle on the ground / Brings thunder, whirlwinds, storm, and lightening' (v. 160–2); Mephostophilis's association between the framing of a circle and a storm has particular resonance in *The Tempest*; yet Prospero has abjured his 'rough magic'. Perhaps Prospero finally conjures another figurative sea or storm in which to drown his book 'deeper than did ever plummet sound', for what follows his circle is a kind of peace that the play has not represented before:

> Their understanding
> Begins to swell, and the approaching tide
> Will shortly fill the reasonable shore
> That now lies foul and muddy.
>
> (v. i. 79–82)

With the 'approaching tide' and 'reasonable shore' comes revelation, as Prospero shows himself 'As I was sometime Milan', and the inhabitants are returned to their 'clearer reason', having never seen his staff, robe, or book. Patience and grace take over from vengeance and trauma. When Prospero tells the company that he 'lost' his daughter 'In this last tempest', 'last' signifies both the most recent one and the final one, putting an end to the art that compelled his enemies into a state of appalling wonder. The sea continues the island's narrative of

---

[30] Shakespeare uses the idea of a circle in a magical way in *Henry V*, when Burgundy says to the king, who is concerned that he cannot 'conjure up the spirit of love' in Catherine: 'If you conjure in her, you must make a circle; if conjure up love in her in his true likeness, he must appear naked and blind' (v. ii. 271–3).

authority. Just before Prospero notices Caliban as 'this thing of darkness I / Acknowledge mine' (v. i. 275–6), he returns him to a sense of place in the image of his mother:

> His mother was a witch, and one so strong
> That could control the moon, make flows and ebbs,
> And deal in her command without her power.
>
> (v. i. 269–71)

Sycorax's control of the sea, its shorelines and tides, confirms a sense of power with which the islanders have now become familiar. It explains Caliban's danger and presence on the island where 'The powers delaying, not forgetting, have / Incensed the seas and shores—yea, all the creatures— / Against your peace' (iii. iii. 73–5). However, when Prospero returns to his original status, it is not through a sense of place, but in the idea of wholeness associated with people rather than possessions:

> My dukedom since you have given me again,
> I will requite you with as good a thing,
> At least bring forth a wonder to content ye
> As much as me my dukedom.
>
> (v. i. 168–71)

This is Prospero's final wondrous act, revealing two people who were thought, although Miranda only briefly, to be dead. But this is not magic; this is Prospero as Duke of Milan, revealing his 'theatre', asserting his power, and staking his claim to the union and the future king. With the book buried deep in the sea, and the spirits free, Prospero leaves the island with the promise of 'calm seas' and 'auspicious gales'. In the assurance of these gentle seas, Prospero suggests that he will no longer raise storms; but in reasserting a right over those seas, he makes a choice to leave his tempest with his drowned book and buried staff.

Why did Peter Greenaway call his film *Prospero's Books*, yet put into the hand of the magus books that belong to themselves, extraordinary, magical, self-creating volumes that fulfil their subject as their pages unfold? Greenaway's books are the product of his brilliant and intellectual eye, which creates a visual montage of humanism, evolution, and the occult. Perhaps one of the most arresting tropes of *Prospero's Books* is that of birth and metamorphosis. The indomitable imperative of time and nature, of birth, of cause and effect, of transformations and growth, are possibly the closest we come to a composite idea of what the book has come to mean. The idea of change and the power that change represents, whether it is parodied in alcohol, celebrated in scholarship, damned in sinning, or imagined in magic, finds an image in the book.

The order of the book, the library, the study, the holy graves of writing voices, and the pages that may be set alight or drowned, will always be theatrically incompatible with heavily vanishing illusions. The structure that roots progression and probability in the unfolding of linear reflection has no place in the representation of mystery and caprice. As magic and illusion, apparitions, and ephemera take over the mimetic structure of the play, symptoms of realistic cognition—plausibility and probability, cause and effect—are confined to absent places of origin. The book may imagine or even endorse change, but it cannot represent it. The mimetic order of representation defies the randomness, the chaos, and, perhaps even, the mystery of art. As the aesthetic art of illusionism emerged in the fifteenth century, the relationship between representing and depicting became crucial to the artist: ' "If painting aims at depicting visible things, we must first of all notice *how* one sees things," writes Leon Battista Alberti in the second book of his treatise *On Painting* (1437).'[31] In *The Tempest*, Prospero's art governs *how* we see things in order to represent the reality of what we see; we do not see the book because we do not know how to see it. The representation of the book is the play's final illusion, and, unlike the rackless actors and pageant, it does not dissolve through the fabric of the stage, but is indeed left behind somewhere, deep buried in the waters we never see.

[31] Norbert Schneider, *Still Life* (London, Cologne, Los Angeles, Madrid, Paris, and Tokyo: Taschen, 2003), 13.

# 7

# Conclusion: 'We turn'd o'er many books together'

*Shakespeare and the Idea of the Book* has not attempted to provide a categorical answer to questions of interpretation, to offer an opinion of William Shakespeare's personal value judgement of the book, or to suggest a clear trajectory of intellectual and dramatic development in the way the plays are written or performed. Nor has it intended to offer Shakespeare's use of the book as a static emblem of dramatic artistry, to function as a decoration or an object of curiosity. What I hope to have demonstrated is not only how important the book is to the evolution of the theatre, an exploration of its limits and the potential of its power, but also how, as an object and an idea, the book moves in conversation with its creation as well as its content. Whilst some of these conversations may be timeless, the dynamic between the body and the mind, the scream of silence, faith, justice, and the thought in motion, others respond to some of the serious discourses of the sixteenth and seventeenth centuries: the Reformation, iconoclasm, scepticism, humanism, and the developing distance between the word and its essence. The book—as a result of both conscious and unconscious processes—was adapting and moving through its cultural production, and this journey was neither passive nor accidental. There is no uniform pattern to Shakespeare's idea of the book; nor does he use it to make any specific claim about the nature of authorship, sectarianism, or personal ambition. The book, in its dependence upon the thinking eye and the writing hand, not only 'offers theatre an image of itself' but challenges those very conditions through which it moves. The book—both material and metaphorical—is strewn throughout Shakespeare's plays: it is held by Hamlet as he turns through revenge to madness, is buried deep in the mudded ooze by Prospero when he has shaken out his art as music and violence; it is forced by Richard II to withstand the mortality of deposition, fetishized by lovers, tormented by pedagogues, lost by kings, written by the alienated, and drawn up in conflict with the blood of lost voices. The book begins and ends Shakespeare's dramatic career as the voice of chance and the image of change, withstanding the distance between violence and hope, between holding and losing.

Across the breadth of Shakespeare's plays, the book performs diverse dramatic and semantic roles, which touch on, with varying importance, the representational limits and commodification of language as it is conducted through both the sign and the image. *Shakespeare and the Idea of the Book* has only begun to address some of the questions that the book proposes: although I have traced the idea of the book thorough the erotic body, the art of memory, the faithless, and the humanist, and although we have seen how the material volume takes to the stage to fragment the playing space, defy the 'reader', translate silence, or betray horror, the nature of the relationship between these media suggests that it is always in discussion with its content and its art. When, in *All Is True*, Buckingham asks whether 'A beggar's book / Outworths a noble's blood' (i. i. 122–3), he uses the idea of the book to confront their time of crisis with tactics over fortune. The 'beggar's book / Outworths a noble's blood' because it recognizes action beyond the whims of justice or hope. Yet, for Westmorland in *2 Henry IV*, war is a betrayal of what 'peace hath tutored', 'Turning your books to graves, your ink to blood' (iv. i. 50). The book moves between what is right and what is expedient, as it holds the conscience and consciousness of those who believe in either something or nothing beyond the time in which they stand.

The book often plays an esoteric role, and the Bible and *The Book of Common Prayer* ostensibly appear most frequently and most consistently throughout Shakespeare's works, touching the action of such diverse plays as *The Merry Wives of Windsor*, *Richard III*, *Measure for Measure*, *King John*, and *The Taming of the Shrew*.[1] Although we are often aware of it in the Histories and the Comedies, the Bible does not specifically appear in any of the Tragedies. Such references to the Bible are notoriously ambiguous, and the Book, even at its most emblematic, does not sustain a stable image or a performative role. In *The Merry Wives*, Mistress Quickly falsely swears 'upon a book' that Fenton is beloved, and, in *Richard III*, Buckingham describes the spectacular entrance of his murderous king:

---

[1] The Bible is nominally mentioned only once, in a mockery of a French accent as a 'Pible' in *The Merry Wives of Windsor* (ii. iii. 6).

Two props of virtue for a Christian prince,
To stay him from the fall of vanity;
And see, a book of prayer in his hand—
True ornaments to know a holy man.

(III. vii. 96–9)

The Bible's relationship to 'virtue' as 'true ornaments to know a holy man' increasingly developed a visual and iconic significance during the Reformation, and John Foxe in his *Acts and Monuments* often sensationalizes the role of the book in his graphic portraits of persecuted Protestants going to their death clutching Tyndale's New Testament or *Obedience of a Christian Man*. In a censored pageant written by Richard Grafton for the entry of Philip II and Mary after her coronation, Henry VIII is depicted holding 'a booke, whereon was written *Verbum Dei*',[2] just as Elizabeth's pre-coronation ceremony is structured around incarnations of Truth and the presentation of the Bible in a conduit in Cheapside. The role of the book in spectacle, the horror of *Titus*, the marvel of *Cymbeline*, or the magic of *The Tempest*, alongside our iconic relationship to structures of ceremony, is deeply suggestive of the way in which the book can accommodate a performative role and enforce a structure of belief. However, the secularization of the theatre, in conjunction with its structural and figurative requisites of realism and illusion, allusion and affinity, provides the fabric for the movement of the book between God and life, truth and imagination. Where in *2 Henry IV* the paradigm of the book of life moves into conflict with the abstract notion of fate and the individual confrontation of a possible self, for Richard II the book of life sustains an existence outside of the requisites of seeing. Yet, as Henry IV's book revolves through an image of the world to find both the king and the 'happiest youth' alike, Henry is confronted by the magnitude of his metaphor: 'O if this were seen', he 'Would shut the book and sit him down and die' (III. i. 52–4). Henry stands beside the image and the idea, both paralysed and personified in its pages. Underlying Shakespeare's historical characters are shadows of a historical past interred by legend, propaganda, spectacle, and story. Thus the book of life serves as a transitional article between analepsis, affecting the future of an already chronicled past, and metamorphosis, the material of change, the medium that can redeploy history, accommodate the imagination, and support

---

[2] Janette Dillon, *Language and Stage in Medieval and Renaissance England* (Cambridge: Cambridge University Press, 1998), 106–7.

the subjective. Such a transition is brilliantly exposed in Richard II's deposition scene, where the blotted book of heaven marks a fissure in the divine order of kings and, by extension, the divine order of things. But, as Richard stands before his accusers, he becomes that defaced book of ordination, an idea he takes up in the form of the book and then transfers to the object of a mirror. Richard's mirror is apposite, because, as much of Shakespeare's use of the book demonstrates, its status is both representative and reflective, signifying a surface that both accepts and denies its form, and offering an image that both elides and endorses its presence.[3]

The sheer representational scope of the book frequently enables discernible processes of translation to occur on-stage. In *As You Like It*, for example, the forest becomes a natural repository for an idea of loving liberty, in textual contrast to the court; a place where the Duke may find 'tongues in trees, books in the running brooks, / Sermons in stones, and good in everything' (II. i. 16–17); Orlando impresses his words upon the wood: 'O Rosalind, these trees shall be my books, / And in their barks my thoughts I'll character' (III. ii. 5–6). Orlando configures his landscape in support of a reciprocal relationship between the text and the eye, which affirms as it sees: 'That every eye which in this forest looks / Shall see thy virtue witnessed everywhere' (III. ii. 7–8). The book of Rosalind's virtue looks out from the trees in order to be seen. Yet, how far the book can support virtue or goodness is always in contention; when Othello exclaims, 'Was this fair paper, this most goodly book, / Made to write "whore" upon?' (IV. ii. 73–4), accusing his wife of adultery, his fatal mistake contaminates the very image he preserves as good. Othello misreads; his wife, the handkerchief, Iago, Cassio, and the image of the book becomes involved, even complicit, in this terrible process. Although the language of the book may turn us to other things—meta-drama or the mirror—it also embraces, by virtue of material contingents, the physical body.[4] The book binds

---

[3] The mirror was a protean metaphor during this period, and was as frequently applied to the book as to the stage. The mind of man as mirror facilitates the mapping of knowledge from the sensory and sensible reflection of the world on the page. Bacon declares that 'God hath framed the mind of man as a mirror or glass capable of the image of the universal world, and joyful to receive the impression thereof': *Advancement of Learning*, Book One, in Brian Vickers (ed.), *Francis Bacon: A Critical Edition of the Major Works* (Oxford and New York: Oxford University Press, 1996), 123.

[4] Carol Chillington Rutter discusses the contest between the 'performative' and 'discursive' body, where the body of the actor and the body of the text 'requires us to read double, both discursively and theatrically, as "the text puts the ideological reading

its pages as the flesh binds the soul. But where as in *Love's Labour's* the idea of the book becomes unhinged from its arcane image to be translated into form, in *The Shrew* the book merely supports a dynamic between subject and object to sanction possession and to open up the beloved. The imperative is reading, and the body is shown to be capable of unfolding in sympathy or under duress in the presence of the book.

### 'HE READS MUCH, / HE IS A GREAT OBSERVER'

What is the idea of the book? Sometimes it is story, 'A pattern, precedent, and lively warrant', for us 'to perform the like' (*Titus*, v. iii. 43); it unfolds myths and tales through which we recognize both action and imagination in the 'history in all men's lives' (*2 Henry IV*, iii. i. 75). Sometimes it is more like 'a dream than an assurance' (*Tempest*, i. ii. 45), tracing the insubstantial or 'airy nothing' of fantasy, fear, magic, or theatre. Or perhaps the book is love, offering its image as analogue to the body, gesturing at the discovery of touch or the secrets of the heart, promising the possibility of reading the beloved and of holding the soul. Or is the book just another actor on-stage, like 'our fangled world' showing things not as they really are, 'a garment / Nobler than it covers' (*Cymbeline*, v. iv. 134–5), reminding us 'that show of such an exercise may colour' (*Hamlet*, iii. i. 47) anything? Perhaps the book is a talisman, an icon of faith, a companion for death, or a ledger of life; or even a form of something substantial beyond the precarious order of state and commonwealth, a hopeful reminder of justice and righteousness amidst the conflicts of human behaviour; or simply a mark of education, Henry VI's bookishness, Young Lucius's study, Lord Saye's book 'which preferred' him 'to the king'; or the drudge from which Romeo's schoolboy flies in his metaphor for love. Whatever Shakespeare's idea of the book, it unfurls on his stage to be read through the eyes, bodies, or words of the speaker as something 'more than that tongue that more hath more expressed' (Sonnet 23). The book demands our attention because it asks us to engage with the vicariousness of thought in conjunction with the vicissitudes of seeing. Theatre is a place

---

into play and at the same time engages it with a theatrical one" ': *Enter the Body: Women and Representation on Shakespeare's Stage* (London and New York: Routledge, 2001), 3–4 (quoting Anthon Dawson).

of seeing; as Antony Munday so feared, the eye has a powerful capacity for recall and impression, and as the theatre begins to accommodate ways of thinking, it moves beyond the requisites of the scaffold to signify 'senseless speaking' in the dynamic relationship between the corporeal and the cognitive that needs more than the body of the actor to perform.

If, as Lukas Erne argues, Shakespeare wrote differently for the stage and the page, including in the text to be read things that would normally be performed (mannerisms, entrances, exits, physical behaviour, expressions), then we might wonder if the book supports what the stage cannot show and the stage performs what the book cannot speak.[5] Where, in a play-text, the page must explain what the eye cannot see, in performed drama does the book support what the ear cannot hear? The journey through the 'mind's eye' that Hamlet travels from the pre-emptory vision of his father to the theatrical disclosure of Claudius simulates a relationship between thinking and seeing. Memory is the locus upon which this journey depends, and from the Ghost's injunction to Claudius's visible guilt, we follow Hamlet's 'mind's eye' in the rejection of 'all saws of books', through 'some dozen or sixteen lines' to his theatre of memory (I. v. 100; II. ii. 529). The radical relationship between seeing and thinking is central to *Hamlet,* to the machinations of Elsinore, madness, dissimulation, the theatre, and the book. The book, as we have seen, may offer the past as a narrative in which 'sad stories chanced in the times of old' (*Titus,* III. ii. 84) proffer their pages to the present, ushering in history as a recursive context for communication, sanctioning action, and restoring the disorder of silence. Here the book forces us to think beyond the visible requisites of the stage; it forces us to move outside the playing space, the language, and the narrative, into further discursive fields: 'the eloquence and dumb presagers of my speaking breast' (Sonnet 23). But we have also seen how the book traces the body, 'every married lineament', which 'in many's eyes doth share the glory / That in gold clasps locks in the golden story' (*Romeo and Juliet,* I. iii. 93–4), or how 'love's stories written in love's richest book' (*Midsummer Night's Dream,* II. ii. 128) may serve the construction of sexual dynamics or disclose 'what obscured in this fair volume lies'. We have seen how the soul can move through a metaphorical landscape between the book and the mirror, imagining the stained conscience or the unmarked victim of treason. Where we cannot see Gertrude's sin,

Hamlet's brain, Richard II's soul, or Imogen's nightmare, we must learn to read 'what silent' pen 'hath writ' (Sonnet 25), and, in 'minding true things by what their mockeries be' (*Henry V*, IV. o. 53), recognize the 'revolutions of the times' (*2 Henry IV*, III. i. 45). Yet, as we travel to the corners of Shakespeare's stage, reading in the shadows of theatre the things we cannot see, the secrets, lies, thoughts, precedents, histories, and desires of the space between thinking and showing, we also learn that 'the purpose of playing, whose end, both at the first and now, was and is to hold as 'twere the mirror up to nature' (*Hamlet*, III. ii. 19–21). If theatre is to reflect nature—indeed, if 'the art itself is nature' (*Winter's Tale*, IV. iv. 97)—then is the book part of that nature if it begins to challenge the representational space in which it lies? What the book explores on-stage is precisely this process of making the imagination, the soul, the mind, performable, making it accountable to the very art it represents. When the soothsayer in *Antony and Cleopatra* describes his skills: 'In nature's infinite book of secrecy / A little I can read', he claims to read the body for its fortune, seeing the lineaments, the margin, and the pen in the brows, palms, and proportions of his companions. 'I make not', he claims, 'but foresee' (I. ii. 7–8, 14). Perhaps this is the closest we come to a single image of Shakespeare's books, wherein the body and nature come together under the auspices of some secret in motion.

When Montaigne claimed of his book and himself that they go 'hand in hand together, and keep one apace,' he supported a dynamic relationship between the body and the book in the act of being. He also claimed, however, that this voice would change, move, develop, and adjust its pace over time and thought. When Shakespeare puts books on-stage or in the semantic range of his plays, he confines those books to the theatre that makes them speak. Although allusions, stories, and a semiotic of epistemology may draw contexts and discourses into the plays' range, Shakespeare's books are, and remain, dependent upon the stage that supports them. Although Erne makes a compelling argument as to the nature of Shakespeare's relationship to the text and the stage, whether the play is read or performed, it remains a dramatic text, and the stage directions, gestured language, and speech-acts refer back to the playing space, whether that is on-stage or in the mind's eye. The book is part of that playing space, and part of the illusion of history, movement, and thought that supports the reciprocal relationship between nature and art. What I hope to have shown is how central the cultural life and imaginative potential of the book is—and how in the presence of the book or the idea of the book, conflicting discourses emerge to compete with the stage's resources and the conversations between the mind and the body.

The book is central to the culture in which Shakespeare evolved, but it also reflects back to us as readers or audiences our own understandings and cultural signs, our own readings and familiarities, our patterns of meaning and our ignorance. Is a modern audience, for example, immune to the impact of Ovid? Do we translate these signs through our own social imperatives to find something new, different, or redundant? If we are always 'reading' bodies, voices, props, symbols, and words, does the nature of the book disrupt or unify that process? These books are always moving and asking us to recognize other readings, whether they are of the body or the prop, the symbol or the sign. Shakespeare uses the book as a token and gesture of exploration that is constantly in transition. Whilst his use of the book points to an often conflicting cultural fabric, one that endorses or rejects its social landscape, the books themselves remain in conversation with the plays in which they appear and the stages from which they emerge.

When, at the beginning of Shakespeare's dramatic career, we see Lavinia fly after her nephew in pursuit of the book of her story, or at the end, Prospero drowning the books he once prized above his dukedom, we realize that the relationship between the book and the stage has come full circle. Where it was once the site of theatre's limitations, condensing history, adumbrating order, and accommodating performative silence, the book ends up as part of the very illusion it once tried to suppress. Tracing the shoreline of Prospero's island or trammelling up the consequences of Posthumus's errors, the book, like 'Bottom's dream', challenges the stage to imagine what 'The eye of man hath not heard, [and] the ear of man hath not seen'.

# Bibliography

## PRIMARY SOURCES

Alighieri, Dante, *The Divine Comedy: Paradiso*, trans. John D. Sinclair (Oxford and New York: Oxford University Press, 1939).

Anonymous, *A Curious Paper of the Time of Queen Elizabeth Respecting the Office of the Revels* (London: Thomas Richards, 1872).

Ascham, Roger, *The Scholemaster, 1570* (Menston, Yorkshire: Scolar Press, 1967).

Atkyns, Richard, *The Original and Growth of Printing Collected out of History, and the Records of this Kingdome: Wherein is also Demonstrated that Printing Appertaineth to the Prerogative Royal; and is a Flower of the Crown of England* (London: John Streater, for the author, 1664).

Ayer, Jakob, *Opus Thaeatricum* (Nuremberg: Balthasar Scherffen, 1618).

Bacon, Francis, *New Atlantis, and The Great Instauration*, rev. edn., ed. Jerry Weinberger (Wheeling, Ill.: Harlan Davidson, Inc., 1989).

___ *The Novum Organum of Sir Francis Bacon, Baron of Verulam, Viscount St Albans epitomiz'd for a clearer understanding of his natural history, translated and taken out of the Latine by M. D.* (London: Thomas Lee, 1676).

Baldwin, William, *The Mirror for Magistrates*, edited from original texts, The Huntingdon Library, Lily B. Campbell (Cambridge: Cambridge University Press, 1938).

Bickersteth, Revd E. (ed.), *The Testimony of The Reformers: Selected from the Writings of Cranmer, Jewell, Tindal, Ridley, Becon, Bradford, etc.* (London: R. B. Seeley and W. Burnside, 1886).

Booth, Stephen (ed.), *Shakespeare's Sonnets* (New Haven and London: Yale Nota Bene, Yale University Press, 2000).

Bowers, Fredson (ed.), *The Dramatic Works of Thomas Dekker*, Vol. ii (Cambridge: Cambridge University Press, 1955).

Braithwait, Richard, *A Survey of History, Or, A Nursery for Gentry* (London: I. Okes, 1638).

Burton, Robert, *The Anatomy of Melancholy*, ed. Holbrook Jackson (New York: New York Review of Books, 2001).

Campbell, Gordon (ed.), *John Milton: Complete English Poems, of Education, Areopagitica* (London: Everyman, J. M. Dent, 2000).

Case, John, *Thesaurus Oeconomiae* (Oxon.: J. Barnes, 1597).

Césaire, Aimé, *A Tempest*, trans. Philip Crispin (London: Oberon Books, 2000).

Cooper, Thomas, *Thesaurus Linguae Romanae & Britannicae* (London, 1578).

Cox, Nicholas, *An Exact Catalogue of Comedies, Tragedies, Tragi-Comedies, Operas, Masks, Pastorals and Interludes, that were yet Printed and Published, till this Present Year 1680* (Oxon.: L. Lichfield, Printer to the University, 1680).

D'Assigny, Marius, *The Art of Memory: A Treatise Useful for such as are to Speak in Publick* (London: Bell, 1697).

Dolan, Frances (ed.), *William Shakespeare's The Taming of the Shrew: Texts and Contexts* (Boston and New York: Bedford Books of St Martin's Press, 1996).

Erasmus, Desiderius, *The Education of a Christian Prince*, trans. Lester K. Born (New York: Columbia University Press, 1986).

Erasmus, Desiderius, *A Playne and Godly Exposition or Declaration of the Commune Crede* (London, 1533).

——— *The Praise of Folly and Other Writings*, ed. Robert M. Adams (London and New York: W. W. Norton and Company, 1989).

Fletcher, John, *The Tamer Tamed*, ed. Gordon McMullen (London: Nick Hern Books, 2003).

Florio, John, *Queen Anna's New World of Words*, facsimile of 1611 (Menston, Yorkshire: Scolar Press Ltd., 1968).

Foakes, R. A. (ed.), *Henslowe's Diary*, 2nd edn. (Cambridge: Cambridge University Press, 2002).

——— and R. T. Ricket (eds.), *Henslowe's Diary* (Cambridge: Cambridge University Press, 1961).

Foxe, John, *Acts and Monuments* (London: John Day, 1576).

Gascoigne, Geo[rge], *Supposes and Jocasta*, two plays translated from the Italian, the first by Geo. Gascoigne, the second by Geo. Gascoigne and F. Kinwelmersh, 1575, ed. John W. Cunliffe (Boston and London: D. C. Heath and Co., 1906).

*The Geneva Bible: A Facsimile of the 1560 Edition*, ed. Lloyd E. Berry (Madison, Milwaukee, and London: University of Wisconsin Press, 1969).

Golding, Arthur, *The XV. Bookes of P. Ovidius Naso, entitled Metamorphosis* (London: Robert Walde-Grave, 1587).

Gosson, Stephen, *The Schoole of Abuse* (1579) (Menston, Yorkshire: Scolar Press, 1972).

——— *The School of Abuse and A Short Apology for the School of Abuse*, ed. Edward Arber (London: Alex. Murray & Son, 1868).

Greenblatt, Stephen, Walter Cohen, Jean E. Howard, and Katherine Eisaman Maus (eds.), *The Norton Shakespeare* (London and New York: W. W. Norton & Company, 1997).

Heywood, Thomas, *An Apology for Actors Containing Three Brief Treatises* (London: Nicholas Okes, 1612).

Hobbes, Thomas, *Leviathan*, ed. C. B. MacPherson (Harmondsworth: Penguin, 1995).

Hopkins, Matthew, *A Juniper Lecture. With the description of all sorts of women, good and bad. From the modest to the maddest, from the most civil, to the*

*Scold Rampant, their praise and dispraise compendiously related. The third Impression, with many new Additions. Also the Author's advice how to tame a Shrew, or vex her* (London, 1652).

Johnson, John, *The Academy of Love* (London: For H. Blunden, 1641).

Johnson, Samuel, *A Dictionary of the English Language; in which the words are deduced from their originals, explained in their different meanings and authorized by the names of the writers in whose work they are found*, 5th edn., corrected and revised (Montrose: Mundel, Doig, and Stevenson; Bell and Bradfute Ednr. W. Anderson, Stirling, and J. and A. Duncan, Glasgow 1809).

Jones, Andrew, *The Black Book of Conscience: or, God's High Court of Justice*, in *The Soul of Man* (London: W.O., 1607).

Jonson, Ben, *Five Plays*, ed. G. A. Wilkes (Oxford and New York: Oxford University Press, 1988).

Kyd, Thomas, *The Spanish Tragedy*, ed. J. R. Mulryne (London: A. & C. Black, 1989).

Lodge, Thomas, *A Defence of Poetry, Music, and Stage-Plays* (London: The Shakespeare Society, 1853).

Machiavelli, Niccolò, *The Prince*, trans. Peter Bondanella and Mark Musa (Oxford and New York: Oxford University Press, 1998).

Mann Phillips, Margaret, *The Adages of Erasmus: A Study with Translations* (Cambridge: Cambridge University Press, 1964).

Marlowe, Christopher, *The Complete Plays*, ed. J. B. Steane (Harmondsworth: Penguin, 1986).

_____ *Doctor Faustus*, ed. John D. Jump (London and New York: Routledge, 1988).

Marston, John, *The Scourge of Villanie*, ed. G. B. Harrison (Edinburgh: Edinburgh University Press, 1966).

McNutty, Robert (ed.), *Ludovico Ariosto's 'Orlando Furioso', Translated into English Heroical Verse by Sir John Harrington* (1591), (Oxford: Clarendon Press, 1972).

Milton, John, 'Areopagitica', in *Complete English Poems, of Education, Areopagitica*, ed. Gordon Campbell (London: Everyman, J. M. Dent, 2000), 575–618.

_____ 'Comus', in *Complete English Poems*, 59–91.

Montaigne, Michel de, *Essays*, trans. J. M. Cohen (Harmondsworth: Penguin, 1983).

More, Thomas, *A Dialogue Concerning Heresies* (1529), ed. Thomas Lawler, Germain More'hadour, and Richard C. Marius (London and New Haven: Yale University Press, 1981).

_____ *Utopia*, trans. Paul Turner (Harmondsworth: Penguin, 1965).

Morrison, Blake, *The Justification of Johann Guttenberg: A Novel* (London: Vintage, 2000).

Osborn, James M. (ed.) [now attributed to Richard Mulcaster], *The Quenes Maisties Passage through the Citie of London to Westiminster the Day before her Coronacion* (facsimile of the publication on 23 January 1559) (New Haven: Yale University Press, 1960).

Ovid, *The Art to Love*, trans. James Michie (London: Folio Society, 1993).

———*Heroides*, trans. Harold Isbell (Harmondsworth: Penguin, 1990).

———*Metamorphoses*, trans. Mary M. Innes (Harmondsworth: Penguin, 1955).

Peacham, Henry, *The Garden of Eloquence* (London: H. Jackson, 1577).

Plato, *Phaedo*, trans. David Gallop (Oxford and New York: Oxford University Press, 1999).

Robortello, Francisco, [*De Arte*] *Francisci Robortelli . . . in librum Aristotelis de Arte Poetica explicatoiones* (Florence: L. Torrentini, 1548).

Salgādo, Gāmini (ed.), *Four Jacobean City Comedies* (Harmondsworth: Penguin, 1975).

Shakespeare, William, *Comedies, Histories, & Tragedies: A Facsimile of the First Folio, 1623*, introduced by Doug Moston (London and New York: Routledge, 1998).

———*Cymbeline*, ed. J. M. Nosworthy, The Arden Shakespeare, 3rd ser. (London: Thomas Learning, 2000).

———*Hamlet*, ed. T. J. B. Spencer (Harmondsworth: Penguin, 1996).

———*Hamlet*, ed. G. R. Hibbard (Oxford and New York: Oxford University Press, 1998).

———*Love's Labour's Lost*, ed. H. R. Woudhuysen, Arden edition, 3rd ser. (Walton-on-Thames: Thomas Nelson, 1998).

———*A Midsummer Night's Dream*, ed. Stanley Wells (Harmondsworth: Penguin, 1986).

———*The Narrative Poems*, ed. Maurice Evans (Harmondsworth: Penguin, 1989).

———*Richard II*, ed. Stanley Wells (Harmondsworth: Penguin, 1997).

———*The Taming of the Shrew*, ed. Robert B. Heilman (London: The New English Library Limited, 1966).

———*The Taming of The Shrew*, ed. G. R. Hibbard (London: Penguin, 1995).

———*The Tempest*, ed. Frank Kermode, Arden edition (London: Methuen and Co. Ltd., 1954).

———*The Tempest*, ed. Virginia Mason Vaughan and Alden T. Vaughan, The Arden Shakespeare, 3rd ser. (Walton-on-Thames: Thomas Nelson, 1999).

———*Titus Andronicus*, ed. Jonathan Bate, The Arden Shakespeare, 3rd ser. (London: Thomas Learning, 2000).

Shirley, James, *Dramatic Works and Poems* (London: John Murray, 1833).

Sidney, Sir Philip, *Selected Writings*, ed. Richard Dutton (Manchester: Carcanet Press, 1987).

Snawsel, Robert, *A Looking Glass for Married Folks* (London, 1610).

Spenser, Edmund, *The Faerie Queene*, ed. Thomas P. Roche Jr.? (Harmondsworth: Penguin, 1978).

Taylor, John, *All the Workes* (London, 1630).

Tilly, Morris Palmer, *A Dictionary of the Proverbs in England in the Sixteenth and Seventeenth Centuries: A Collection of the Proverbs Found in English Literature and the Dictionaries of the Period* (Ann Arbor: University of Michigan Press, 1950).

Tilney, Edmund, *Briefe and Pleasant Discourse of Duties in Marriage*, ed. Valerie Wayne (Ithaca, NY, and London: Cornell University Press, 1992).

Vickers, Brian (ed.), *Francis Bacon: A Critical Edition of the Major Works* (Oxford and New York: Oxford University Press, 1996).

Watson, Foster (ed.), 'J. L. Vives: Instruction of a Christian Woman, Translated into English by Richard Hyrde in 1540', in *Vives and the Renascence Education of Women* (London: Edward Arnold, 1912).


SECONDARY SOURCES

Ackroyd, Peter, *The Life of Thomas More* (London: Vintage, 1999).

Anderson, Randall, 'The Rhetoric of Paratext in Early Printed Books', in Barnard *et al.* (eds.), *Cambridge History of the Book*, 636–47.

Appert, Lucile G., 'Towards a British Academy: The Poet, The King and The Commonwealth of Learning', *Renaissance Papers* (1998), 115–24.

Artaud, Antonin, *The Theatre and its Double*, trans. Victor Corti (Montreuil, London, and New York: Calder, 1999).

Ashley, Robert, and Edwin M. Moseley, *Elizabethan Fiction* (New York and Toronto: Rinehart & Co. Inc., 1953).

Auerbach, Eric, *Mimesis: The Representation of Reality in Western Literature*, trans. Willard R. Trask (Princeton: Princeton University Press, 1974).

Ayers, P. K., 'Reading, Writing, and Hamlet', *Shakespeare Quarterly*, 44 (1993), 423–39.

Backhouse, Janet, *The Illuminated Manuscript* (London: Phaidon Press Ltd., 1999).

Baldwin, T. W., *William Shakespeare's Small Latine & Lesse Greeke*, i (Urbana, Ill.: University of Illinois Press, 1944).

Barkan, Leonard, 'What did Shakespeare Read?', in de Grazia and Wells (eds.), *Cambridge Companion to Shakespeare*, 31–47.

Barker, Francis, and Peter Hulme, 'Nymphs and Reapers Heavily Vanish: The Discursive Con-Texts of *The Tempest*', in Drakakis (ed.), *Alternative Shakespeares* 191–205.

Barnard, John, D. F. McKenzie, and Maureen Bell (eds.), *The Cambridge History of the Book in Britain*, iv: *1557–1695* (Cambridge: Cambridge University Press, 2002).

Barthes, Roland, 'The Death of the Author', in Finkelstein and McCleery (eds.), *Book History Reader*, 221–4.

Bate, Jonathan, 'Caliban and Ariel Write Back', *Shakespeare Survey*, 48 (1995), 155–62.

—— *The Genius of Shakespeare* (Basingstoke and Oxford: Picador, 1997).

—— 'The Humanist Tempest', in Claude Peltrault (ed.), *Shakespeare, La Tempête: Études critiques* (Besançon Cedex: Université de Franche-Comté, 1993), 5–20.

—— *Shakespeare and Ovid* (Oxford: Clarendon Press, 1994).

Bates, Catherine, *The Rhetoric of Courtship in Elizabethan Language and Literature* (Cambridge: Cambridge University Press, 1992).

Bath, Michael, *Speaking Pictures: English Emblem Books and Renaissance Culture* (London and New York: Longman, 1994).

Bell, Maureen, 'Women Writing and Women Written', in Barnard *et al.* (eds.), *Cambridge History of the Book*, iv. 431–51.

Benjamin, Walter, *One-Way Street*, trans. Edmund Jephcott and Kingsley Shorter (London and New York: Verso, 2000).

Bennett, H. S., *English Books and Readers 1558–1603: Being a Study of the History of the Book Trade in the Reign of Elizabeth I* (London and New York: Cambridge University Press, 1965).

The Bibliographical Society, *The Bibliographical Society 1892–1942: Studies in Retrospect* (London: Bibliographical Society, 1945).

Blayney, Peter W. M., 'The Publication of Playbooks', in Cox and Kastan (eds.), *New History of Early English Drama*, 383–418.

Bourdieu, Pierre, 'The Field of Cultural Production', in Finkelstein and McCleery (eds.), *Book History Reader*, 77–99.

Bragg, Melvyn, *The Adventure of English: 500 AD to 2000, The Biography of a Language* (London: Hodder & Stoughton, 2003).

Brewer, John, 'Authors, Publishers and the Making of Literary Culture', in Finkelstein and McCleery (eds.), *Book History Reader*, 241–9.

Brown, Georgia, *Redefining Elizabethan Literature* (Cambridge: Cambridge University Press, 2004).

Brown, John Russell, and Bernard Harris (eds.), *Elizabethan Theatre* (London: Edward Arnold, 1966).

Brown, Paul, 'This thing of darkness I acknowledge mine', in Dollimore and Sinfield (eds.), *Political Shakespeare*, 48–71.

Bruster, Douglas, *Shakespeare and the Question of Culture: Early Modern Literature and the Cultural Turn* (Basingstoke and New York: Palgrave Macmillan, 2003).

—— 'The Structural Transformation of Print in Late Elizabethan England', in Marotti and Bristol (eds.), *Print, Manuscript and Performance*, 49–90.

Burckhardt, Jacob, *The Civilisation of the Renaissance in Italy*, 2 vols. (New York: Harper & Row, 1958).

Calderwood, James L., *Shakespearean Metadrama: The Argument of the Play in 'Titus Andronicus', 'Love's Labour's Lost', Romeo and Juliet', 'A Midsummer Night's Dream', and 'Richard II'* (Minneapolis: University of Minnesota Press, 1971).

Carpi, Daniela, '*Prospero's Books* and *The Tempest*: Science, Magic and Painting', in Kennan and Tempera (eds.), *Metamorphosing Shakespeare*, 109–19.

Carroll, William C., *The Great Feast of Language in 'Love's Labour's Lost'* (Princeton: Princeton University Press, 1976).

_____ 'The Virgin Not: Language and Sexuality in Shakespeare', *Shakespeare Survey*, 46 (1993), 107–19.

Carruthers, Mary, 'Reading with Attitude, Remembering the Book', in Frese and O'Keefe (eds.), *The Book and the Body*, Ind., and London: 1–33.

Cave, Terence, *The Cornucopian Text: Problems of Writing the French Renaissance* (Oxford: Clarendon Press, 1979).

Chappell, W., *Popular Music of the Olden Time: A Collection of Ancient Songs, Ballads, and Dance Tunes, Illustrative of the National Music of England*, 2 vols. (London: Cramer, Beale, & Chappell, 1893).

Chartier, Roger, 'Labourers and Voyagers: From the Text to the Reader', in Finkelstein and McCleery (eds.), *Book History Reader*, 47–58.

_____ 'The Practical Impact of Writing', in Finkelstein and McCleery (eds.), *Book History Reader*, 118–42.

_____ *Publishing Drama in Early Modern Europe*, Panizzi Lectures (London: British Library, 1998).

Cheney, Patrick, *Shakespeare, National Poet-Playwright* (Cambridge: Cambridge University Press, 2004).

Chillington Rutter, Carol, *Enter the Body: Women and Representation on Shakespeare's Stage* (London and New York: Routledge, 2001).

Corfield, Cosmo, 'Why Does Prospero Abjure his "Rough Magic"?', *Shakespeare Quarterly*, 36 (1985), 31–48.

Cover, J. A., and Mark Kulstad (eds.), *Central Themes in Early Modern Philosophy* (Indianapolis and Cambridge: Hackett Publishing Company, Inc., 1990).

Cox, John D., and David Scott Kastan (eds.), *A New History of Early English Drama*, (New York and Chichester: Columbia University Press, 1997).

Crane, Nicholas, *Mercator: The Man who Mapped the Planet* (London: Weidenfeld & Nicolson, 2002).

Cressy, David, *Society and Culture in Early Modern England*, 2 vols. (Aldershot and Burlington, Vt.: Ashgate Publishing Company, 2003).

Crystal, David, and Ben Crystal, *Shakespeare's Words: A Glossary & Language Companion* (London: Penguin Books, 2002).

Curtius, Ernst Robert, *European Literature and the Latin Middle Ages*, trans. Willard R. Trask (London and Henley: Routledge & Kegan Paul, 1953).

Danby, John F., *Shakespeare's Doctrine of Nature: A Study of King Lear* (London: Faber & Faber, 1961).

Daniell, David, 'The Good Marriage of Katherine and Petruchio', *Shakespeare Survey*, 37 (1984), 23–31.

——— 'Shakespeare and the Protestant Mind', *Shakespeare Survey*, 54 (2001), 1–12.

——— 'William Tyndale, the English Bible, and the English Language', in O'Sullivan (ed.), *Bible as Book: The Reformation*, 39–50.

Danson Brown, Robert, and David Johnson (eds.), *A Shakespeare Reader: Sources and Criticism* (Basingstoke and London: Macmillan, 2000).

Darnton, Robert, 'What is the History of Books?', in Finkelstein and McCleery (eds.), *Book History Reader*, 9–26.

Davies, Tony, *Humanism* (London and New York: Routledge, 1997).

Dawson, Anthony B., and Paul Yachnin, *The Culture of Playgoing in Shakespeare's England: A Collaborative Debate* (Cambridge: Cambridge University Press, 2001).

De Grazia, Margreta, and Peter Stallybrass, 'The Materiality of the Shakespearean Text', *Shakespeare Quarterly*, 44 (1993), 255–84.

——— and Stanley Wells (eds.), *The Cambridge Companion to Shakespeare* (Cambridge: Cambridge University Press, 2001).

——— Maureen Quilligan, and Peter Stallybrass (eds.), *Subject and Object in Renaissance Culture* (Cambridge: Cambridge University Press, 1996).

De Ricci, Seymour, *A Census of Caxtons* (Oxford: Oxford University Press and Bibliographical Society, 1909).

Diehl, Huston, *An Index of Icons in English Emblem Books 1500–1700* (Norman, Okla., and London: University of Oklahoma Press, 1986).

Dillon, Janette, *Language and Stage in Medieval and Renaissance England* (Cambridge: Cambridge University Press, 1998).

——— *Theatre, Court, and City, 1595–1610: Drama and Social Space in London* (Cambridge: Cambridge University Press, 2000).

Dobson, Michael, and Stanley Wells (eds.), *The Oxford Companion to Shakespeare* (Oxford: Oxford University Press, 2001).

Doebler, John, *Shakespeare's Speaking Pictures: Studies in Iconic Imagery* (Albuquerque, N. Mex.: University of New Mexico Press, 1974).

Dollimore, Jonathan, and Alan Sinfield (eds.), *Political Shakespeare: Essays in Cultural Materialism* (Manchester: Manchester University Press, 1994).

Donaldson, Ian, 'The Destruction of the Book', in Greenspan and Rose (eds.), *Book History*, i. 1–11.

Drakakis, John (ed.), *Alternative Shakespeares* (London and New York: Routledge, 1996).

Duffy, Eamon, *The Stripping of the Altars: Traditional Religion in England 1400–1580* (New Haven and London: Yale University Press, 1992).

Dutton, Richard, Alison Findlay, and Richard Wilson (eds.), *Theatre and Religion: Lancastrian Shakespeare* (Manchester and New York: Manchester University Press, 2003).

Eagleton, Terry, *William Shakespeare* (Oxford and Manchester: Blackwell, 2000).

*Early Modern English Dictionary*, <chass.utoronto.ca/English/emed/emedd. html>.

Eisenstein, Elizabeth L., *The Printing Press as an Agent of Change*, 2 vols. (Cambridge: Cambridge University Press, 1979).

_____ *The Printing Revolution in Early Modern Europe* (Cambridge: Cambridge University Press, 2000).

Eistein, Lewis, *The Italian Renaissance in England: Studies in Comparative Literature* (New York: Columbia University Press, 1907).

Elam, Keir, *Shakespeare's Universe of Discourse: Language-Games in the Comedies* (Cambridge: Cambridge University Press, 1984).

Empson, William, *Essays on Renaissance Literature, i: Donne and the New Philosophy*, ed. John Haffenden (Cambridge: Cambridge University Press, 1995).

_____ *Essays on Shakespeare*, ed. David B. Pirie (Cambridge: Cambridge University Press, 1994).

Enterline, Lynn, *The Rhetoric of the Body from Ovid to Shakespeare* (Cambridge: Cambridge University Press, 2000).

Erne, Lukas, *Shakespeare as Literary Dramatist* (Cambridge: Cambridge University Press, 2003).

Evans, Malcolm, 'Deconstructing Shakespeare's Comedies', in Drakakis (ed.), *Alternative Shakespeares*, 67–94.

Febvre, Lucien, and Henri-Jean Martin, *The Coming of the Book: The Impact of Printing 1450–1800*, trans. David Gerad (London and New York: Verso, 1997).

Fergerson, F. S., 'English Books before 1640', in *The Bibliographical Society 1892–1942: Studies in Retrospect* (London: Bibliographical Society, 1945), 42–75.

Fineman, Joel, *The Subjectivity Effect in Western Literary Tradition: Essays toward the Release of Shakespeare's Will* (Cambridge, Mass., and London: October Books, 1991).

Finkelstein, David, and Alistair McCleery (eds.), *The Book History Reader* (London and New York: Routledge, 2002).

Fletcher, Angus, *Allegory: The Theory of the Symbolic Mode* (Ithaca, NY: Cornell University Press, 1964).

Foucault, Michel, *The Order of Things: An Archaeology of the Human Sciences* (London and New York: Routledge, 2000).

_____ 'What is an Author?', in Finkelstein and McCleery (eds.), *Book History Reader*, 225–30.

Fowler, Alistair, *Renaissance Realism: Narrative Images in Literature and Art* (Oxford and New York: Oxford University Press, 2003).

Fox, Adam, *Oral and Literate Culture in England 1500–1700* (Oxford: Clarendon Press, 2000).

Freeman, Charles, *The Closing of the Western Mind: The Rise of Faith and the Fall of Reason* (London: William Heinemann, 2002).

Frese, Warwick Dolores, and Katherine O'Brien O'Keefe, *The Book and the Body* (Notre Dame, Ind., and London: University of Notre Dame Press, 1979).

Garber, Marjorie, *Shakespeare's Ghost Writers: Literature as Uncanny Causality* (London and New York: Routledge, 1987).

Gellrich, Jesse M., *The Idea of the Book in the Middle Ages: Language, Mythology, and Fiction* (Ithaca, NY, and London: Cornell University Press, 1985).

Goldberg, Jonathan, *Writing Matter: From the Hands of the English Renaissance* (Stanford, Calif.: Stanford University Press, 1990).

Grady, Hugh, 'Shakespeare Studies, 2005: A Situated Overview', *Shakespeare*, 1 & 2 (2005), 102–20.

Grafton, Anthony, *Commerce with the Classics: Ancient Books and Renaissance Readers*, Jerome Lectures, 20 (Ann Arbor: University of Michigan Press, 1997).

_____ *New Worlds, Ancient Texts: The Power of Tradition and the Shock of Discovery* (Cambridge, Mass., and London: The Belknap Press of Harvard University Press, 1995).

_____ and Lisa Jardine, *From Humanism to the Humanities: Education and Liberal Arts in Fifteenth- and Sixteenth-Century Europe* (London: Gerald Duckworth & Co. Ltd., 1986).

Greenaway, Peter, *Prospero's Books: A Film of Shakespeare's* The Tempest (London: Chatto & Windus, 1991).

Greenblatt, Stephen, *Renaissance Self-Fashioning: From More to Shakespeare* (Chicago and London: University of Chicago Press, 1984).

_____ *Shakespearean Negotiations* (Oxford: Oxford University Press, 1999).

_____ *Will in The World: How Shakespeare Became Shakespeare* (New York and London: W. W. Norton and Company, 2004).

Greenspan, Ezra, and Jonathan Rose (eds.), *Book History: Society for the History of Authorship, Reading and Publishing* (University Park, Pa.: The Pennsylvania State University Press), i (1998) and ii (1999).

Greg, W. W., *Collected Papers*, ed. J. C. Maxwell (Oxford: Clarendon Press, 1966).

Gross, John (ed.), *After Shakespeare: Writing Inspired by the World's Greatest Author* (Oxford and New York: Oxford University Press, 2002).

Gurr, Andrew, *The Shakespearean Stage 1574–1642*, 3rd edn. (Cambridge: Cambridge University Press, 2003).

Hadfield, Andrew, *The English Renaissance 1500–1620* (Oxford and Malden, Mass. Blackwell, 2001).

——— 'The Revelation and Early English Colonial Ventures', in O'Sullivan (ed.), *Bible as Book: The Reformation*, 145–56.

Hamilton, Donna B., 'Re-Engineering Virgil: *The Tempest* and the Printed English *Aeneid*', in Hulme and Sherman (eds.), *The Tempest and Its Travels* 114–20.

Hardison Londré, Felicia (ed.), *Love's Labour's Lost: Critical Essays* (New York and London: Routledge, 2001).

Harrier, Richard, 'Ceremony and Politics in *Richard II*', in *Shakespeare: Text, Language, Criticism: Essays in Honour of Marvin Spevack*, ed. Bernhaud Fabian and Kurt Tetzeh Von Rosador (Hildesheim, Zurich, and New York: Olms-Weidmann, 1987), 80–97.

Hattaway, Michael, 'Fleshing his Will, the Spoil of her Honour': Desire, Misogyny, and the Perils of Chivalry', *Shakespeare Survey*, 46 (1993), 121–35.

Hawkes, Terence, *Shakespeare's Talking Animals: Language and Drama in Society* (London: Edward Arnold, 1973).

Hill, Christopher, *The English Bible and the Seventeenth-Century Revolution* (Harmondsworth: Penguin, 1994).

Holden, Anthony, *William Shakespeare: His Life and Work* (London: Abacus, 1999).

Holmes, George, *Renaissance* (London: Phoenix Illustrated, Orion Publishing Group, 1998).

Honan, Park, *Shakespeare: A Life* (Oxford and New York: Oxford University Press, 1999).

Honigmann, E. A. J., 'The Play of Thomas More and Some Contemporary Events', *Shakespeare Survey*, 42 (1990), 77–84.

Howard, Maurice, *The Tudor Image* (London: Tate Publishing Ltd., 1995).

Howard-Hill, T. H., ' "Nor Stage, nor stationers stall can showe": The Circulation of Plays in Manuscripts in the Early Seventeenth Century', in Greenspan and Rose (eds.), *Book History*, ii. 28–39.

Hucks Gibbs, Henry, *A Catalogue of Some Printed Books and Manuscripts at St. Dunstans, Regents Park and Aldenham House, Herts* (London, 1888).

Hull, Suzanne W., *Chaste, Silent and Obedient: English Books for Women 1475–1640* (San Marino, Calif.: Huntingdon Library, 1982).

Hulme, Peter, and William H. Sherman (eds.), *The Tempest and its Travels* (London: Reaktion Books Ltd., 2000).

Iser, Wolfgang, 'Interaction between Text and Reader', in Finkelstein and McCleery (eds.), *Book History Reader*, 291–6.

Jager, Eric, *The Book of the Heart* (Chicago and London: University of Chicago Press, 2000).

Jagodzinsk, Cecile M., *Privacy and Print: Reading and Writing in Seventeenth-Century England* (Charlottesville, Va., and London: University Press of Virginia, 1999).

James, Heather, *Shakespeare's Troy: Drama, Politics, and the Translation of Empire* (Cambridge and New York: Cambridge University Press, 1997).

Jardine, Lisa, *Reading Shakespeare Historically* (London and New York: Routledge, 1996).

Johns, Adrian, 'The Book of Nature and the Nature of the Book', in Finkelstein and McCleery (eds.), *Book History Reader*, 59–76.

—— *The Nature of the Book: Print and Knowledge in the Making* (Chicago and London: University of Chicago Press, 1998).

Jones, Marian, 'The Court and the Dramatists', in Brown and Harris (eds.), *Elizabethan Theatre*, 169–95.

Kahn, Coppélia, *Roman Shakespeare* (London and New York: Routledge, 1997).

Kegel, Rosemary, *The Rhetoric of Concealment: Figuring Gender and Class in Renaissance Literature* (Ithaca, NY, and London: Cornell University Press, 1994).

Kennan, Patricia, and Mariangela Tempera (eds.), *Metamorphosing Shakespeare: Mutual Illuminations of the Arts* (Bologna: CLUEB, 2004).

Kermode, Frank, *Shakespeare's Language* (London: Penguin, 2000).

Kerrigan, John, 'Keats and Lucrece', *Shakespeare Survey*, 41 (1989), 103–18.

Kiefer Lewalski, Barbara (ed.), *Renaissance Genres: Essays on Theory, History, and Interpretation* (Cambridge, Mass., and London: Harvard University Press, 1986).

Kingsley-Smith, Jane, 'The Tempest's Forgotten Exile', *Shakespeare Survey*, 54 (2001), 223–33.

Kinney, Arthur F., *Shakespeare's Web: Networks of Meaning in Renaissance Drama* (London and New York: Routledge, 2004).

Knapp, Jeffrey, *Shakespeare's Tribe: Church, Nation and Theatre in Renaissance England* (Chicago and London: University of Chicago Press, 2002).

Knapp, Robert S., ' "Is it appropriate for a man to fear his wife?": John Case on Marriage', *English Literary Renaissance*, 28 (1998), 387–415.

—— *Shakespeare: The Theatre and the Book* (Princeton: Princeton University Press, 1989).

Langbaine, Gerard, *An Account of the English Dramatic Poets, 1691* (Menston, Yorkshire: Scolar Press, 1971).

Lechner, Sister Joan Marie, OSU, *Renaissance Concepts of the Commonplaces* (Westport, Conn.: Greenwood Press, 1962).

Lesser, Zachary, *Renaissance Drama and the Politics of Publication* (Cambridge: Cambridge University Press, 2004).

Levi, Peter, *The Life and Times of William Shakespeare* (London: Macmillan, 1998).

Lewis, C. S., *English Literature in the Sixteenth Century, Excluding Drama* (London, Oxford and New York: Oxford, University Press, 1973).

Livingstone, E. A., *The Concise Oxford Dictionary of the Christian Church* (Oxford and New York: Oxford University Press, 2000).

Magnusson, Lynne, *Shakespeare and Social Dialogue: Dramatic Language and Elizabethan Letters* (Cambridge: Cambridge University Press, 1999).

Maguire, Laurie E., *Shakespearean Suspect Texts: The 'Bad' Quartos and their Contexts* (Cambridge: Cambridge University Press, 1996).

\_\_\_\_ *Studying Shakespeare: A Guide to the Plays* (Oxford: Blackwell, 2004).

Man, John, *The Gutenberg Revolution: The Story of a Genius and an Invention that Changed the World* (London: Review, 2002).

Manguel, Alberto, *A History of Reading* (London: Flamingo, 1997).

Margolies, David, *Novel and Society in Elizabethan England* (Totowa, NJ: Barnes and Noble Books, 1985).

Marotti, Arthur F., and Michael D. Bristol (eds.), *Print, Manuscript and Performance: The Changing Relations of the Media in Early Modern England* (Columbus, Oh.: Ohio State University Press, 2000).

Martin, John, 'Inventing Sincerity, Refashioning Prudence: The Discovery of the Individual in Renaissance Europe', in Whitlock (ed.), *The Renaissance in Europe*, 11–31.

Maus, Katherine, Eisaman, *Inwardness and Theater in the English Renaissance* (Chicago and London: University of Chicago Press, 1995).

McDonald, Russ, *Shakespeare and the Art of Language* (Oxford and New York: Oxford University Press, 2001).

\_\_\_\_ (ed.), *Shakespeare: An Anthology of Criticism and Theory 1945–2000* (Oxford: Blackwell, 2004).

McGann, Jerome, 'The Socialisation of Texts', in Finkelstein and McCleery (eds.), *Book History Reader*, 39–46.

McKenzie, D. F., 'The Book as an Expressive Form', in Finkelstein and McCleery (eds.), *Book History Reader*, 27–38.

McKerrow, Ronald Brunless, *Notes on Bibliographical Evidence for Literary Students and Editors of English Works of the Sixteenth and Seventeenth Centuries* (London: Blades, 1914).

McMullen, Gordon (ed.), *Renaissance Configurations: Voices, Bodies, Spaces, 1580–1690* (Basingstoke and New York: Palgrave, 2001).

Mead, Philip, and Marion Campbell (eds.), *Shakespeare's Books: Contemporary Cultural Politics and the Persistence of Empire* (Parkville, Victoria: Department of English, University of Melbourne, 1993).

Miles, Pliny, *Mnemotechny, or Art of Memory, Theoretical and Practical with a Mnemotechnic Dictionary* (London: E. Charton, 1850).

Miller, Jonathan, *On Reflection* (London: National Gallery Publications Ltd., distributed by Yale University Press, 1998).

Miola, Robert S., 'Jesuit drama in early modern England', in Dutton *et al.* (eds.), *Theatre and Religion: Lancastrian Shakespeare*, 71–86.

―― *Shakespeare's Reading* (Oxford: Oxford University press, 2000).

Monta, Susannah Brietz, *Martyrdom and Literature in Early Modern England* (Cambridge: Cambridge University Press, 2005).

Morgan, Paul, 'Frances Wolfreston and "Hor Bouks": A Seventeenth-Century Woman Book Collector', in B. Fabian and K. T. Von Rosador (eds.), *Shakespeare: Text, Language, Criticism: Essays in Honour of Marvin Spevack* (Hildesheim, Zurich, and New York: Olms-Weidmann, 1987), 193–211.

Morrison, Paul G., *Index of Printers, Publishers and Booksellers in A. W. Pollard and G. R. Redgrave: A Short-Title Catalogue of Books Printed in England, Scotland and Ireland and of English Books Printed Abroad, 1475–1640* (Charlottesville, Va.: Bibliographical Society of the University of Virginia, 1961).

Moss, Ann, *Printed Commonplace-Books and the Structuring of Renaissance Thought* (Oxford: Clarendon Press, 1996).

Mowat, Barbara, ' "Knowing I loved my Books": Reading *The Tempest* Intertextually', in Hulme and Sherman (eds.), *The Tempest and its Travels*, 27–36.

Moynahan, Brian, *If God Spare My Life: William Tyndale, the English Bible and Sir Thomas More: A Story of Martyrdom and Betrayal* (London: Little, Brown, 2002).

Mullaney, Steven, *The Place of the Stage: License, Play, and Power in Renaissance England* (Chicago: University of Chicago Press, 1988).

Muller, Jan-Dirk, 'The Body of the Book: The Media Transition from Manuscript to Print', in Finkelstein and McCleery (eds.), *Book History Reader*, 143–50.

Murphy, Andrew (ed.), *The Renaissance Text: Theory, Editing, Textuality* (Manchester and New York: Manchester University Press, 2000).

Murray, Penelope (trans.), *Classical Literary Criticism* (Harmondsworth: Penguin, 2000).

Myers, Robin, 'The Records of the Worshipful Company of Stationers and Newspaper Makers (1554–1912)', in *Publishing History: The Social, Economic, and Literary History of the Book, Newspaper and Magazine Publishing*, xiii. 89–105.

Neu Watkins, Renée (trans.), *Humanism and Liberty: Writings on Freedom from Fifteenth-Century Florence* (Columbia, SC: University of South Carolina Press, 1978).

Norton, Glyn P. (ed.), *The Cambridge History of Literary Criticism*, iii: *The Renaissance* (Cambridge: Cambridge University Press, 1999).

Nuttall, A. D., *The Alternative Trinity: Gnostic Heresy in Marlowe, Milton, and Blake* (Oxford: Clarendon Press, 1998).

O'Connell, Michael, *The Idolatrous Eye: Iconoclasm and Theatre in Early Modern England* (New York and Oxford: Oxford University Press, 2000).

Olson, David. R., *The World on Paper: The Conceptual and Cognitive Implications of Writing and Reading* (Cambridge: Cambridge University Press, 1994).

Ong, Walter J., *Orality and Literacy: The Technologising of the Word* (London and New York: Routledge, 2000).

Orgel, Stephen, *The Illusion of Power* (Berkeley: University of California Press, 1975).

_____ *Imagining Shakespeare: A History of Texts and Visions* (Basingstoke and New York: Palgrave, 2003).

O'Sullivan, Orlaith (ed.), *The Bible as Book: The Reformation* (London and New Castle, Del.: British Library and Oak Knoll Press, 2000).

Palfrey, Simon, *Late Shakespeare: A New World of Words* (Oxford: Clarendon Press, 1997).

Petcher, Edward (ed.), *Textual and Theoretical Shakespeare: Questions of Evidence* (Iowa City: University of Iowa Press, 1969).

Peters Stone, Julie, *Theatre of the Book 1480–1880: Print, Text, and Performance in Europe* (Oxford: Oxford University Press, 2000).

Picard, Liza, *Elizabeth's London: Everyday Life in Elizabethan England* (London: Weidenfeld & Nicolson, 2003).

Pitcher, John, 'Literature, the Playhouse and the Public', in Barnard *et al.* (eds.), *Cambridge History of the Book in Britain*, iv. 351–75.

Plumb, J. H., *The Penguin Book of the Renaissance* (Harmondsworth: Penguin, 1961).

Pollard, Alfred, and G. R. Redgrave, *A Short-Title Catalogue of Books Printed in England, Scotland, and Ireland and of English Books Printed Abroad, 1475–1640* (London: Bibliographical Society, 1950).

Ramage, David (ed.), *A Finding-List of English Books to 1640 in Libraries of the British Isles (excluding the National Libraries of Oxford and Cambridge), based on the numbers in Pollard & Redgraves 'Short-Title Catalogue of Books Printed in England, Scotland and Ireland & English Books Printed Abroad, 1475–1640* (Durham: The Council of Durham Colleges, 1958).

Rhodes, Neil, and Jonathan Sawday (eds.), *The Renaissance Computer* (London and New York: Routledge, 2000).

Righter, Anne, *Shakespeare and the Idea of the Play* (London: Chatto & Windus, 1962).

Rigolot, François, 'The Rhetoric of Presence: Art, Literature, and Illusion', in Norton (ed.), *Cambridge History of Literary Criticism*, iii. 161–7.

Roberts, Sasha, 'Shakespeare "creepes into womens closets about bedtime": Women Reading in a Room of their Own', in McMullen (ed.), *Renaissance Configurations*, 30–63.

Roesen, Bobbyann (Anne Barton), 'Love's Labour's Lost', in Hardison Londré (ed.), *Love's Labour's Lost*, 125–44.

Rossiter, A. P., *Angel with Horns: Fifteen Lectures on Shakespeare* (London and New York: Longman, 1989).

Rowe, Katherine A., 'Dismembering and Forgetting', *Shakespeare Quarterly*, 45 (1994), 279–304.

Rowse, A. L., *The England of Elizabeth: The Structure of Society* (London: Macmillan and Co. Ltd., 1950).

Saunders, Eve Rachele, *Gender and Literacy on Stage in Early Modern England* (Cambridge: Cambridge University Press, 1998).

Schalkwyk, David, *Speech and Performance in Shakespeare's Sonnets and Plays* (Cambridge: Cambridge University Press, 2002).

Schleiner, Louise, *Tudor and Stewart Women Writers* (Bloomington, Ind., and Indianapolis: Indiana University Press, 1994).

Schneider, Norbert, *Still Life* (London, Cologne, Los Angeles, Madrid, Paris, and Tokyo: Taschen, 2003).

Schwyzer, Philip, *Literature, Nationalism, and Memory in Early Modern England and Wales* (Cambridge: Cambridge University Press, 2004).

Scott Kastan, David, *Shakespeare and the Book* (Cambridge: Cambridge University Press, 2001).

Shaheen, Naseeb, *Biblical References in Shakespeare's Plays* (Newark, NJ: University of Delaware Press; London: Associated University Press, 1999).

Shapiro, Marianne, *De Vulgari Eloquentia: Dante's Book of Exile* (Lincoln, Nebr., and London: University of Nebraska Press, 1990).

Sharpe, Kevin, *Reading Revolutions: The Politics of Reading in Early Modern England* (New Haven and London: Yale University Press, 2000).

Siemon, James R., *Word against Word: Shakespearean Utterance* (Amherst, Mass., and Boston: University of Massachusetts Press, 2002).

Slights, William W. E., *Managing Readers: Printed Marginalia in English Renaissance Books* (Ann Arbor: University of Michigan Press, 2001).

Smith, Nigel, 'Non-Conformist Voices and Books', in Barnard *et al.* (eds.), *Cambridge History of the Book*, iv. 410–30.

Spevack, Marvin, *The Harvard Concordance to Shakespeare* (Hildesheim: George Olms, 1970).

Sponsler, Claire, *Drama and Resistance: Bodies, Goods, and Theatricality in Late Medieval England* (Minneapolis and London: University of Minnesota Press, 1997).

Spufford, Margaret, *Small Books and Pleasant Histories: Popular Fiction and its Readership in Seventeenth-Century England* (Cambridge: Cambridge University Press, 1985).

Stallybrass, Peter, Roger Chartier, J. Franklin Mowery, and Heather Wolfe, 'Hamlet's Tables and the Technologies of Writing in Renaissance England', *Shakespeare Quarterly*, 55 (2004), 379–419.

Steinburg, S. H., *Five Hundred Years of Printing* (Harmondsworth: Penguin, 1961).

Stern, Tiffany, *Making Shakespeare: From Stage to Page* (London: Routledge, 2004).

Straznicky, Marta, *Privacy, Playreading, and Women's Closet Drama, 1550–1700* (Cambridge: Cambridge University Press, 2004).

Tillyard, E. M. W., *The Elizabethan World Picture* (London: Pimlico, 1998).

Tracy, James D., *Europe's Reformations 1450–1650* (London, Boulder, Colo., New York, and Oxford: Rowan & Littlefield, 1999).

Tribble, Evelyn B., *Margins and Marginality: The Printed Page in Early Modern England* (Charlottesville, Va., and London: University Press of Virginia, 1993).

Trousdale, Marion, 'Reading and the Early Modern Text', *Shakespeare Survey*, 50 (1997), 135–45.

Vandiver, Elizabeth, Ralph Keen, and Thomas D. Frazel (eds.), *Luther's Lives: Two Contemporary Accounts of Martin Luther* (Manchester: Manchester University Press, 2002).

Walker, Lewis, 'Chaucer's Contribution to *The Tempest*: A Reappraisal', *Renaissance Papers* (2000), 119–35.

Waso, Richard, 'Theories of Language', in Norton (ed.), *Cambridge History of Literary Criticism*, iii. 25–35.

Weimann, Robert, *Author's Pen and Actor's Voice: Playing and Writing in Shakespeare's Theatre* (Cambridge: Cambridge University Press, 2000).

_____ 'Mimesis in *Hamlet*' in Parker and Hartman (eds.), *Shakespeare and the Question of Theory* (New York: Methuen, 1985), 275–91.

_____ 'Playing with Difference. Revising Pen and "Voice" in Shakespeare's Theatre', *Shakespeare Quarterly*, 50 (1999), 414–33.

Wells, Stanley, Gary Taylor, John Jowett, and William Montgomery (eds.), *William Shakespeare: A Textual Companion* (Oxford: Clarendon Press, 1987).

West, Grace Starry, 'Going by the Book: Classical Allusions in Shakespeare's *Titus Andronicus*', *Studies in Philology*, 79 (1982), 62–77.

Whitaker, Virgil K., *Shakespeare's Use of Learning: An Inquiry into the Growth of his Mind and Art* (San Marino, Calif.: The Huntingdon Library, 1969).

Whitfield White, Paul, *Theatre and Reformation: Protestantism, Patronage, and Playing in Tudor England* (Cambridge: Cambridge University Press, 1993).

Whitlock, Keith (ed.), *The Renaissance: A Reader* (New Haven and London: Yale University Press in association with The Open University, 2000).

Williams, Gordon, *Shakespeare, Sex, and the Print Revolution* (London and Atlantic Highlands, NJ: Athlone, 1996).

Wilson, F. P., *Shakespeare and the New Bibliography*, rev. and ed. Helen Gardner (Oxford: Clarendon Press, 1970).

Wilson, Richard, 'Introduction: A Torturing Hour: Shakespeare and the Martyrs', in Dutton *et al.* (eds.), *Theatre and Religion: Lancastrian Shakespeare*, 1–39.

Woolf, D. R., *Reading History in Early Modern England* (Cambridge: Cambridge University Press, 2000).

Yates, Frances, A., *The Art of Memory* (London: Pimlico, 1992).

\_\_\_\_ *The Occult Philosophy in the Elizabethan Age* (London and New York: Routledge Classics, 2001).

# Index